Software Security Engineering

Software Security Engineering

A Guide for Project Managers

Julia H. Allen
Sean Barnum
Robert J. Ellison
Gary McGraw
Nancy R. Mead

✦✦ Addison-Wesley

Upper Saddle River, NJ • Boston • Indianapolis • San Francisco
New York • Toronto • Montreal • London • Munich • Paris • Madrid
Capetown • Sydney • Tokyo • Singapore • Mexico City

Carnegie Mellon
Software Engineering Institute
The SEI Series in Software Engineering

The Addison-Wesley Software Security Series

Many of the designations used by manufacturers and sellers to distinguish their products are claimed as trademarks. Where those designations appear in this book, and the publisher was aware of a trademark claim, the designations have been printed with initial capital letters or in all capitals.

CMM, CMMI, Capability Maturity Model, Capability Maturity Modeling, Carnegie Mellon, CERT, and CERT Coordination Center are registered in the U.S. Patent and Trademark Office by Carnegie Mellon University.

ATAM; Architecture Tradeoff Analysis Method; CMM Integration; COTS Usage-Risk Evaluation; CURE; EPIC; Evolutionary Process for Integrating COTS Based Systems; Framework for Software Product Line Practice; IDEAL; Interim Profile; OAR; OCTAVE; Operationally Critical Threat, Asset, and Vulnerability Evaluation; Options Analysis for Reengineering; Personal Software Process; PLTP; Product Line Technical Probe; PSP; SCAMPI; SCAMPI Lead Appraiser; SCAMPI Lead Assessor; SCE; SEI; SEPG; Team Software Process; and TSP are service marks of Carnegie Mellon University.

Special permission to reproduce portions of Build Security In, © 2005–2007 by Carnegie Mellon University, in this book is granted by the Software Engineering Institute.

Special permission to reproduce portions of Build Security In, © 2005–2007 by Cigital, Inc., in this book is granted by Cigital, Inc.

Special permission to reprint excerpts from the article "Software Quality at Top Speed," © 1996 Steve McConnell, in this book is granted by Steve McConnell.

The authors and publisher have taken care in the preparation of this book, but make no express or implied warranty of any kind and assume no responsibility for errors or omissions. No liability is assumed for incidental or consequential damages in connection with or arising out of the use of the information or programs contained herein.

The publisher offers excellent discounts on this book when ordered in quantity for bulk purchases or special sales, which may include electronic versions and/or custom covers and content particular to your business, training goals, marketing focus, and branding interests. For more information, please contact: U.S. Corporate and Government Sales, (800) 382-3419, corpsales@pearsontechgroup.com.

For sales outside the United States, please contact: International Sales, international@pearsoned.com.

Visit us on the Web: informit.com/aw

Library of Congress Cataloging-in-Publication Data
Software security engineering : a guide for project managers / Julia H. Allen ... [et al.].
    p. cm.
  Includes bibliographical references and index.
  ISBN 978-0-321-50917-8 (pbk. : alk. paper) 1. Computer security. 2. Software engineering. 3. Computer networks—Security measures. I. Allen, Julia H.

  QA76.9.A25S654 2008
  005.8—dc22

                                                                              2008007000

ISBN-13: 978-0-321-50917-8
ISBN-10:   0-321-50917-X
This product is printed digitally on demand.
First printing, April 2008

Contents

Foreword

Everybody knows that software is riddled with security flaws. At first blush, this is surprising. We know how to write software in a way that provides a moderately high level of security and robustness. So why don't software developers practice these techniques?

This book deals with two of the myriad answers to this question. The first is the meaning of secure software. In fact, the term "secure software" is a misnomer. Security is a product of software *plus environment*. How a program is used, under what conditions it is used, and what security requirements it must meet determine whether the software is secure. A term like "security-enabled software" captures the idea that the software was designed and written to meet specific security requirements, but in other environments where the assumptions underlying the software—and any implied requirements—do not hold, the software may not be secure. In a way that is easy to understand, this book presents the need for accurate and meaningful security requirements, as well as approaches for developing them. Unlike many books on the subject of secure software, this book does not assume the requirements are given *a priori*, but instead discusses requirements derivation and analysis. Equally important, it describes their validation.

The second answer lies in the roles of the executives, managers, and technical leaders of projects. They must support the introduction of security enhancements in software, as well as robust coding practices (which is really a type of security enhancement). Moreover, they must understand the processes and make allowances for it in their scheduling, budgeting, and staffing plans. This book does an excellent job of laying out the process for the people in these roles, so they can realistically assess its impact. Additionally, the book points out where the state of the art is too new or lacks enough experience to have approaches that are proven to work, or are not generally accepted to work. In those cases, the authors suggest ways to think about the issues in order to develop effective approaches. Thus, executives, managers, and technical leaders can figure out what should work best in their environment.

An additional, and in fact crucial, benefit of designing and implementing security in software from the very beginning of the project is the increase in assurance that the software will meet its requirements. This will greatly reduce the need to patch the software to fix security holes—a process that is itself fraught with security problems, undercuts the reputation of the vendor, and adversely impacts the vendor financially. Loss of credibility, while intangible, has tangible repercussions. Paying the extra cost of developing software correctly from the start reduces the cost of fixing it after it is deployed—and produces a better, more robust, and more secure product.

This book discusses several ways to develop software in such a way that security considerations play a key role in its development. It speaks to executives, to managers at all levels, and to technical leaders, and in that way, it is unique. It also speaks to students and developers, so they can understand the process of developing software with security in mind and find resources to help them do so.

The underlying theme of this book is that the software we all use could be made much better. The information in this book provides a foundation for executives, project managers, and technical leaders to improve the software they create and to improve the quality and security of the software we all use.

Matt Bishop
Davis, California
March 2008

Preface

The Problem Addressed by This Book

Software is ubiquitous. Many of the products, services, and processes that organizations use and offer are highly dependent on software to handle the sensitive and high-value data on which people's privacy, livelihoods, and very lives depend. For instance, national security—and by extension citizens' personal safety—relies on increasingly complex, interconnected, software-intensive information systems that, in many cases, use the Internet or Internet-exposed private networks as their means for communication and transporting data.

This ubiquitous dependence on information technology makes software security a key element of business continuity, disaster recovery, incident response, and national security. Software vulnerabilities can jeopardize intellectual property, consumer trust, business operations and services, and a broad spectrum of critical applications and infrastructures, including everything from process control systems to commercial application products.

The integrity of critical digital assets (systems, networks, applications, and information) depends on the reliability and security of the software that enables and controls those assets. However, business leaders and informed consumers have growing concerns about the scarcity of practitioners with requisite competencies to address software security [Carey 2006]. Specifically, they have doubts about suppliers' capabilities to build and deliver secure software that they can use with confidence and without fear of compromise. Application software is the primary gateway to sensitive information. According to a Deloitte survey of 169 major global financial institutions, titled *2007 Global Security Survey: The Shifting Security Paradigm* [Deloitte 2007], current application software countermeasures are no longer adequate. In the survey, Gartner identifies application security as the number one issue for chief information officers (CIOs).

Selected content in this preface is summarized and excerpted from *Security in the Software Lifecycle: Making Software Development Processes—and Software Produced by Them—More Secure* [Goertzel 2006].

The absence of security discipline in today's software development practices often produces software with exploitable weaknesses. Security-enhanced processes and practices—and the skilled people to manage them and perform them—are required to build software that can be trusted to operate more securely than software being used today.

That said, there is an economic counter-argument, or at least the perception of one: Some business leaders and project managers believe that developing secure software slows the software development process and adds to the cost while not offering any apparent advantage. In many cases, when the decision reduces to "ship now" or "be secure and ship later," "ship now" is almost always the choice made by those who control the money but have no idea of the risks. The opposite side of this argument, including how software security can potentially reduce cost and schedule, is discussed in Chapter 1 (Section 1.6, "The Benefits of Detecting Software Security Defects Early") and Chapter 7 (Section 7.5.3, in the "Knowledge and Expertise" subsection discussing Microsoft's experience with its Security Development Lifecycle) in this book.

Software's Vulnerability to Attack

The number of threats specifically targeting software is increasing, and the majority of network- and system-level attacks now exploit vulnerabilities in application-level software. According to CERT analysts at Carnegie Mellon University,[1] most successful attacks result from targeting and exploiting known, unpatched software vulnerabilities and insecure software configurations, a significant number of which are introduced during software design and development.

These conditions contribute to the increased risks associated with software-enabled capabilities and exacerbate the threat of attack. Given this atmosphere of uncertainty, a broad range of stakeholders need justifiable confidence that the software that enables their core business operations can be trusted to perform as intended.

Why We Wrote This Book: Its Purpose, Goals, and Scope
The Challenge of Software Security Engineering

Software security engineering entails using practices, processes, tools, and techniques to address security issues in every phase of the software

---

1. CERT (www.cert.org) is registered in the U.S. Patent and Trademark Office by Carnegie Mellon University.

development life cycle (SDLC). Software that is developed with security in mind is typically more resistant to both intentional attack and unintentional failures. One view of secure software is software that is engineered "so that it continues to function correctly under malicious attack" [McGraw 2006] and is able to recognize, resist, tolerate, and recover from events that intentionally threaten its dependability. Broader views that can overlap with software security (for example, software safety, reliability, and fault tolerance) include the notion of proper functioning in the face of unintentional failures or accidents and inadvertent misuse and abuse, as well as reducing software defects and weaknesses to the greatest extent possible regardless of their cause. This book addresses the narrower view.

The goal of software security engineering is to build better, defect-free software. Software-intensive systems that are constructed using more securely developed software are better able to do the following:

- Continue operating correctly in the presence of most attacks by either *resisting* the exploitation of weaknesses in the software by attackers or *tolerating* the failures that result from such exploits
- Limit the damage resulting from any failures caused by attack-triggered faults that the software was unable to resist or tolerate and recover as quickly as possible from those failures

No single practice offers a universal "silver bullet" for software security. With this caveat in mind, *Software Security Engineering: A Guide for Project Managers* provides software project managers with sound practices that they can evaluate and selectively adopt to help reshape their own development practices. The objective is to increase the security and dependability of the software produced by these practices, both during its development and during its operation.

What Readers Can Expect

Readers will increase their awareness and understanding of the security issues in the design and development of software. The book's content will help readers recognize how software development practices can either contribute to or detract from the security of software.

The book (and material referenced on the Build Security In Web site described later in this preface) will enable readers to identify and compare potential new practices that can be adapted to augment a project's current software development practices, thereby greatly increasing the likelihood of producing more secure software and meeting specified security requirements. As one example, assurance cases can be used to assert and specify desired security properties, including the extent to which security practices have been successful in satisfying security requirements. Assurance cases are discussed in Chapter 2 (Section 2.4, "How to Assert and Specify Desired Security Properties").

Software developed and assembled using the practices described in this book should contain significantly fewer exploitable weaknesses. Such software can then be relied on to more capably resist or tolerate and recover from attacks and, therefore, to function more securely in an operational environment. Project managers responsible for ensuring that software and systems adequately address their security requirements throughout the SDLC should review, select, and tailor guidance from this book, the Build Security In Web site, and the sources cited throughout this book as part of their normal project management activities.

The five key take-away messages for readers of this book are as follows:

1. Software security is about more than eliminating vulnerabilities and conducting penetration tests. Project managers need to take a systematic approach to incorporate the sound practices discussed in this book into their development processes (all chapters).

2. Network security mechanisms and IT infrastructure security services do not sufficiently protect application software from security risks (Chapters 1 and 2).

3. Software security initiatives should follow a risk management approach to identify priorities and determine what is "good enough," while understanding that software security risks will inevitably change throughout the SDLC (Chapters 1, 4, and 7).

4. Developing secure software depends on understanding the operational context in which it will be used (Chapter 6).

5. Project managers and software engineers need to learn to think like an attacker to address the range of things that software should *not* do and identify how software can better resist, tolerate, and recover when under attack (Chapters 2, 3, 4, and 5). *limit*

Who Should Read This Book

Software Security Engineering: A Guide for Project Managers is primarily intended for project managers who are responsible for software development and the development of software-intensive systems. Lead requirements analysts, experienced software and security architects and designers, system integrators, and their managers should also find this book useful. It provides guidance for those involved in the management of secure, software-intensive systems, either developed from scratch or through the assembly, integration, and evolution of acquired or reused software.

This book will help readers understand the security issues associated with the engineering of software and should help them identify practices that can be used to manage and develop software that is better able to withstand the threats to which it is increasingly subjected. It presumes that readers are familiar with good general systems and software engineering management methods, practices, and technologies.

How This Book Is Organized

This book is organized into two introductory chapters, four technical chapters, a chapter that describes governance and management considerations, and a concluding chapter on how to get started.

Chapter 1, Why Is Security a Software Issue?, identifies threats that target most software and the shortcomings of the software development process that can render software vulnerable to those threats. It describes the benefits of detecting software security defects early in the SDLC, including the current state of the practice for making the business case for software security. It closes by introducing some pragmatic solutions that are further elaborated in the chapters that follow.

Chapter 2, What Makes Software Secure?, examines the core and influential properties of software that make it secure and the defensive and attacker perspectives in addressing those properties, and discusses how desirable traits of software can contribute to its security. The chapter introduces and defines the key resources of attack patterns and assurance cases and explains how to use them throughout the SDLC.

Chapter 3, Requirements Engineering for Secure Software, describes practices for security requirements engineering, including processes that are specific to eliciting, specifying, analyzing, and validating security requirements. This chapter also explores the key practice of misuse/abuse cases.

Chapter 4, Secure Software Architecture and Design, presents the practice of architectural and risk analysis for reviewing, assessing, and validating the specification, architecture, and design of a software system with respect to software security, and reliability.

Chapter 5, Considerations for Secure Coding and Testing, summarizes key practices for performing code analysis to uncover errors in and improve the quality of source code, as well as practices for security testing, white-box testing, black-box testing, and penetration testing. Along the way, this chapter references recently published works on secure coding and testing for further details.

Chapter 6, Security and Complexity: System Assembly Challenges, describes the challenges and practices inherent in the design, assembly, integration, and evolution of trustworthy systems and systems of systems. It provides guidelines for project managers to consider, recognizing that most new or updated software components are typically integrated into an existing operational environment.

Chapter 7, Governance, and Managing for More Secure Software, describes how to motivate business leaders to treat software security as a governance and management concern. It includes actionable practices for risk management and project management and for establishing an enterprise security framework.

Chapter 8, Getting Started, summarizes all of the recommended practices discussed in the book and provides several aids for determining which practices are most relevant and for whom, and where to start.

The book closes with a comprehensive bibliography and glossary.

Notes to the Reader

Navigating the Book's Content

As an aid to the reader, we have added descriptive icons that mark the book's sections and key practices in two practical ways:

- Identifying the content's relative "maturity of practice":

    L1 The content provides guidance for how to think about a topic for which there is no proven or widely accepted approach. The intent of the description is to raise awareness and aid the reader in thinking about the problem and candidate solutions. The content may also describe promising research results that may have been demonstrated in a constrained setting.

L2 The content describes practices that are in early (pilot) use and are demonstrating some successful results.

L3 The content describes practices that are in limited use in industry or government organizations, perhaps for a particular market sector.

L4 The content describes practices that have been successfully deployed and are in widespread use. Readers can start using these practices today with confidence. Experience reports and case studies are typically available.

- Identifying the designated audiences for which each chapter section or practice is most relevant:

  E Executive and senior managers

  M Project and mid-level managers

  L Technical leaders, engineering managers, first-line managers, and supervisors

As the audience icons in the chapters show, we urge executive and senior managers to read all of Chapters 1 and 8, plus the following sections in other chapters: 2.1, 2.2, 2.5, 3.1, 3.7, 4.1, 5.1, 5.6, 6.1, 6.6, 7.1, 7.3, 7.4, 7.6, and 7.7.

Project and mid-level managers should be sure to read all of Chapters 1, 2, 4, 5, 6, 7, and 8, plus these sections in Chapter 3: 3.1, 3.3, and 3.7.

Technical leaders, engineering managers, first-line managers, and supervisors will find useful information and guidance throughout the entire book.

Build Security In: A Key Resource

Since 2004, the U.S. Department of Homeland Security Software Assurance Program has sponsored development of the Build Security In (BSI) Web site (https://buildsecurityin.us-cert.gov/), which was one of the significant resources used in writing this book. BSI content is based on the principle that software security is fundamentally a software engineering problem and must be managed in a systematic way throughout the SDLC.

BSI contains and links to a broad range of information about sound practices, tools, guidelines, rules, principles, and other knowledge to help project managers deploy software security practices and build secure and reliable software. Contributing authors to this book and the articles appearing on the BSI Web site include senior staff from the Carnegie Mellon Software Engineering Institute (SEI) and Cigital, Inc., as well as other experienced software and security professionals.

Several sections in the book were originally published as articles in *IEEE Security & Privacy* magazine and are reprinted here with the permission of IEEE Computer Society Press. Where an article occurs in the book, a statement such as the following appears in a footnote:

> This section was originally published as an article in *IEEE Security & Privacy* [citation]. It is reprinted here with permission from the publisher.

These articles are also available on the BSI Web site.

Articles on BSI are referenced throughout this book. Readers can consult BSI for additional details, book errata, and ongoing research results.

Start the Journey

A number of excellent books address secure systems and software engineering. *Software Security Engineering: A Guide for Project Managers* offers an engineering perspective that has been sorely needed in the software security community. It puts the entire SDLC in the context of an integrated set of sound software security engineering practices.

As part of its comprehensive coverage, this book captures both standard and emerging software security practices and explains why they are needed to develop more security-responsive and robust systems. The book is packed with reasons for taking action early and revisiting these actions frequently throughout the SDLC.

This is not a book for the faint of heart or the neophyte software project manager who is confronting software security for the first time. Readers need to understand the SDLC and the processes in use within their organizations to comprehend the implications of the various techniques presented and to choose among the recommended practices to determine the best fit for any given project.

Other books are available that discuss each phase of secure software engineering. Few, however, cover all of the SDLC phases in as concise and usable a format as we have attempted to do here. Enjoy the journey!

Acknowledgments

We are pleased to acknowledge the support of many people who helped us through the book development process. Our organizations, the CERT Program at the Software Engineering Institute (SEI) and Cigital, Inc., encouraged our authorship of the book and provided release time as well as other support to make it possible. Pamela Curtis, our SEI technical editor, diligently read and reread each word of the entire manuscript and provided many valuable suggestions for improvement, as well as helping with packaging questions and supervising development of figures for the book. Jan Vargas provided SEI management support, tracked schedules and action items, and helped with meeting agendas and management. In the early stages of the process, Petra Dilone provided SEI administrative support as well as configuration management for the various chapters and iterations of the manuscript.

We also appreciate the encouragement of Joe Jarzombek, the sponsor of the Department of Homeland Security Build Security In (BSI) Web site. The Build Security In Web site content is a key resource for this book.

Much of the material in this book is based on articles published with other authors on the BSI Web site and elsewhere. We greatly appreciated the opportunity to collaborate with these authors, and their names are listed in the individual sections that they contributed to, directly or indirectly.

We had many reviewers, whose input was extremely valuable and led to many improvements in the book. Internal reviewers included Carol Woody and Robert Ferguson of the SEI. We also appreciate the inputs and thoughtful comments of the Addison-Wesley reviewers: Chris Cleeland, Jeremy Epstein, Ronda R. Henning, Jeffrey A. Ingalsbe, Ron Lichty, Gabor Liptak, Donald Reifer, and David Strom. We would like to give special recognition to Steve Riley, one of the Addison-Wesley reviewers who reviewed our initial proposal and all iterations of the manuscript.

We would like to recognize the encouragement and support of our contacts at Addison-Wesley. These include Peter Gordon, publishing partner; Kim Boedigheimer, editorial assistant; Julie Nahil, full-service production manager; and Jill Hobbs, freelance copyeditor. We also appreciate the efforts of the Addison-Wesley and SEI artists and designers who assisted with the cover design, layout, and figures.

About the Authors

Julia H. Allen

Julia H. Allen is a Senior Member of the Technical Staff within the CERT Program at the Software Engineering Institute (SEI), a unit of Carnegie Mellon University in Pittsburgh, Pennsylvania. In addition to her work in software security and assurance, Allen is engaged in developing and transitioning executive outreach programs in enterprise security and governance. Prior to this technical assignment, Allen served as Acting Director of the SEI for an interim period of six months as well as Deputy Director/Chief Operating Officer for three years. She formalized the SEI's relationship with industry organizations and created the Customer Relations team.

Before joining the SEI, Allen was a Vice President at Science Applications International Corporation (SAIC), responsible for starting a new software division specializing in embedded systems software. Allen led SAIC's initial efforts in software process improvement. Allen also worked at TRW (now Northrop Grumman), tackling a range of assignments from systems integration, testing, and field site support to managing major software development programs.

Her degrees include a B.S. in Computer Science from the University of Michigan and an M.S. in Electrical Engineering from the University of Southern California. Allen is the author of *The CERT® Guide to System and Network Security Practices* (Addison-Wesley, 2001), *Governing for Enterprise Security* (CMU/SEI-2005-TN-023, 2005), and the CERT Podcast Series: Security for Business Leaders (2006–2008).

Sean Barnum

Sean Barnum is a Principal Consultant at Cigital, Inc., and is Technical Lead for Cigital's federal services practice. He has more than twenty years of experience in the software industry in the areas of development, software quality assurance, quality management, process architecture and improvement, knowledge management, and security. Barnum is a frequent contributor and speaker for regional and national software security and software quality publications, conferences, and events. He is very active in the software assurance community and is involved in numerous knowledge standards-defining efforts, including the Common Weakness Enumeration (CWE), the Common Attack Pattern Enumeration and Classification (CAPEC), and other elements of the Software Assurance Programs of the Department of Homeland Security and the Department of Defense. He is also the lead technical subject matter expert for the Air Force Application Software Assurance Center of Excellence.

Robert J. Ellison

As a member of the Survivable Systems Engineering Team within the CERT Program at the Software Engineering Institute, Robert J. Ellison has served in a number of technical and management roles. He was a project leader for the evaluation of software engineering development environments and associated software development tools. He was also a member of the Carnegie Mellon University team that wrote the proposal for the SEI; he joined the new FFRDC in 1985 as a founding member.

Before coming to Carnegie Mellon, Ellison taught mathematics at Brown University, Williams College, and Hamilton College. At Hamilton College, he directed the creation of the computer science curriculum. Ellison belongs to the Association for Computing Machinery (ACM) and the IEEE Computer Society.

Ellison regularly participates in the evaluation of software architectures and contributes from the perspective of security and reliability measures. His research draws on that experience to integrate security issues into the overall architecture design process. His current work explores developing reasoning frameworks to help architects select and refine design tactics to mitigate the impact of a class of cyberattacks. He continues to work on refinements to the Survivability Analysis Framework.

Gary McGraw

Gary McGraw is the Chief Technology Officer at Cigital, Inc., a software security and quality consulting firm with headquarters in the Washington, D.C., area. He is a globally recognized authority on software security and the author of six best-selling books on this topic. The latest book is *Exploiting Online Games* (Addison-Wesley, 2008). His other books include *Java Security*, *Building Secure Software*, *Exploiting Software*, and *Software Security*; he is also editor of the Addison-Wesley Software Security series. Dr. McGraw has written more than ninety peer-reviewed scientific publications, authors a monthly security column for darkreading.com, and is frequently quoted in the press as an expert on software security.

Besides serving as a strategic counselor for top business and IT executives, Dr. McGraw is on the advisory boards of Fortify Software and Raven White. He received a dual Ph.D. in Cognitive Science and Computer Science from Indiana University, where he serves on the Dean's Advisory Council for the School of Informatics. Dr. McGraw is also a member of the IEEE Computer Society Board of Governors and produces the monthly Silver Bullet Security Podcast for *IEEE Security & Privacy* magazine.

Nancy R. Mead

Nancy R. Mead is a Senior Member of the Technical Staff in the Survivable Systems Engineering Group, which is part of the CERT Program at the Software Engineering Institute. She is also a faculty member in the Master of Software Engineering and Master of Information Systems Management programs at Carnegie Mellon University. Her research interests are in the areas of information security, software requirements engineering, and software architectures.

Prior to joining the SEI, Mead was Senior Technical Staff Member at IBM Federal Systems, where she spent most of her career in the development and management of large real-time systems. She also worked in IBM's software engineering technology area and managed IBM Federal Systems' software engineering education department. She has developed and taught numerous courses on software engineering topics, both at universities and in professional education courses.

To date, Mead has more than one hundred publications and invited presentations. She is a fellow of the Institute of Electrical and Electronic Engineers (IEEE) and the IEEE Computer Society, and is also a member of the Association for Computing Machinery (ACM). Mead received her Ph.D. in Mathematics from the Polytechnic Institute of New York and received a B.A. and an M.S. in Mathematics from New York University.

Chapter 1

Why Is Security a Software Issue?

1.1 Introduction

Software is everywhere. It runs your car. It controls your cell phone. It's how you access your bank's financial services; how you receive electricity, water, and natural gas; and how you fly from coast to coast [McGraw 2006]. Whether we recognize it or not, we all rely on complex, interconnected, software-intensive information systems that use the Internet as their means for communicating and transporting information.

Building, deploying, operating, and using software that has not been developed with security in mind can be high risk—like walking a high wire without a net (Figure 1–1). The degree of risk can be compared to the distance you can fall and the potential impact (no pun intended).

This chapter discusses why security is increasingly a software problem. It defines the dimensions of software assurance and software security. It identifies threats that target most software and the shortcomings of the

---

Selected content in this chapter is summarized and excerpted from *Security in the Software Lifecycle: Making Software Development Processes—and Software Produced by Them—More Secure* [Goertzel 2006]. An earlier version of this material appeared in [Allen 2007].

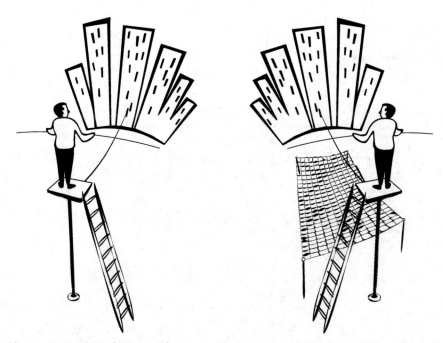

Figure 1–1: *Developing software without security in mind is like walking a high wire without a net*

software development process that can render software vulnerable to those threats. It closes by introducing some pragmatic solutions that are expanded in the chapters to follow. This entire chapter is relevant for executives (E), project managers (M), and technical leaders (L).

1.2 The Problem

Organizations increasingly store, process, and transmit their most sensitive information using software-intensive systems that are directly connected to the Internet. Private citizens' financial transactions are exposed via the Internet by software used to shop, bank, pay taxes, buy insurance, invest, register children for school, and join various organizations and social networks. The increased exposure that comes with global connectivity has made sensitive information and the software systems that handle it more vulnerable to unintentional and unauthorized use. In short, software-intensive systems and other software-enabled capabilities have provided more open, widespread access to sensitive information—including personal identities—than ever before.

Concurrently, the era of information warfare [Denning 1998], cyberterrorism, and computer crime is well under way. Terrorists, organized crime, and other criminals are targeting the entire gamut of software-intensive systems and, through human ingenuity gone awry, are being successful at gaining entry to these systems. Most such systems are not attack resistant or attack resilient enough to withstand them.

In a report to the U.S. president titled *Cyber Security: A Crisis of Prioritization* [PITAC 2005], the President's Information Technology Advisory Committee summed up the problem of nonsecure software as follows:

> Software development is not yet a science or a rigorous discipline, and the development process by and large is not controlled to minimize the vulnerabilities that attackers exploit. Today, as with cancer, vulnerable software can be invaded and modified to cause damage to previously healthy software, and infected software can replicate itself and be carried across networks to cause damage in other systems. Like cancer, these damaging processes may be invisible to the lay person even though experts recognize that their threat is growing.

Software defects with security ramifications—including coding bugs such as buffer overflows and design flaws such as inconsistent error handling—are ubiquitous. Malicious intruders, and the malicious code and botnets[1] they use to obtain unauthorized access and launch attacks, can compromise systems by taking advantage of software defects. Internet-enabled software applications are a commonly exploited target, with software's increasing complexity and extensibility making software security even more challenging [Hoglund 2004].

The security of computer systems and networks has become increasingly limited by the quality and security of their software. Security defects and vulnerabilities in software are commonplace and can pose serious risks when exploited by malicious attacks. Over the past six years, this problem has grown significantly. Figure 1–2 shows the number of vulnerabilities reported to CERT from 1997 through 2006. Given this trend, "[T]here is a clear and pressing need to change the

---

1. http://en.wikipedia.org/wiki/Botnet

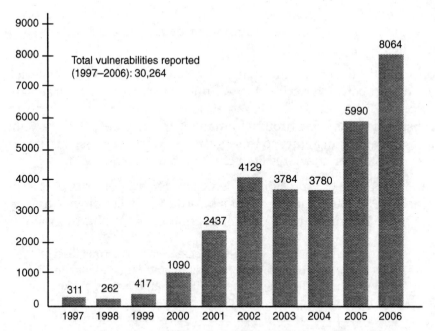

Figure 1–2: *Vulnerabilities reported to CERT*

way we (project managers and software engineers) approach computer security and to develop a disciplined approach to software security" [McGraw 2006].

In Deloitte's *2007 Global Security Survey*, 87 percent of survey respondents cited poor software development quality as a top threat in the next 12 months. "Application security means ensuring that there is secure code, integrated at the development stage, to prevent potential vulnerabilities and that steps such as vulnerability testing, application scanning, and penetration testing are part of an organization's software development life cycle [SDLC]" [Deloitte 2007].

The growing Internet connectivity of computers and networks and the corresponding user dependence on network-enabled services (such as email and Web-based transactions) have increased the number and sophistication of attack methods, as well as the ease with which an attack can be launched. This trend puts software at greater risk. Another risk area affecting software security is the degree to which systems accept updates and extensions for evolving capabilities. Extensible systems are attractive because they provide for the addition of new features and services, but each new extension adds new capabilities, new interfaces, and thus new risks. A final software security risk area is the unbridled growth in the size and complexity of software systems (such as the Microsoft Windows operating system). The unfortunate reality is that in general more lines of code produce more bugs and vulnerabilities [McGraw 2006].

1.2.1 System Complexity: The Context within Which Software Lives

Building a trustworthy software system can no longer be predicated on constructing and assembling discrete, isolated pieces that address static requirements within planned cost and schedule. Each new or updated software component joins an existing operational environment and must merge with that legacy to form an operational whole. Bolting new systems onto old systems and Web-enabling old systems creates systems of systems that are fraught with vulnerabilities. With the expanding scope and scale of systems, project managers need to reconsider a number of development assumptions that are generally applied to software security:

- Instead of centralized control, which was the norm for large stand-alone systems, project managers have to consider multiple and often independent control points for systems and systems of systems.

- Increased integration among systems has reduced the capability to make wide-scale changes quickly. In addition, for independently managed systems, upgrades are not necessarily synchronized. Project managers need to maintain operational capabilities with appropriate security as services are upgraded and new services are added.

- With the integration among independently developed and operated systems, project managers have to contend with a heterogeneous collection of components, multiple implementations of common interfaces, and inconsistencies among security policies.

- With the mismatches and errors introduced by independently developed and managed systems, failure in some form is more likely to be the norm than the exception and so further complicates meeting security requirements.

There are no known solutions for ensuring a specified level or degree of software security for complex systems and systems of systems, assuming these could even be defined. This said, Chapter 6, Security and Complexity: System Assembly Challenges, elaborates on these points and provides useful guidelines for project managers to consider in addressing the implications.

1.3 Software Assurance and Software Security

The increasing dependence on software to get critical jobs done means that software's value no longer lies solely in its ability to enhance or sustain productivity and efficiency. Instead, its value also derives from its ability to continue operating dependably even in the face of events that threaten it. The ability to trust that software will remain dependable under all circumstances, with a justified level of confidence, is the objective of software assurance.

Software assurance has become critical because dramatic increases in business and mission risks are now known to be attributable to exploitable software [DHS 2003]. The growing extent of the resulting risk exposure is rarely understood, as evidenced by these facts:

- Software is the weakest link in the successful execution of interdependent systems and software applications.
- Software size and complexity obscure intent and preclude exhaustive testing.
- Outsourcing and the use of unvetted software supply-chain components increase risk exposure.
- The sophistication and increasingly more stealthy nature of attacks facilitates exploitation.
- Reuse of legacy software with other applications introduces unintended consequences, increasing the number of vulnerable targets.
- Business leaders are unwilling to make risk-appropriate investments in software security.

According to the U.S. Committee on National Security Systems' "National Information Assurance (IA) Glossary" [CNSS 2006], software assurance is

> the level of confidence that software is free from vulnerabilities, either intentionally designed into the software or accidentally

inserted at any time during its life cycle, and that the software functions in the intended manner.

Software assurance includes the disciplines of software reliability[2] (also known as software fault tolerance), software safety,[3] and software security. The focus of *Software Security Engineering: A Guide for Project Managers* is on the third of these, software security, which is the ability of software to resist, tolerate, and recover from events that intentionally threaten its dependability. The main objective of software security is to build more-robust, higher-quality, defect-free software that continues to function correctly under malicious attack [McGraw 2006].

Software security matters because so many critical functions are completely dependent on software. This makes software a very high-value target for attackers, whose motives may be malicious, criminal, adversarial, competitive, or terrorist in nature. What makes it so easy for attackers to target software is the virtually guaranteed presence of known vulnerabilities with known attack methods, which can be exploited to violate one or more of the software's security properties or to force the software into an insecure state. Secure software remains dependable (i.e., correct and predictable) despite intentional efforts to compromise that dependability.

The objective of software security is to field software-based systems that satisfy the following criteria:

- The system is as vulnerability and defect free as possible.
- The system limits the damage resulting from any failures caused by attack-triggered faults, ensuring that the effects of any attack are not propagated, and it recovers as quickly as possible from those failures.
- The system continues operating correctly in the presence of most attacks by either *resisting* the exploitation of weaknesses in the software by the attacker or *tolerating* the failures that result from such exploits.

---

2. Software reliability means the probability of failure-free (or otherwise satisfactory) software operation for a specified/expected period/interval of time, or for a specified/expected number of operations, in a specified/expected environment under specified/expected operating conditions. Sources for this definition can be found in [Goertzel 2006], appendix A.1.

3. Software safety means the persistence of dependability in the face of accidents or mishaps—that is, unplanned events that result in death, injury, illness, damage to or loss of property, or environmental harm. Sources for this definition can be found in [Goertzel 2006], appendix A.1.

Software that has been developed with security in mind generally reflects the following properties throughout its development life cycle:

- *Predictable execution.* There is justifiable confidence that the software, when executed, functions as intended. The ability of malicious input to alter the execution or outcome in a way favorable to the attacker is significantly reduced or eliminated.
- *Trustworthiness.* The number of exploitable vulnerabilities is intentionally minimized to the greatest extent possible. The goal is no exploitable vulnerabilities.
- *Conformance.* Planned, systematic, and multidisciplinary activities ensure that software components, products, and systems conform to requirements and applicable standards and procedures for specified uses.

These objectives and properties must be interpreted and constrained based on the practical realities that you face, such as what constitutes an adequate level of security, what is most critical to address, and which actions fit within the project's cost and schedule. These are risk management decisions.

In addition to predictable execution, trustworthiness, and conformance, secure software and systems should be as attack resistant, attack tolerant, and attack resilient as possible. To ensure that these criteria are satisfied, software engineers should design software components and systems to recognize both legitimate inputs and known attack patterns in the data or signals they receive from external entities (humans or processes) and reflect this recognition in the developed software to the extent possible and practical.

To achieve attack resilience, a software system should be able to recover from failures that result from successful attacks by resuming operation at or above some predefined minimum acceptable level of service in a timely manner. The system must eventually recover full service at the specified level of performance. These qualities and properties, as well as attack patterns, are described in more detail in Chapter 2, What Makes Software Secure?

1.3.1 The Role of Processes and Practices in Software Security

A number of factors influence how likely software is to be secure. For instance, software vulnerabilities can originate in the processes and practices used in its creation. These sources include the decisions made by software engineers, the flaws they introduce in specification and design, and the faults and other defects they include in developed code, inadvertently or intentionally. Other factors may include the choice of programming languages and development tools used to develop the software, and the configuration and behavior of software components in their development and operational environments. It is increasingly observed, however, that *the most critical difference between secure software and insecure software lies in the nature of the processes and practices used to specify, design, and develop the software* [Goertzel 2006].

The return on investment when security analysis and secure engineering practices are introduced early in the development cycle ranges from 12 percent to 21 percent, with the highest rate of return occurring when the analysis is performed during application design [Berinato 2002; Soo Hoo 2001]. This return on investment occurs because there are fewer security defects in the released product and hence reduced labor costs for fixing defects that are discovered later.

A project that adopts a security-enhanced software development process is adopting a set of practices (such as those described in this book's chapters) that initially should reduce the number of exploitable faults and weaknesses. Over time, as these practices become more codified, they should decrease the likelihood that such vulnerabilities are introduced into the software in the first place. More and more, research results and real-world experiences indicate that *correcting potential vulnerabilities as early as possible in the software development life cycle, mainly through the adoption of security-enhanced processes and practices, is far more cost-effective* than the currently pervasive approach of developing and releasing frequent patches to operational software [Goertzel 2006].

1.4 Threats to Software Security

In information security, the threat—the source of danger—is often a person intending to do harm, using one or more malicious software agents. Software is subject to two general categories of threats:

- *Threats during development* (mainly insider threats). A software engineer can sabotage the software at any point in its development life cycle through intentional exclusions from, inclusions in, or modifications of the requirements specification, the threat models, the design documents, the source code, the assembly and integration framework, the test cases and test results, or the installation and configuration instructions and tools. The secure development practices described in this book are, in part, designed to help reduce the exposure of software to insider threats during its development process. For more information on this aspect, see "Insider Threats in the SDLC" [Cappelli 2006].

* *Threats during operation* (both insider and external threats). Any software system that runs on a network-connected platform is likely to have its vulnerabilities exposed to attackers during its operation. Attacks may take advantage of publicly known but unpatched vulnerabilities, leading to memory corruption, execution of arbitrary exploit scripts, remote code execution, and buffer overflows. Software flaws can be exploited to install spyware, adware, and other malware on users' systems that can lie dormant until it is triggered to execute.[4]

Weaknesses that are most likely to be targeted are those found in the software components' external interfaces, because those interfaces provide the attacker with a direct communication path to the software's vulnerabilities. A number of well-known attacks target software that incorporates interfaces, protocols, design features, or development faults that are well understood and widely publicized as harboring inherent weaknesses. That software includes Web applications (including browser and server components), Web services, database management systems, and operating systems. Misuse (or abuse) cases can help project managers and software engineers see their software from the perspective of an attacker by anticipating and defining unexpected or abnormal behavior through which a software feature could be unintentionally misused or intentionally abused [Hope 2004]. (See Section 3.2.)

Today, most project and IT managers responsible for system operation respond to the increasing number of Internet-based attacks by relying on operational controls at the operating system, network, and database or Web server levels while failing to directly address the insecurity

---

4. See the Common Weakness Enumeration [CWE 2007], for additional examples.

of the application-level software that is being compromised. This approach has two critical shortcomings:

1. The security of the application depends completely on the robustness of operational protections that surround it.
2. Many of the software-based protection mechanisms (controls) can easily be misconfigured or misapplied. Also, they are as likely to contain exploitable vulnerabilities as the application software they are (supposedly) protecting.

The wide publicity about the literally thousands of successful attacks on software accessible from the Internet has merely made the attacker's job easier. Attackers can study numerous reports of security vulnerabilities in a wide range of commercial and open-source software programs and access publicly available exploit scripts. More experienced attackers often develop (and share) sophisticated, targeted attacks that exploit specific vulnerabilities. In addition, the nature of the risks is changing more rapidly than the software can be adapted to counteract those risks, regardless of the software development process and practices used. To be 100 percent effective, defenders must anticipate *all* possible vulnerabilities, while attackers need find only *one* to carry out their attack.

1.5 Sources of Software Insecurity

Most commercial and open-source applications, middleware systems, and operating systems are extremely large and complex. In normal execution, these systems can transition through a vast number of different states. These characteristics make it particularly difficult to develop and operate software that is consistently correct, let alone consistently secure. The unavoidable presence of security threats and risks means that project managers and software engineers need to pay attention to software security even if explicit requirements for it have not been captured in the software's specification.

A large percentage of security weaknesses in software could be avoided if project managers and software engineers were routinely trained in how to address those weaknesses systematically and consistently. Unfortunately, these personnel are seldom taught how to design and develop secure applications and conduct quality assurance to test for insecure coding errors and the use of poor development techniques. They do not generally understand which practices are effective in recognizing and removing faults and defects or in handling vulnerabilities when software is exploited by attackers. They are often unfamiliar with the security implications of certain software requirements (or their absence). Likewise, they rarely learn about the security implications of how software is architected, designed, developed, deployed, and operated. The absence of this knowledge means that security requirements are likely to be inadequate and that the resulting software is likely to deviate from specified (and unspecified) security requirements. In addition, this lack of knowledge prevents the manager and engineer from recognizing and understanding how mistakes can manifest as exploitable weaknesses and vulnerabilities in the software when it becomes operational.

Software—especially networked, application-level software—is most often compromised by exploiting weaknesses that result from the following sources:

- Complexities, inadequacies, and/or changes in the software's processing model (e.g., a Web- or service-oriented architecture model).
- Incorrect assumptions by the engineer, including assumptions about the capabilities, outputs, and behavioral states of the software's execution environment or about expected inputs from external entities (users, software processes).
- Flawed specification or design, or defective implementation of
    - The software's interfaces with external entities. Development mistakes of this type include inadequate (or nonexistent) input validation, error handling, and exception handling.
    - The components of the software's execution environment (from middleware-level and operating-system-level to firmware- and hardware-level components).
- Unintended interactions between software components, including those provided by a third party.

Mistakes are unavoidable. Even if they are avoided during requirements engineering and design (e.g., through the use of formal methods) and development (e.g., through comprehensive code reviews and extensive testing), vulnerabilities may still be introduced into software during its assembly, integration, deployment, and operation. No matter how faithfully a security-enhanced life cycle is followed, as long as software continues to grow in size and complexity, some number of exploitable faults and other weaknesses are sure to exist.

In addition to the issues identified here, Chapter 2, What Makes Software Secure?, discusses a range of principles and practices, the absence of which contribute to software insecurity.

1.6 The Benefits of Detecting Software Security Defects Early[5]

Limited data is available that discusses the return on investment (ROI) of reducing security flaws in source code (refer to Section 1.6.1 for more on this subject). Nevertheless, a number of studies have shown that significant cost benefits are realized through improvements to reduce software defects (including security flaws) throughout the SDLC [Goldenson 2003]. The general software quality case is made in this section, including reasonable arguments for extending this case to include software security defects.

Proactively tackling software security is often under-budgeted and dismissed as a luxury. In an attempt to shorten development schedules or decrease costs, software project managers often reduce the time spent on secure software practices during requirements analysis and design. In addition, they often try to compress the testing schedule or reduce the level of effort. Skimping on software quality[6] is one of the worst decisions an organization that wants to maximize development speed can make; higher quality (in the form of lower defect rates) and reduced development time go hand in hand. Figure 1–3 illustrates the relationship between defect rate and development time.

Projects that achieve lower defect rates typically have shorter schedules. But many organizations currently develop software with defect levels that result in longer schedules than necessary. In the 1970s,

---

5. This material is extracted and adapted from a more extensive article by Steven Lavenhar of Cigital, Inc. [BSI 18]. That article should be consulted for more details and examples. In addition, this article has been adapted with permission from "Software Quality at Top Speed" by Steve McConnell. For the original article, see [McConnell 1996]. While some of the sources cited in this section may seem dated, the problems and trends described persist today.

6. A similar argument could be made for skimping on software security if the schedule and resources under consideration include software production and operations, when security patches are typically applied.

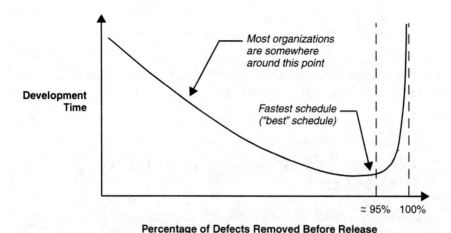

Figure 1–3: *Relationship between defect rate and development time*

studies performed by IBM demonstrated that software products with lower defect counts also had shorter development schedules [Jones 1991]. After surveying more than 4000 software projects, Capers Jones [1994] reported that poor quality was one of the most common reasons for schedule overruns. He also reported that poor quality was a significant factor in approximately 50 percent of all canceled projects. A Software Engineering Institute survey found that more than 60 percent of organizations assessed suffered from inadequate quality assurance [Kitson 1993]. On the curve in Figure 1–3, the organizations that experienced higher numbers of defects are to the left of the "95 percent defect removal" line.

The "95 percent defect removal" line is significant because that level of prerelease defect removal appears to be the point at which projects achieve the shortest schedules for the least effort and with the highest levels of user satisfaction [Jones 1991]. If more than 5 percent of defects are found after a product has been released, then the product is vulnerable to the problems associated with low quality, and the organization takes longer to develop its software than necessary. Projects that are completed with undue haste are particularly vulnerable to short-changing quality assurance at the individual developer level. Any developer who has been pushed to satisfy a specific deadline or ship a product quickly knows how much pressure there can be to cut corners because "we're only three weeks from the deadline." As many as four times the average number of defects are reported for released software products that were developed under excessive schedule pressure. Developers participating in projects that are in schedule trouble often become obsessed with working harder rather than working smarter, which gets them into even deeper schedule trouble.

One aspect of quality assurance that is particularly relevant during rapid development is the presence of error-prone modules—that is, modules that are responsible for a disproportionate number of defects. Barry Boehm reported that 20 percent of the modules in a program are typically responsible for 80 percent of the errors [Boehm 1987]. On its IMS project, IBM found that 57 percent of the errors occurred in 7 percent of the modules [Jones 1991]. Modules with such high defect rates are more expensive and time-consuming to deliver than less error-prone modules. Normal modules cost about $500 to $1000 per function point to develop, whereas error-prone modules cost about $2000 to $4000 per function point to develop [Jones 1994]. Error-prone modules tend to be more complex, less structured, and significantly larger than other modules. They often are developed under excessive schedule pressure and are not fully tested. If development speed is important, then identification and redesign of error-prone modules should be a high priority.

If an organization can prevent defects or detect and remove them early, it can realize significant cost and schedule benefits. Studies have found that reworking defective requirements, design, and code typically accounts for 40 to 50 percent of the total cost of software development [Jones 1986b]. As a rule of thumb, every hour an organization spends on defect prevention reduces repair time for a system in production by three to ten hours. In the worst case, reworking a software requirements problem once the software is in operation typically costs 50 to 200 times what it would take to rework the same problem during the requirements phase [Boehm 1988]. It is easy to understand why this phenomenon occurs. For example, a one-sentence requirement could expand into 5 pages of design diagrams, then into 500 lines of code, then into 15 pages of user documentation and a few dozen test cases. It is cheaper to correct an error in that one-sentence requirement at the time requirements are specified (assuming the error can be identified and corrected) than it is after design, code, user documentation, and test cases have been written. Figure 1–4 illustrates that the longer defects persist, the more expensive they are to correct.

The savings potential from early defect detection is significant: Approximately 60 percent of all defects usually exist by design time

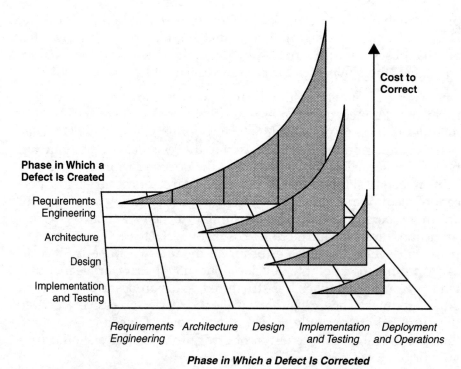

Figure 1–4: *Cost of correcting defects by life-cycle phase*

[Gilb 1988]. A decision early in a project to exclude defect detection amounts to a decision to postpone defect detection and correction until later in the project, when defects become much more expensive and time-consuming to address. That is not a rational decision when time and development dollars are at a premium. According to software quality assurance empirical research, $1 required to resolve an issue during the design phase grows into $60 to $100 required to resolve the same issue after the application has shipped [Soo Hoo 2001].

When a software product has too many defects, including security flaws, vulnerabilities, and bugs, software engineers can end up spending more time correcting these problems than they spent on developing the software in the first place. Project managers can achieve the shortest possible schedules with a higher-quality product by addressing security throughout the SDLC, especially during the early phases, to increase the likelihood that software is more secure the first time.

1.6.1 Making the Business Case for Software Security: Current State[7]

As software project managers and developers, we know that when we want to introduce new approaches in our development processes, we have to make a cost–benefit argument to executive management to convince them that this move offers a business or strategic return on investment. Executives are not interested in investing in new technical approaches simply because they are innovative or exciting. For profit-making organizations, we need to make a case that demonstrates we will improve market share, profit, or other business elements. For other types of organizations, we need to show that we will improve our software in a way that is important—in a way that adds to the organization's prestige, that ensures the safety of troops in the battlefield, and so on.

In the area of software security, we have started to see some evidence of successful ROI or economic arguments for security administrative operations, such as maintaining current levels of patches, establishing organizational entities such as computer security incident response teams (CSIRTs) to support security investment, and so on [Blum 2006, Gordon 2006, Huang 2006, Nagaratnam 2005]. In their article "Tangible ROI through Secure Software Engineering," Kevin Soo Hoo and his colleagues at @stake state the following:

> Findings indicate that significant cost savings and other advantages are achieved when security analysis and secure engineering practices are introduced early in the development cycle. The return on investment ranges from 12 percent to 21 percent, with the highest rate of return occurring when analysis is performed during application design.
>
> Since nearly three-quarters of security-related defects are design issues that could be resolved inexpensively during the early stages, a significant opportunity for cost savings exists when secure software engineering principles are applied during design.

However, except for a few studies [Berinato 2002; Soo Hoo 2001], we have seen little evidence presented to support the idea that investment during software development in software security will result in commensurate benefits across the entire life cycle.

---

7. Updated from [BSI 45].

Results of the Hoover project [Jaquith 2002] provide some case study data that supports the ROI argument for investment in software security early in software development. In his article "The Security of Applications: Not All Are Created Equal," Jaquith says that "the best-designed e-business applications have one-quarter as many security defects as the worst. By making the right investments in application security, companies can out-perform their peers—and reduce risk by 80 percent."

In their article "Impact of Software Vulnerability Announcements on the Market Value of Software Vendors: An Empirical Investigation," the authors state that "On average, a vendor loses around 0.6 percent value in stock price when a vulnerability is reported. This is equivalent to a loss in market capitalization values of $0.86 billion per vulnerability announcement." The purpose of the study described in this article is "to measure vendors' incentive to develop secure software" [Telang 2004].

We believe that in the future Microsoft may well publish data reflecting the results of using its Security Development Lifecycle [Howard 2006, 2007]. We would also refer readers to the business context discussion in chapter 2 and the business climate discussion in chapter 10 of McGraw's recent book [McGraw 2006] for ideas.

1.7 Managing Secure Software Development

The previous section put forth useful arguments and identified emerging evidence for the value of detecting software security defects as early in the SDLC as possible. We now turn our attention to some of the key project management and software engineering practices to aid in accomplishing this goal. These are introduced here and covered in greater detail in subsequent chapters of this book.

1.7.1 Which Security Strategy Questions Should I Ask?

Achieving an adequate level of software security means more than complying with regulations or implementing commonly accepted best practices. You and your organization must determine your own definition of "adequate." The range of actions you must take to reduce software security risk to an acceptable level depends on what the product, service, or system you are building needs to protect and what it needs to prevent and manage.

Consider the following questions from an enterprise perspective. Answers to these questions aid in understanding security risks to achieving project goals and objectives.

- What is the value we must protect?
- To sustain this value, which assets must be protected? Why must they be protected? What happens if they're not protected?
- What potential adverse conditions and consequences must be prevented and managed? At what cost? How much disruption can we stand before we take action?
- How do we determine and effectively manage residual risk (the risk remaining after mitigation actions are taken)?
- How do we integrate our answers to these questions into an effective, implementable, enforceable security strategy and plan?

Clearly, an organization cannot protect and prevent everything. Interaction with key stakeholders is essential to determine the project's risk tolerance and its resilience if the risk is realized. In effect, security in the context of risk management involves determining what could go wrong, how likely such events are to occur, what impact they will have if they do occur, and which actions might mitigate or minimize both the likelihood and the impact of each event to an acceptable level.

The answers to these questions can help you determine how much to invest, where to invest, and how fast to invest in an effort to mitigate software security risk. In the absence of answers to these questions (and a process for periodically reviewing and updating them), you (and your business leaders) will find it difficult to define and deploy an effective security strategy and, therefore, may be unable to effectively govern and manage enterprise, information, and software security.[8]

The next section presents a practical way to incorporate a reasoned security strategy into your development process. The framework

---

8. Refer to *Managing Information Security Risks: The OCTAVE Approach* [Alberts 2003] for more information on managing information security risk; "An Introduction to Factor Analysis of Information Risk (FAIR)" [Jones 2005] for more information on managing information risk; and "Risk Management Approaches to Protection" [NIAC 2005] for a description of risk management approaches for national critical infrastructures.

described is a condensed version of the Cigital Risk Management Framework, a mature process that has been applied in the field for almost ten years. It is designed to manage software-induced business risks. Through the application of five simple activities (further detailed in Section 7.4.2), analysts can use their own technical expertise, relevant tools, and technologies to carry out a reasonable risk management approach.

1.7.2 A Risk Management Framework for Software Security[9]

A necessary part of any approach to ensuring adequate software security is the definition and use of a continuous risk management process. Software security risk includes risks found in the outputs and results produced by each life-cycle phase during assurance activities, risks introduced by insufficient processes, and personnel-related risks. The risk management framework (RMF) introduced here and expanded in Chapter 7 can be used to implement a high-level, consistent, iterative risk analysis that is deeply integrated throughout the SDLC.

Figure 1–5 shows the RMF as a closed-loop process with five activity stages. Throughout the application of the RMF, measurement and reporting activities occur. These activities focus on tracking, displaying, and understanding progress regarding software risk.

1.7.3 Software Security Practices in the Development Life Cycle

Managers and software engineers should treat all software faults and weaknesses as potentially exploitable. Reducing exploitable weaknesses begins with the specification of software security requirements, along with considering requirements that may have been overlooked (see Chapter 3, Requirements Engineering for Secure Software). Software that includes security requirements (such as security constraints on process behaviors and the handling of inputs, and resistance to and tolerance of intentional failures) is more likely to be engineered to remain dependable and secure in the face of an attack. In addition, exercising misuse/abuse cases that anticipate abnormal and unexpected behavior can aid in gaining a better understanding of how to create secure and reliable software (see Section 3.2).

---

9. This material is extracted and adapted from a more extensive article by Gary McGraw, Cigital, Inc. [BSI 33].

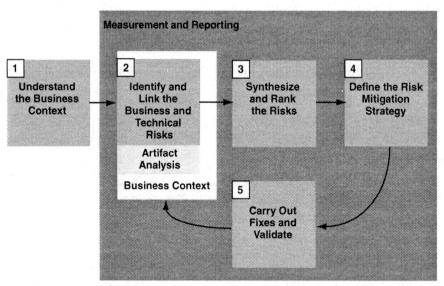

Figure 1–5: *A software security risk management framework*

Developing software from the beginning with security in mind is more effective by orders of magnitude than trying to validate, through testing and verification, that the software is secure. For example, attempting to demonstrate that an implemented system will *never* accept an unsafe input (that is, proving a negative) is impossible. You can prove, however, using approaches such as formal methods and function abstraction, that the software you are designing will never accept an unsafe input. In addition, it is easier to design and implement the system so that input validation routines check *every* input that the software receives against a set of predefined constraints. Testing the input validation function to demonstrate that it is consistently invoked and correctly performed every time input enters the system is then included in the system's functional testing.

Analysis and modeling can serve to better protect your software against the more subtle, complex attack patterns involving externally forced sequences of interactions among components or processes that were never intended to interact during normal software execution. Analysis and modeling can help you determine how to strengthen the security of the software's interfaces with external entities and increase its tolerance of all faults. Methods in support of analysis and modeling during each life-cycle phase such as attack patterns, misuse and abuse cases, and architectural risk analysis are described in subsequent chapters of this book.

If your development organization's time and resource constraints prevent secure development practices from being applied to the entire software system, you can use the results of a business-driven risk assessment (as introduced earlier in this chapter and further detailed in Section 7.4.2) to determine which software components should be given highest priority.

A security-enhanced life-cycle process should (at least to some extent) compensate for security inadequacies in the software's requirements by adding risk-driven practices and checks for the adequacy of those practices during all software life-cycle phases. Figure 1–6 depicts one example of how to incorporate security into the SDLC using the concept of touchpoints [McGraw 2006; Taylor 2005]. Software security best practices (touchpoints shown as arrows) are applied to a set of software artifacts (the boxes) that are created during the software development process. The intent of this particular approach is that it is

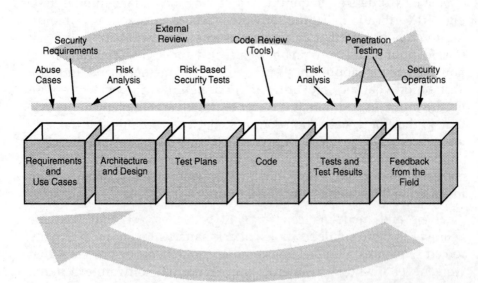

Figure 1–6: *Software development life cycle with defined security touchpoints [McGraw 2006]*

process neutral and, therefore, can be used with a wide range of software development processes (e.g., waterfall, agile, spiral, Capability Maturity Model Integration [CMMI]).

Security controls in the software's life cycle should not be limited to the requirements, design, code, and test phases. It is important to continue performing code reviews, security tests, strict configuration control, and quality assurance during deployment and operations to ensure that updates and patches do not add security weaknesses or malicious logic to production software.[10] Additional considerations for project managers, including the effect of software security requirements on project scope, project plans, estimating resources, and product and process measures, are detailed in Chapter 7.

1.8 Summary

It is a fact of life that software faults, defects, and other weaknesses affect the ability of software to function securely. These vulnerabilities can be exploited to violate software's security properties and force the software into an insecure, exploitable state. Dealing with this possibility is a particularly daunting challenge given the ubiquitous connectivity and explosive growth and complexity of software-based systems.

Adopting a security-enhanced software development process that includes secure development practices will reduce the number of exploitable faults and weaknesses in the deployed software. Correcting potential vulnerabilities as early as possible in the SDLC, mainly through the adoption of security-enhanced processes and practices, is far more cost-effective than attempting to diagnose and correct such problems after the system goes into production. It just makes good sense.

Thus, the goals of using secure software practices are as follows:

- Exploitable faults and other weaknesses are eliminated to the greatest extent possible by well-intentioned engineers.
- The likelihood is greatly reduced or eliminated that malicious engineers can intentionally implant exploitable faults and weaknesses, malicious logic, or backdoors into the software.

---

10. See the Build Security In Deployment & Operations content area for more information [BSI 01].

- The software is attack resistant, attack tolerant, and attack resilient to the extent possible and practical in support of fulfilling the organization's mission.

To ensure that software and systems meet their security requirements throughout the development life cycle, review, select, and tailor guidance from this book, the BSI Web site, and the sources cited throughout this book as part of normal project management activities.

Chapter 2

What Makes Software Secure?

2.1 Introduction   Ⓔ Ⓜ Ⓛ

To answer the question, "What makes software secure?" it is important to understand the meaning of software security in the broader context of software assurance.

As described in Chapter 1, software assurance is the domain of working toward software that exhibits the following qualities:

- Trustworthiness, whereby no exploitable vulnerabilities or weaknesses exist, either of malicious or unintentional origin

- Predictable execution, whereby there is justifiable confidence that the software, when executed, functions as intended

- Conformance, whereby a planned and systematic set of multidisciplinary activities ensure that software processes and products conform to their requirements, standards, and procedures

We will focus primarily on the dimension of trustworthiness—that is, which properties can be identified, influenced, and asserted to characterize the trustworthiness, and thereby the security, of software. To be effective, predictable execution must be interpreted with an appropriately broader brush than is typically applied. Predictable execution must imply not only that software effectively does what it is expected to do, but also that it is robust under attack and does not do anything that it is *not* expected to do. This may seem to some to be splitting hairs, but it is an important distinction between what makes for high-quality software versus what makes for secure software.

To determine and influence the trustworthiness of software, it is necessary to define the properties that characterize secure software, identify mechanisms to influence these properties, and leverage structures and tools for asserting the presence or absence of these properties in communication surrounding the security of software.

This chapter draws on a diverse set of existing knowledge to present solutions to these challenges and provide you with resources to explore for more in-depth coverage of individual topics.

2.2 Defining Properties of Secure Software[1] 🄴🄼🄻🄛

Before we can determine the security characteristics of software and look for ways to effectively measure and improve them, we must first define the properties by which these characteristics can be described. These properties consist of (1) a set of core properties whose presence (or absence) are the ground truth that makes software secure (or not) and (2) a set of influential properties that do not directly make software secure but do make it possible to characterize how secure software is.

2.2.1 Core Properties of Secure Software

Several fundamental properties may be seen as attributes of security as a software property, as shown in Figure 2–1:

• *Confidentiality.* The software must ensure that any of its characteristics (including its relationships with its execution environment and its users), its managed assets, and/or its content are obscured or hidden from *unauthorized* entities. This remains appropriate for cases such as open-source software; its characteristics and content are available to the public (authorized entities in this case), yet it still must maintain confidentiality of its managed assets.

---

1. Much of this section is excerpted from *Security in the Software Lifecycle* [Goertzel 2006].

- *Integrity.* The software and its managed assets must be resistant and resilient to subversion. Subversion is achieved through unauthorized modifications to the software code, managed assets, configuration, or behavior by authorized entities, or any modifications by unauthorized entities. Such modifications may include overwriting, corruption, tampering, destruction, insertion of unintended (including malicious) logic, or deletion. Integrity must be preserved both during the software's development and during its execution.

- *Availability.* The software must be operational and accessible to its intended, authorized users (humans and processes) whenever it is needed. At the same time, its functionality and privileges must be inaccessible to unauthorized users (humans and processes) at all times.

Two additional properties commonly associated with human users are required in software entities that act as users (e.g., proxy agents, Web services, peer processes):

- *Accountability.* All security-relevant actions of the software-as-user must be recorded and tracked, with attribution of responsibility. This tracking must be possible both while and after the recorded actions occur. The audit-related language in the security policy for the software system should indicate which actions are considered "security relevant."

- *Non-repudiation.* This property pertains to the ability to prevent the software-as-user from disproving or denying responsibility for actions it has performed. It ensures that the accountability property cannot be subverted or circumvented.

These core properties are most typically used to describe network security. However, their definitions have been modified here slightly to map these still valid concepts to the software security domain. The effects of a security breach in software can, therefore, be described in terms of the effects on these core properties. A successful SQL injection attack on an application to extract personally identifiable information from its database would be a violation of its confidentiality property. A successful cross-site scripting (XSS) attack against a Web application could result in a violation of both its integrity and availability properties. And a successful buffer overflow[2] attack that injects malicious

---

2. See the glossary for definitions of SQL injection, cross-site scripting, and buffer overflow.

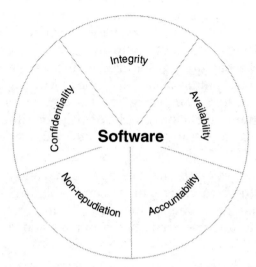

Figure 2–1: *Core security properties of secure software*

code in an attempt to steal user account information and then alter logs to cover its tracks would be a violation of all five core security properties. While many other important characteristics of software have implications for its security, their relevance can typically be described and communicated in terms of how they affect these core properties.

2.2.2 Influential Properties of Secure Software

Some properties of software, although they do not directly make software secure, nevertheless make it possible to characterize how secure software is (Figure 2–2):

- Dependability
- Correctness
- Predictability
- Reliability
- Safety

These influential properties are further influenced by the size, complexity, and traceability of the software. Much of the activity of software security engineering focuses on addressing these properties and thus targets the core security properties themselves.

Figure 2–2: *Influential properties of secure software*

Dependability and Security

In simplest terms, dependability is the property of software that ensures that the software always operates as intended. It is not surprising that security as a property of software and dependability as a property of software share a number of subordinate properties (or attributes). The most obvious, to security practitioners, are availability and integrity. However, according to Algirdas Avizienis et al. in "Basic Concepts and Taxonomy of Dependable and Secure Computing," a number of other properties are shared by dependability and security, including reliability, safety, survivability, maintainability, and fault tolerance [Avizienis 2004].

To better understand the relationship between security and dependability, consider the nature of risk to security and, by extension, dependability. A variety of factors affect the defects and weaknesses that lead to increased risk related to the security or dependability of software. But are they human-made or environmental? Are they intentional or unintentional? If they are intentional, are they malicious? Nonmalicious intentional weaknesses often result from bad judgment. For example, a software engineer may make a tradeoff between performance and usability on the one hand and security on the other hand that results in a design decision that includes weaknesses. While many defects and weaknesses have the ability to affect both the security and the dependability of software, it is typically the intentionality, the exploitability, and the resultant impact if exploited that determine whether a defect or weakness actually constitutes a vulnerability leading to security risk.

Note that while dependability directly implies the core properties of integrity and availability, it does not necessarily imply confidentiality, accountability, or non-repudiation.

Correctness and Security

From the standpoint of quality, correctness is a critical attribute of software that should be consistently demonstrated under all anticipated operating conditions. Security requires that the attribute of correctness be maintained under unanticipated conditions as well. One of the mechanisms most commonly used to attack the security of software seeks to cause the software's correctness to be violated by forcing it into unanticipated operating conditions, often through unexpected input or exploitation of environmental assumptions.

Some advocates for secure software engineering have suggested that good software engineering is all that is needed to ensure that the software produced will be free of exploitable faults and other weaknesses. There is a flaw in this thinking—namely, good software engineering typically fails to proactively consider the behavior of the software under unanticipated conditions. These unanticipated conditions are typically determined to be out of scope as part of the requirements process. Correctness under anticipated conditions (as it is typically interpreted) is not enough to ensure that the software is secure, because the conditions that surround the software when it comes under attack are very likely to be unanticipated. Most software specifications do not include explicit requirements for the software's functions to continue operating correctly under unanticipated conditions. Software engineering that focuses only on achieving correctness under anticipated conditions, therefore, does not ensure that the software will remain correct under unanticipated conditions.

If explicit requirements for secure behavior are not specified, then requirements-driven engineering, which is used frequently to increase the correctness of software, will do nothing to ensure that correct software is also secure. In requirements-driven engineering, correctness is assured by verifying that the software operates in strict accordance with its specified requirements. If the requirements are deficient, the software still may strictly be deemed correct as long as it satisfies those requirements that do exist.

The requirements specified for the majority of software are limited to functional, interoperability, and performance requirements. Determining that such requirements have been satisfied will do nothing to ensure that the software will also behave securely even when it operates correctly. Unless a requirement exists for the software to contain a particular security property or attribute, verifying correctness will indicate nothing about security. A property or attribute that is not captured as a requirement will not be the subject of any verification effort that seeks to discover whether the software contains that function or property.

Security requirements that define software's expected behavior as adhering to a desired security property are best elicited through a documented process, such as the use of misuse/abuse cases (see Section 3.2). Misuse/abuse cases are descriptive statements of the undesired, nonstandard conditions that the software is likely to face during its operation from either unintentional misuse or intentional and malicious misuse/abuse. Misuse/abuse cases are effectively captured by analyzing common approaches to attack that the software is likely to face. Attack patterns, as discussed later in this chapter, are a physical representation of these common approaches to attack. Misuse/abuse cases, when explicitly captured as part of the requirements process, provide a measurable benchmark against which to assess the completeness and quality of the defined security requirements to achieve the desired security properties in the face of attack and misuse.

It is much easier to specify and satisfy functional requirements stated in positive terms ("The software will perform such-and-such a function"). Security properties and attributes, however, are often nonfunctional ("This process must be non-bypassable"). Even "positively" stated requirements may reflect inherently negative concerns. For example, the requirement "If the software cannot handle a fault, the software must release all of its resources and then terminate execution" is, in fact, just a more positive way of stating the requirement that "A crash must not leave the software in an insecure state."

Moreover, it is possible to specify requirements for functions, interactions, and performance attributes that result in insecure software behavior. By the same token, it is possible to implement software that deviates from its functional, interoperability, and performance requirements (that is, software that is incorrect only from a requirements engineering perspective) without that software actually behaving insecurely.

Software that executes correctly under anticipated conditions cannot be considered secure when it is used in an operating environment characterized by unanticipated conditions that lead to unpredictable behavior. However, it may be possible to consider software that is *in*correct but completely predictable to be secure *if* the incorrect portions of the software are not manifested as vulnerabilities. Thus it does not follow that correctness will necessarily help assure security, or that incorrectness will necessarily become manifest as insecurity. Nevertheless, correctness in software is just as important a property as security. Neither property should ever have to be achieved at the expense of the other.

A number of vulnerabilities in software that can be exploited by attackers can be avoided by engineering for correctness. By reducing the total number of defects in software, the subset of those defects that are exploitable (that is, are vulnerabilities) will be coincidentally reduced. However, some complex vulnerabilities may result from a sequence or combination of interactions among individual components; each interaction may be perfectly correct yet, when combined with other interactions, may result in incorrectness and vulnerability. Engineering for correctness will not eliminate such complex vulnerabilities.

For the purposes of requirements-driven engineering, no requirement for a software function, interface, performance attribute, or any other attribute of the software should ever be deemed "correct" if that requirement can only be satisfied in a way that allows the software to behave insecurely or that makes it impossible to determine or predict whether the software will behave securely. Instead, every requirement should be specified in a way that ensures that the software will always and only behave securely when the requirement is satisfied.

"Small" Faults, Big Consequences

There is a conventional wisdom espoused by many software engineers that says vulnerabilities which fall within a specified range of speculated impact ("size") can be tolerated and allowed to remain in the software. This belief is based on the underlying assumption that small faults have small consequences. In terms of defects with security implications, however, this conventional wisdom is wrong. Nancy Leveson suggests that vulnerabilities in large software-intensive systems with significant human interaction will increasingly result from multiple minor defects, each insignificant by itself, thereby collectively placing the system into a vulnerable state [Leveson 2004].

Consider a classic stack-smashing attack that relies on a combination of multiple "small" defects that individually may have only minor impact, yet together represent significant vulnerability [Aleph One 1996]. An input function writes data to a buffer without first performing a bounds check on the data. This action occurs in a program that runs with root privilege. If an attacker submits a very long string of input data that includes both malicious code and a return address pointer to that code, because the program does not do bounds checking, the input will be accepted by the program and will overflow the stack buffer that receives it. This outcome will allow the malicious code to be loaded onto the program's execution stack and overwrite the subroutine return address so that it points to that malicious code. When the subroutine terminates, the program will jump to the malicious code, which will be executed, operating with root privilege. This particular malicious code is written to call the system shell, enabling the attacker to take control of the system. (Even if the original program had not operated with root privileges, the malicious code may have contained a privilege escalation exploit to gain those privileges.)

Obviously, when considering software security, the *perceived size* of a vulnerability is not a reliable predictor of the magnitude of that vulnerability *impact*. For this reason, the risks of every known vulnerability—regardless of whether it is detected during design review, implementation, or testing—should be explicitly analyzed and mitigated or accepted by authoritative persons in the development organization. Assumption is a primary root of insecurity anywhere, but especially so in software.

For high-assurance systems, there is no justification for tolerating known vulnerabilities. True software security is achievable only when all known aspects of the software are understood and verified to be predictably correct. This includes verifying the correctness of the software's behavior under a wide variety of conditions, including hostile conditions. As a consequence, software testing needs to include observing the software's behavior under the following circumstances:

- Attacks are launched against the software itself
- The software's inputs or outputs (e.g., data files, arguments, signals) are compromised
- The software's interfaces to other entities are compromised
- The software's execution environment is attacked

Predictability and Security

Predictability means that the software's functionality, properties, and behaviors will always be what they are expected to be as long as the conditions under which the software operates (i.e., its environment, the inputs it receives) are also predictable. For dependable software, this means the software will never deviate from correct operation under anticipated conditions.

Software security extends predictability to the software's operation under unanticipated conditions—specifically, under conditions in which attackers attempt to exploit faults in the software or its environment. In such circumstances, it is important to have confidence in precisely how the software will behave when faced with misuse or attack. The best way to ensure predictability of software under unanticipated conditions is to minimize the presence of vulnerabilities and other weaknesses, to prevent the insertion of malicious logic, and to isolate the software to the greatest extent possible from unanticipated environmental conditions.

Reliability, Safety, and Security[3]

The focus of reliability for software is on preserving predictable, correct execution despite the presence of unintentional defects and other weaknesses and unpredictable environment state changes. Software that is highly reliable is often referred to as high-confidence software (implying that a high level of assurance of that reliability exists) or fault-tolerant software (implying that fault tolerance techniques were used to achieve the high level of reliability).

---

3. This section's use of the term *reliability* is consistent with the definition of the term found in IEEE Standard 610.12-1990, *Standard Glossary of Software Engineering Terminology* [IEEE 1990], which defines reliability as "the ability of a system or component to perform its required functions under stated conditions for a specified period of time." Nevertheless, it is more closely aligned with the definition of the term in the National Research Council's study *Trust in Cyberspace* [Schneider 1999], which defines reliability as "the capability of a computer, or information or telecommunications system, to perform consistently and precisely according to its specifications and design requirements, and to do so with high confidence."

Software safety depends on reliability and typically has very real and significant implications if the property is not met. The consequences, if reliability is not preserved in a safety-critical system, can be catastrophic: Human life may be lost, or the sustainability of the environment may be compromised.

Software security extends the requirements of reliability and safety to the need to preserve predictable, correct execution even in the face of *malicious* attacks on defects or weaknesses and environmental state changes. It is this *maliciousness* that makes the requirements of software security somewhat different from the requirements of safety and reliability. Failures in a reliability or safety context are expected to be random and unpredictable. Failures in a security context, by contrast, result from human effort (direct, or through malicious code). Attackers tend to be persistent, and once they successfully exploit a vulnerability, they tend to continue exploiting that vulnerability on other systems as long as the vulnerability is present and the outcome of the attack remains satisfactory.

Until recently, many software reliability and safety practitioners have not concerned themselves with software security issues. Indeed, the two domains have traditionally been viewed as separate and distinct. The truth is that safety, as a property of software, is directly dependent on security properties such as dependability. A failure in the security of software, especially one that is intentional and malicious, can directly change the operational and environmental presumptions on which safety is based, thereby compromising any possible assurance in its safety properties. Any work toward assuring the safety of software that does not take security properties into consideration is incomplete and unreliable.

Size, Complexity, Traceability, and Security

Software that satisfies its requirements through simple functions that are implemented in the smallest amount of code that is practical, with process flows and data flows that are easily followed, will be easier to comprehend and maintain. The fewer the dependencies in the software, the easier it will be to implement effective failure detection and to reduce the *attack surface*.[4]

---

4. A system's attack surface is the set of ways in which an attacker can enter and potentially cause damage to the system.

Size and complexity should be not only properties of the software's implementation, but also properties of its design, as they will make it easier for reviewers to discover design flaws that could be manifested as exploitable weaknesses in the implementation. Traceability will enable the same reviewers to ensure that the design satisfies the specified security requirements and that the implementation does not deviate from the secure design. Moreover, traceability provides a firm basis on which to define security test cases.

2.3 How to Influence the Security Properties of Software

Once you understand the properties that determine the security of software, the challenge becomes acting effectively to influence those properties in a positive way. The ability of a software development team to manipulate the security properties of software resolves to a balance between engaging in defensive action and thinking like an attacker. The primary perspective is that of a defender, where the team works to build into the software appropriate security features and characteristics to make the software more resistant to attack and to minimize the inherent weaknesses in the software that may make it more vulnerable to attack. The balancing perspective is that of the attacker, where the team strives to understand the exact nature of the threat that the software is likely to face so as to focus defensive efforts on areas of highest risk. These two perspectives, working in combination, guide the actions taken to make software more secure.

Taking action to address these perspectives requires knowledge resources (prescriptive, diagnostic, and historical) covering the various aspects of software assurance combined with security best practices called *touchpoints* integrated throughout the SDLC; all of this must then be deployed under an umbrella of applied risk management [McGraw 2006]. For the discussion here, we use these definitions for best practices and touchpoints:

> Best practices are the most efficient (least amount of effort) and effective (best results) way of accomplishing a task,

> based on repeatable procedures that have proven themselves over time for large numbers of people.[5]
>
> Touchpoints are lightweight software security best practice activities that are applied to various software artifacts. [McGraw 2006]

Project managers who are concerned with the security of the software they are developing must proactively select the appropriate practices and knowledge to ensure that both the defensive and attacker's perspectives are appropriately represented and understood by the development team. This chapter, and the rest of this book, presents several of the most effective options (though they vary in their level of adoption) for knowledge resources and security practices and guidance on how to select and use them.

2.3.1 The Defensive Perspective

Assuming the defensive perspective involves looking at the software from the inside out. It requires analyzing the software for vulnerabilities and opportunities for the security of the software to be compromised through inadvertent misuse and, more importantly, through malicious attack and abuse. Doing so requires the software development team to perform the following steps:

- Address expected issues through the application of appropriate security architecture and features
- Address unexpected issues through the avoidance, removal, and mitigation of weaknesses that could lead to security vulnerabilities
- Continually strive to improve and strengthen the attack resistance, tolerance, and resilience of the software in everything they do

Addressing the Expected: Security Architecture and Features

When most people think of making software secure, they think in terms of the architecture and functionality of security features. Security features and functionality alone are insufficient to ensure software security, but they are a necessary facet to consider. As shown in Figure 2–3, security features aim to address expected security issues with software such as authentication, authorization, access control,

---

5. http://en.wikipedia.org/wiki/Best_practice

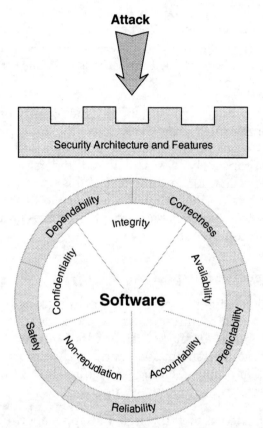

Figure 2–3: *Addressing expected issues with security architecture and features*

permissions, privileges, and cryptography. Security architecture is the overall framework that holds these security functionalities together and provides the set of interfaces that integrates them with the broader software architecture.[6]

Without security architecture and features, adequate levels of confidentiality, integrity, accountability, and non-repudiation may be unattainable. However, fully addressing these properties (as well as availability) requires the development team not only to provide

---

6. In-depth discussions of and best practices for these very technical considerations can be found in other books and forums. This book focuses on providing guidance to the software project manager on software security engineering practices and knowledge that will help improve the security assurance of the software being developed regardless of its functionality or features.

functionality to manage the security behavior of the software, but also to ensure that the functionality and architecture of the software do not contain weaknesses that could render the software vulnerable to attack in potentially unexpected ways.

Addressing the Unexpected: Avoiding, Removing, and Mitigating Weaknesses

Many activities and practices are available across the life cycle of software systems that can help reduce and mitigate weaknesses present in software. These activities and practices can typically be categorized into two approaches: application defense and software security.

Application Defense

Employing practices focused at detecting and mitigating weaknesses in software systems after they are deployed is often referred to as *application defense* (see Figure 2–4), which in many cases is mislabeled as *application security*. Application defense techniques typically focus on the following issues:

- Establishing a protective boundary around the application that enforces rules defining valid input or recognizes and either blocks or filters input that contains recognized patterns of attack
- Constraining the extent and impact of damage that might result from the exploit of a vulnerability in the application
- Discovering points of vulnerability in the implemented application through black-box testing so as to help developers and administrators identify necessary countermeasures (see the description of black-box testing in Section 5.5.4)

Reactive application defense measures are often similar to the techniques and tools used for securing networks, operating systems, and middleware services. They include things such as vulnerability scanners, intrusion detection tools, and firewalls or security gateways. Often, these measures are intended to strengthen the boundaries *around* the application rather than address the actual vulnerabilities *inside* the application.

In some cases, application defense measures are applied as stopgaps for from-scratch application software until a security patch or new version is released. In other cases, these measures provide ongoing defense in depth to counter vulnerabilities in the application. In software systems

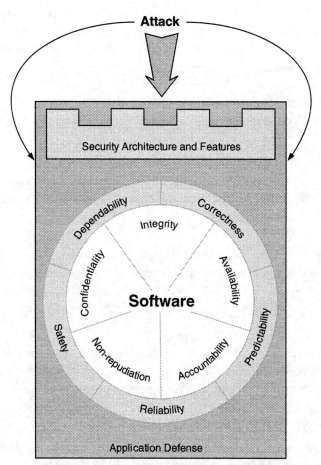

Figure 2–4: *Addressing the unexpected through application defense*

that include acquired or reused (commercial, government off-the-shelf, open-source, shareware, freeware, or legacy) binary components, application defense techniques and tools may be the only cost-effective countermeasures to mitigate vulnerabilities in those components.

Application defense as typically practiced today incorporates few, if any, techniques and tools that will aid the developer in producing software that has very few vulnerabilities in the first place. These practices often provide valuable guidance in identifying and mitigating more obvious security vulnerabilities, especially those associated with the deployment configuration and environment. Most serious weaknesses, including both design flaws and implementation bugs, are not typically detectable in this manner, however; when they are, they are usually much more expensive to remedy so late in the life cycle. A software security perspective, by contrast, not only incorporates protective, post-implementation techniques, but also addresses the need to specify, design, and implement an application with a minimal attack surface.

The point to take away is that a disciplined, repeatable, security-enhanced development process should be instituted that ensures application defense measures are used only because they are determined in the design process to be the best approach to solving a software security problem, not because they are the only possible approach after the software is deployed.

That said, using secure systems engineering approaches can be helpful to further protect securely engineered software in deployment by reducing its exposure to threats in various operational environments. These measures may be particularly useful for reducing risk for software, such as commercial and open-source software, that is intended to be deployed in a wide variety of threat environments and operational contexts.

Software Security

While application defense takes a somewhat after-the-fact approach, practices associated with "software security" and its role in secure software engineering processes focus on preventing weaknesses from entering the software in the first place or, if that is unavoidable, at least removing them as early in the life cycle as possible and before the software is deployed (see Figure 2–5). These weaknesses, whether unintentional or maliciously inserted, can enter the software at any point in the development process through inadequate or incorrect requirements; ambiguous, incomplete, unstable, or improper architecture and design; implementation errors; incomplete or inappropriate testing; or insecure configuration and deployment decisions.

Contrary to a common misconception, software security cannot be the sole responsibility of the developers who are writing code, but rather requires the involvement of the entire development team and the organization supporting it. Luckily, a wide variety of security-focused practices are available to software project managers and their development teams that can be seamlessly integrated throughout any typical software engineering SDLC. Among other things, these practices include security requirements engineering with misuse/abuse cases,

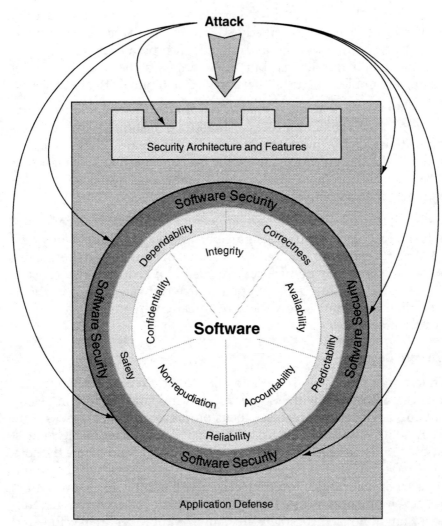

Figure 2–5: *Addressing the unexpected through software security*

architectural risk analysis, secure code review, risk-based security testing, and software penetration testing. These practices of software security, which are collectively referred to as "building security in," are the
primary focus of this book. The chapters that follow outline software
security practices and knowledge associated with various phases of
the SDLC that are of value to development teams looking to minimize
weaknesses and thereby build more secure software that is resistant,
tolerant, and resilient to attack.

Attack Resistance, Attack Tolerance, and Attack Resilience

The ultimate goal of defensive software security efforts can be most clearly seen in their ability to maintain security properties in the face of motivated and intentional attempts to subvert them. The ability of software to function in the face of attack can be broken down into three primary characteristics: attack resistance, attack tolerance, and attack resilience.

- *Attack resistance* is the ability of the software to prevent the capability of an attacker to execute an attack against it. The most critical of the three characteristics, it is nevertheless often the most difficult to achieve, as it involves minimizing exploitable weaknesses at all levels of abstraction, from architecture through detailed implementation and deployment. Indeed, sometimes attack resistance is impossible to fully achieve.
- *Attack tolerance* is the ability of the software to "tolerate" the errors and failure that result from successful attacks and, in effect, to continue to operate as if the attacks had not occurred.
- *Attack resilience* is the ability of the software to isolate, contain, and limit the damage resulting from any failures caused by attack-triggered faults that the software was unable to resist or tolerate and to recover as quickly as possible from those failures.[7]

Attack tolerance and attack resilience are often a result of effective architectural and design decisions rather than implementation wizardry. Software that can achieve attack resistance, attack tolerance, and attack resilience is implicitly more capable of maintaining its core security properties.

2.3.2 The Attacker's Perspective[8]

Assuming the attacker's perspective involves looking at the software from the outside in. It requires thinking like attackers think, and analyzing and understanding the software the way they would to attack it. Through better understanding of how the software is likely to be

---

7. See Bruce Schneier's discussion of resilient systems in chapter 9 of his book *Beyond Fear* [Schneier 2003].

8. The majority of the content provided in this section is adapted from the Attack Patterns content area on the Build Security In Web site authored by Sean Barnum and Amit Sethi of Cigital, Inc. [BSI 02]. For deeper understanding, see the full and more detailed content available there.

attacked, the software development team can better harden and secure it against attack.

The Attacker's Advantage

The primary challenge in building secure software is that it is much easier to find vulnerabilities in software than it is to make software secure. As an analogy, consider a bank vault. Its designers need to ensure that it is safe against many different types of attacks, not just the seemingly obvious ones. It must generally be safe against mechanical attacks (e.g., using bulldozers), explosives, and safecracking, to name a few, while still maintaining usability (e.g., allowing authorized personnel to enter, having sufficient ventilation and lighting). This is clearly not a trivial task. However, the attacker may simply need to find one exploitable vulnerability to achieve his or her goal of entering the vault. The attacker may try to access the vault through various potential means, including through the main entrance by cracking the safe combination, through the ceiling, by digging underground, by entering through the ventilation system, by bribing an authorized employee to open the vault, or by creating a small fire in the bank while the vault is open to cause all employees to flee in panic. Given these realities, it is evident that building and maintaining bank vault security is typically much more difficult than breaking into a vault.

Building secure software has similar issues, but the problem is exacerbated by the virtual (rather than physical) nature of software. With many systems, the attacker may actually possess the software (obtaining a local copy to attack is often trivial) or could attack it from anywhere in the world through networks. Given attackers' ability to attack remotely and without physical access, vulnerabilities become much more widely exposed to attack. Audit trails may not be sufficient to catch attackers after an attack takes place, because attackers could leverage the anonymity of an unsuspecting user's wireless network or public computers to launch attacks.

The attackers' advantage is further strengthened by the fact that attackers have been learning how to exploit software for several decades, but the general software development community has not kept up-to-date with the knowledge that attackers have gained. This knowledge gap is also evident in the difference of perspective evident between attackers, with their cynical deconstructive view, and developers, with their happy-go-lucky "You're not supposed to do that" view. The problem continues to grow in part because of the traditional fear that teaching how software is exploited could actually reduce the security of software by helping the existing attackers and even potentially creating new ones. In the past, the software development community hoped that obscurity would keep the number of attackers relatively small. This assumption has been shown to be a poor one, and some elements of the community are now beginning to look for more effective methods of addressing this problem.

To identify and mitigate vulnerabilities in software, the development community needs more than just good software engineering and analytical practices, a solid grasp of software security features, and a powerful set of tools. All of these things are necessary but not sufficient. To be effective, the community needs to think creatively and to have a firm grasp of the attacker's perspective and the approaches used to exploit software [Hoglund 2004; Koizol 2004].

Finding a Way to Represent the Attacker's Perspective

For software development teams to take advantage of the attacker's perspective in building security into software, there first must be a mechanism for capturing and communicating this perspective from knowledgeable experts and communicating it to teams. A powerful resource for providing such a mechanism is the *attack pattern*.

Design patterns are a familiar tool used by the software development community to help solve recurring problems encountered during software development [Alexander 1964, 1977, 1979; Gamma 1995]. These patterns attempt to tackle head-on the thorny problems of secure, stable, and effective software architecture and design. Since the introduction of design patterns, the pattern construct has been applied to many other areas of software development. One of these areas is software security and representation of the attacker's perspective in the form of attack patterns. The term *attack patterns* was coined in discussions among software security experts starting around 2001, was introduced in the paper *Attack Modeling for Information Security and Survivability* [Moore 2001], and was brought to the broader industry in greater detail and with a solid set of specific examples by Greg Hoglund and Gary McGraw in their book *Exploiting Software: How to Break Code* [Hoglund 2004].

Attack patterns apply the problem–solution paradigm of design patterns in a destructive—rather than constructive—context. Here, the common problem targeted by the pattern represents the objective of the software attacker, and the pattern's solution represents common methods for performing the attack. In short, attack patterns describe the techniques that attackers might use to break software.

The incentive behind using attack patterns is that they give software developers a structured representation of how attackers think, which enables them to anticipate attacks and hence take more effective steps to mitigate the likelihood or impact of attacks. Attack patterns help to categorize attacks in a meaningful way so that problems and solutions can be discussed effectively. They can identify the types of known attacks to which an application could be exposed so that mitigations can be built into the application. Another benefit of attack patterns is that they contain sufficient detail about how attacks are carried out to enable developers to help prevent them. Owing to the omission of information about software security in many curricula and the traditional shroud of secrecy surrounding exploits, software developers are often ill informed about the field of software security and especially software exploit. The concept of attack patterns can be used to teach the software development community both how software is exploited in reality and how to avoid such attacks.

Since the publication of *Exploiting Software*, several individuals and groups in the industry have tried to push the concept of attack patterns forward, with varying levels of success. These efforts have faced challenges such as the lack of a common definition and schema for attack patterns, a lack of diversity in the targeted areas of analysis by the various groups involved, and a lack of any independent body to act as the collector and disseminator of common attack pattern catalogues. The two most significant advances in this regard have been the recent publication of the detailed attack pattern articles on the Build Security In Web site sponsored by the U.S. Department of Homeland Security (DHS) and the initial launch of the ongoing DHS-sponsored Common Attack Pattern Enumeration and Classification (CAPEC) [CAPEC 2007] initiative content. Content released as part of the initial launch of CAPEC includes a formal attack pattern schema, a draft attack classification taxonomy, and 101 actual detailed attack patterns. All of this content is freely available to the public to use for software security engineering.

MITRE Security Initiatives

In addition to the Common Attack Pattern Enumeration and Classification (CAPEC), the Making Security Measurable program sponsored by the Department of Homeland Security and led by MITRE Corporation produces *Common Vulnerabilities and Exposures* (CVE), a dictionary of publicly known information security vulnerabilities and exposures, and *Common Weakness Enumeration* (CWE), a dictionary of software weakness types. Links to all three can be found on MITRE's Making Security Measurable site, along with links to other information security enumerations, languages, and repositories.

http://measurablesecurity.mitre.org/

What Does an Attack Pattern Look Like?

An attack pattern at a minimum should fully describe what the attack looks like, what sort of skill or resources are required to successfully execute it, and in which contexts it is applicable and should provide enough information to enable defenders to effectively prevent or mitigate it.

We propose that a simple attack pattern should typically include the information shown in Table 2–1.

Table 2–1: *Attack Pattern Components*

Pattern name and classification	A unique, descriptive identifier for the pattern.
Attack prerequisites	Which conditions must exist or which functionality and which characteristics must the target software have, or which behavior must it exhibit, for this attack to succeed?
Description	A description of the attack, including the chain of actions taken.

Continues

Table 2–1: *Attack Pattern Components (Continued)*

Related vulnerabilities or weaknesses	Which specific vulnerabilities or weaknesses does this attack leverage? Specific vulnerabilities should reference industry-standard identifiers such as Common Vulnerabilities and Exposures (CVE) number [CVE 2007] or US-CERT[a] number. Specific weaknesses (underlying issues that may cause vulnerabilities) should reference industry-standard identifiers such as the Common Weakness Enumeration (CWE) [CWE 2007].
Method of attack	What is the vector of attack used (e.g., malicious data entry, maliciously crafted file, protocol corruption)?
Attack motivation— consequences	What is the attacker trying to achieve by using this attack? This is not the end business/mission goal of the attack within the target context, but rather the specific technical result desired that could be used to achieve the end business/mission objective. This information is useful for aligning attack patterns to threat models and for determining which attack patterns from the broader set available are relevant for a given context.
Attacker skill or knowledge required	What level of skill or specific knowledge must the attacker have to execute such an attack? This should be communicated on a rough scale (e.g., low, moderate, high) as well as in contextual detail of which type of skills or knowledge are required.
Resources required	Which resources (e.g., CPU cycles, IP addresses, tools, time) are required to execute the attack?
Solutions and mitigations	Which actions or approaches are recommended to mitigate this attack, either through resistance or through resiliency?

Table 2–1: *Attack Pattern Components (Continued)*

Context description	In which technical contexts (e.g., platform, operating system, language, architectural paradigm) is this pattern relevant? This information is useful for selecting a set of attack patterns that are appropriate for a given context.
References	What other sources of information are available to describe this attack?

a. http://www.us-cert.gov

A simplified example of an attack pattern written to this basic schema is provided in Table 2–2. The idea for this pattern came from Hoglund and McGraw's book *Exploiting Software,* and a more detailed version is now available as CAPEC attack pattern #22.[9]

Table 2–2: *Example Attack Pattern*

Pattern name and classification	Make the Client Invisible
Attack prerequisites	The application must have a multitiered architecture with a division between the client and the server.
Description	This attack pattern exploits client-side trust issues that are apparent in the software architecture. The attacker removes the client from the communication loop by communicating directly with the server. This could be done by bypassing the client or by creating a malicious impersonation of the client.

Continues

9. http://capec.mitre.org/data/definitions/22.html

Table 2–2: *Example Attack Pattern (Continued)*

Related vulnerabilities or weaknesses	Man-in-the-Middle (MITM) (CWE #300), Origin Validation Error (CWE #346), Authentication Bypass by Spoofing (CWE #290), No Authentication for Critical Function (CWE #306), Reflection Attack in an Authentication Protocol (CWE #301).
Method of attack	Direct protocol communication with the server.
Attack motivation— consequences	Potentially information leak, data modification, arbitrary code execution, and so on. These can all be achieved by bypassing authentication and filtering accomplished with this attack pattern.
Attacker skill or knowledge required	Finding and initially executing this attack requires a moderate skill level and knowledge of the client/server communications protocol. Once the vulnerability is found, the attack can be easily automated for execution by far less skilled attackers. Skill levels for follow-on attacks can vary widely depending on the nature of the attack.
Resources required	None, although protocol analysis tools and client impersonation tools such as netcat can greatly increase the ease and effectiveness of the attack.
Solutions and mitigations	Increase attack resistance: Use strong two-way authentication for all communication between the client and the server. This option could have significant performance implications. Increase attack resilience: Minimize the amount of logic and filtering present on the client; place it on the server instead. Use white lists on the server to filter and validate client input.

Attack patterns can be an invaluable resource for helping to identify both positive and negative security requirements. They have obvious direct benefit in defining the software's expected reaction to the attacks they describe. When put into the context of the other functional requirements for the software and when considering the underlying weaknesses targeted by the attack, they can help identify both negative requirements describing potential undesired behaviors and positive functional requirements for avoiding—or at least mitigating—the potential attack. For instance, if a customer provides the requirement "The application must accept ASCII characters," then the attack pattern "Using Unicode Encoding to Bypass Validation Logic" (CAPEC #71)[10] can be used to ask the question, "What should the application do if Unicode characters or another unacceptable, non-ASCII character set is encountered?" From this question, misuse/abuse cases can be defined, such as "Malicious user provides Unicode characters to the data entry field." By having a specific definition for this negative requirement, the designers, implementers, and testers will have a clear idea of the type of hostile environment with which the software must deal and will build the software accordingly. This information can also help define positive requirements, such as "The system shall translate all input into the ASCII character set before processing that input." If these sorts of requirements are overlooked, the developed application may unknowingly accept Unicode characters in some instances, and an attacker could use that fact to bypass input filters for ASCII characters.

Many vulnerabilities result from vague specifications and requirements. In general, attack patterns allow the requirements engineer to ask "what if" questions in a structured and bounded way to make the requirements more specific. If an attack pattern states "Condition X can be leveraged by an attacker to cause Y," then a valid question may be "What should the application do if it encounters condition X?" Of course, one of the great challenges with any "what if" session is knowing when to stop. There is no hard-and-fast answer to this question, as it is very dependent on context. Using attack patterns, however, can help minimize this risk by offering a method to ask the appropriate "what if" questions within a defined rather than boundless scope.

Software security requirements as an element of software security engineering are discussed further in Chapter 3.

10. http://capec.mitre.org/data/definitions/71.html

Table 2–2: *Example Attack Pattern (Continued)*

Context description	"Any raw data that exist outside the server software cannot and should not be trusted. Client-side security is an oxymoron. Simply put, all clients will be hacked. Of course, the real problem is one of client-side trust. Accepting anything blindly from the client and trusting it through and through is a bad idea, and yet this is often the case in server-side design."
References	*Exploiting Software: How to Break Code*, p. 150.

Note that an attack pattern is not overly generic or theoretical. The following is not an attack pattern: "Writing outside array boundaries in an application can allow an attacker to execute arbitrary code on the computer running the target software." This statement does not identify which type of functionality and specific weakness is targeted or how malicious input is provided to the application. Without that information, the statement is not particularly useful and cannot be considered an attack pattern.

An attack pattern is also not an overly specific attack that applies only to a particular application, such as "When the PATH environment variable is set to a string of length greater than 128, the application foo executes the code at the memory location pointed to by characters 132, 133, 134, and 135 in the environment variable." This amount of specificity is of limited benefit to the software development community because it does not help its members discover and fix vulnerabilities in other applications or even fix other similar vulnerabilities in the same application.

Although not broadly required or typical, it can be valuable to adorn attack patterns where possible and appropriate with other useful reference information such as that listed in Table 2–3.

Table 2–3: *Optional Attack Pattern Components*

Examples— instances	Explanatory examples or demonstrative exploit instances of this type of attack. They are intended to help the reader understand the nature, context, and variability of the attack in more practical and concrete terms.
Source exploits	From which specific exploits (e.g., malware, cracks) was this pattern derived, and which shows an example?
Related attack patterns	Which other attack patterns affect or are affected by this pattern?
Relevant design patterns	Which specific design patterns are recommended as providing resistance or resilience against this attack, or which design patterns are not recommended because they are particularly susceptible to this attack?
Relevant security patterns	Which specific security patterns are recommended as providing resistance or resilience against this attack?
Related guidelines or rules	Which existing security guidelines or secure coding rules are relevant to identifying or mitigating this attack?
Relevant security requirements	Have specific security requirements relevant to this attack been identified that offer opportunities for reuse?
Probing techniques	Which techniques are typically used to probe and reconnoiter a potential target to determine vulnerability and/or to prepare for an attack?
Indicators— warnings of attack	Which activities, events, conditions, or behaviors could serve as indicators that an attack of this type is imminent, is in progress, or has occurred?
Obfuscation techniques	Which techniques are typically used to disguise the fact that an attack of this type is imminent, is in progress, or has occurred?

Table 2–3: *Optional Attack Pattern Components (Continued)*

Injection vector	What is the mechanism and format for this input-driven attack? Injection vectors must take into account the grammar of an attack, the syntax accepted by the system, the position of various fields, and the acceptable ranges of data.
Payload	What is the code, configuration, or other data to be executed or otherwise activated as part of this injection-based attack?
Activation zone	What is the area within the target software that is capable of executing or otherwise activating the payload of this injection-based attack? The activation zone is where the intent of the attacker is put into action. It may be a command interpreter, some active machine code in a buffer, a client browser, a system API call, or other element.
Payload activation impact	What is the typical impact of the attack payload activation for this injection-based attack on the confidentiality, integrity, or availability of the target software?

Leveraging Attack Patterns in All Phases of the Software Development Life Cycle

Unlike many of the defensive touchpoint activities and knowledge with a narrowly focused area of impact within the SDLC, attack patterns as a resource provide potential value to the development team during all phases of software development regardless of the SDLC chosen, including requirements, architecture, design, coding, testing and even deploying the system.

Leveraging Attack Patterns in Positive and Negative Security Requirements

Security-focused requirements are typically split between positive requirements, which specify functional behaviors the software must exhibit (often security features), and negative requirements (typically in the form of misuse/abuse cases), which describe behaviors that software must not exhibit if it is to operate securely.

Leveraging Attack Patterns in Architecture and Design

Once requirements have been defined, all software must go through some level of architecture and design. Regardless of the formality of the process followed, the results of this activity will form the foundation for the software and drive all remaining development activities. During architecture and design, decisions must be made about how the software will be structured, how the various components will be integrated and interact, which technologies will be used, and how the requirements defining how the software will function will be interpreted. Careful consideration is necessary during this activity, given that as much as 50 percent of software defects leading to security problems are design flaws [McGraw 2006]. In the example depicted in Figure 2–6, a potential architecture could consist of a three-tier system with the client (a Web browser leveraging JavaScript/HTML), a Web server (leveraging Java servlets), and a database server (leveraging Oracle 10i). Decisions made at this level can have significant implications for the overall security profile of the software.

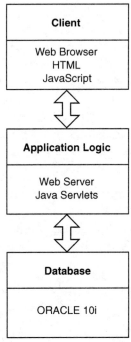

Figure 2–6: *Example architecture*

Attack patterns can be valuable during planning of the software's architecture and design in two ways. First, some attack patterns describe attacks that directly exploit architecture and design flaws in software. For instance, the Make the Client Invisible attack pattern (briefly described earlier in this chapter) exploits client-side trust issues that are apparent in the software architecture. Second, attack patterns at all levels can provide a useful context for the threats that the software is likely to face and thereby determine which architectural and design features to avoid or to specifically incorporate. The Make the Client Invisible attack pattern, for example, tells us that absolutely nothing sent back by the client can be trusted, regardless of which network security mechanisms (e.g., SSL) are used. The client is untrusted, and an attacker can send back literally any information that he or she desires. All input validation, authorization checks, and other security assessments must be performed on the server side. In addition, any data sent to the client should be considered visible by the client regardless of its intended presentation (that is, data that the client should not see should never be sent to the client). Performing authorization checks on the client side to determine which data to display is unacceptable.

The Make the Client Invisible attack pattern instructs the architects and designers that they must ensure that absolutely no security-critical business logic is performed on the client side. In fact, depending on the system requirements and the threats and risks faced by the system, the architects and designers may even want to define an input validator through which all input to the server must pass before being sent to the other classes. Such decisions must be made at the architecture and design phase, and attack patterns provide some guidance regarding what issues should be considered.

It is essential to document any attack patterns used in the architecture and design phase so that the application can be tested using those attack patterns. Tests must be created to validate that mitigations for the attack patterns considered during this phase were implemented properly.

Software architecture and design as an element of software security engineering is discussed further in Chapter 4.

Leveraging Attack Patterns in Implementation and Coding

If the architecture and design have been performed properly, each developer implementing the design should be writing well-defined components with well-defined interfaces.

Attack patterns can be useful during implementation because they enumerate the specific weaknesses targeted by relevant attacks and allow developers to ensure that these weaknesses do not occur in their code. These weaknesses could take the form of implementation bugs or simply valid coding constructs that can have security implications if used improperly. Unfortunately, implementation bugs are not always easy to avoid or to catch and fix. Even after applying basic review techniques, they can still remain abundant and can make software vulnerable to extremely dangerous exploits. It is important to extend basic review techniques by including more focused security-relevant concerns. Failure to properly check an array bound, for example, might permit an attacker to execute arbitrary code on the target host, whereas failure to perform proper input validation might enable an attacker to destroy an entire database.

Underlying security issues in non-buggy valid code are typically more difficult to identify. They cannot be identified with simple black-box scanning or testing, but instead require specialized knowledge of what these weaknesses look like. Here, we focus on how attack patterns can be used to identify specific weaknesses for targeting and mitigation through informing the developer ahead of time about those issues to avoid and through providing a list of issues (security coding rules) to look for in code reviews; the latter step can often be automated through the use of security scanning tools. It is important to determine precisely which attack patterns are applicable for a particular project. In some instances, different attack patterns may be applicable for different components of a product.

Good architecture and design, as well as developer awareness, enhanced with attack patterns can help to minimize security weaknesses. Nevertheless, it is also essential to ensure that all source code, once written, is reviewed with processes that have been shown to be capable of detecting the targeted weaknesses. Given the sometimes daunting size and sheer monotony of this task, it is typically performed using an automated analysis tool (e.g., those from Fortify, Ounce Labs,

Klocwork, or Coverity). Even though analysis tools cannot find all security weaknesses, they can help weed out many potential issues. Using attack patterns as guidance, specific subsets of the tools' search rules can be selected and custom rules can be created for organizations to help find specific security weaknesses or instances of failure to follow security standards. For example, to deal with the Simple Script Injection (CAPEC #63)[11] attack pattern, an organization may establish a security standard in which all untrusted input is passed through an input filter and all output of data obtained from an untrusted source is passed through an encoder. An organization can develop a variety of such filters and encoders, and static source code analysis tools can help find occurrences in code where developers may have neglected to adhere to standards and opted to use Java's input/output features directly.

Software implementation and coding as an element of software security engineering is discussed further in Chapter 5.

Leveraging Attack Patterns in Software Security Testing

The testing phase differs from the previous phases in the SDLC in that its goal is not necessarily constructive; the goal of risk-based security testing is typically to break software so that the discovered issues can be fixed before an attacker can find them [Whittaker 2003]. The purpose of using attack patterns in this phase is to have the individuals performing the various levels and types of testing act as attackers attempting to break the software. In unit testing, applicable attack patterns should be used to identify relevant targeted weaknesses and to generate test cases for each component, thereby ensuring that each component avoids or at least resists these weaknesses. For example, to test for shell command injection using command delimiters, malicious input strings containing delimiter-separated shell commands should be crafted and input to the applicable component(s) to confirm that the software demonstrates the proper behavior when provided with this type of malicious data. In integration testing, a primary security issue to consider is whether the individual components make differing assumptions that affect security, such that the integrated whole may contain conflicts or ambiguities. Attack patterns documented in the architecture and design phase should be used to create integration tests exploring such ambiguities and conflicts.

In system testing, the entire system is exercised and probed to ensure that it meets all of its functional and nonfunctional requirements. If

---

11. http://capec.mitre.org/data/definitions/63.html

attack patterns were used in the requirements-gathering phase to generate security requirements, system testing will have a solid foundation for identifying test cases that validate secure behavior. These security requirements should be tested during system testing. For example, the Using Unicode Encoding to Bypass Validation attack pattern can be used to generate test cases that ensure that the application behaves properly when provided with unexpected characters as input. Testers should input characters that the application is not supposed to accept to see how the application behaves under these conditions. The application's actual behavior when under attack should be compared with the desired behavior defined in the security requirements.

Even if security is considered throughout the SDLC when building software, and even if extensive testing is performed, vulnerabilities will likely still exist in the software after deployment, simply because no useful software is 100 percent secure [Viega 2001]. Software can be designed and developed to be extremely secure, but if it is deployed and operated in an insecure fashion, many vulnerabilities can be introduced. For example, a piece of software might provide strong encryption and proper authentication before allowing access to encrypted data, but if an attacker can obtain valid authentication credentials, he or she can subvert the software's security. Nothing is 100 percent secure, which means that the environment must always be secured and monitored to thwart attacks.

Given these caveats, it is extremely important to perform security testing of the software in its actual operational environment. Vulnerabilities present in software can sometimes be masked by environmental protections such as network firewalls and application firewalls, and environmental conditions can sometimes create new vulnerabilities. Such issues can often be discovered using a mix of white-box and black-box analysis of the deployed environment. White-box analysis of deployed software involves performing security analysis of the software, including its deployed environment, with knowledge of the architecture, design, and implementation of the software. Black-box analysis (typically in the form of penetration testing) involves treating the deployed software as a "black box" and attempting to attack it without any knowledge of its inner workings. Black-box testing is good for finding the specific implementation issues you know to look for, whereas detailed and structured white-box testing can uncover unexpected architecture and design and implementation issues that you may not have known to look for. Both types of testing are important, and attack patterns can be leveraged for both.

Black box testing of Web applications is generally performed using tools such as application security testers like those from companies such as Watchfire that automatically run predefined tests. Attack patterns can be used as models to create the tests (simulated attacks) these tools perform, thereby giving them more significant relevance and effectiveness. These tools typically test for a large variety of attacks, but they generally cannot find subtle architectural vulnerabilities. Although they may effectively identify vulnerabilities that script kiddies and other relatively unskilled attackers would likely exploit, a skilled attacker would be able to find many issues that a vulnerability scanning tool simply could not detect. For instance, a lack of encryption for transmitting Social Security numbers would not be detected using an automated tool because the fact that Social Security numbers are unencrypted is not a purely technical flaw. The black-box testing tool cannot determine which information is a Social Security number and cannot apply business logic. Attack patterns that are useful for creating black-box tests include those that can be executed remotely without requiring many steps.

White-box testing is typically more thorough than black-box testing. It involves extensive analysis performed by security experts who have access to the software's requirements, architecture, design, and code. Because of the deeper understanding of the code involved, white-box security testing is often capable of finding more obscure implementation bugs that are not uncovered in black-box testing and, occasionally, some architecture and design flaws. Attack patterns can be leveraged to determine areas posing system risks, which can then be scrutinized by the system white-box analysis. Attack patterns that are effective guides for white-box analysis include those that focus on architecture and design weaknesses or implementation weaknesses. For example, an attack pattern that could be used in white-box testing of a deployed system is sniffing sensitive data on an insecure channel. Those with knowledge of data sensitivity classifications and an understanding of the business context around various types of data can determine whether some information that should always be communicated over an encrypted channel is actually being sent over an insecure channel. Such issues are often specific to a deployed environment; thus, analysis of the actual deployed software is required.

Software testing as an element of software security engineering is discussed further in Chapter 5.

2.4 How to Assert and Specify Desired Security Properties[12]

Identifying and describing the properties that determine the security profile of software gave us the common language and objectives for building secure software. Outlining mechanisms for how these properties can be influenced gave us the ability to take action and effect positive change in regard to the security assurance of the software we build. Taken in combination, these achievements lay a foundation for understanding what makes software secure. Unfortunately, without a mechanism for clearly communicating the desired or attained security assurance of software in terms of these properties and activities, this understanding is incomplete. What is needed is a mechanism for asserting and specifying desired security properties and using them as a basis for planning, communicating, and assuring compliance. These assertions and specifications are typically captured and managed in an artifact known as an *assurance case*.

Elsewhere in this book and on the BSI Web site, you can learn about best practices, tools, and techniques that can help in building security into software. Nevertheless, the mere existence or claimed use of one or more of these best practices, tools, or techniques does not constitute an adequate assurance case. For example, in support of an overarching security claim (e.g., that a system is acceptably secure), security assurance cases must provide evidence that particular best practices, tools, and techniques were properly applied and must indicate by whom they were applied and how extensive their coverage is. Moreover, unlike many product certifications that quickly grow stale because they are merely snapshots in time of an infrequently applied certification process, a security assurance case should provide evidence that the practices, tools, or techniques being used to improve security were actually applied to the currently released version of the software (or

---

12. The majority of the content provided in this section is adapted from the Assurance Cases content area of the Build Security In Web site authored by Howard Lipson, John Goodenough, and Chuck Weinstock of the Software Engineering Institute [BSI 03].

that the results were invariant to any of the code changes that subsequently occurred).

2.4.1 Building a Security Assurance Case

A security assurance case uses a structured set of arguments and a corresponding body of evidence to demonstrate that a system satisfies specific claims with respect to its security properties. This case should be amenable to review by a wide variety of stakeholders. Although tool support is available for development of these cases, the creation and documentation of a security assurance case can be a demanding and time-consuming process. Even so, similarities may exist among security cases in the structure and other characteristics of the claims, arguments, and evidence used to construct them. A catalog of patterns (templates) for security assurance cases can facilitate the process of creating and documenting an individual case. Moreover, assurance case patterns offer the benefits of reuse and repeatability of process, as well as providing some notion of coverage or completeness of the evidence.

A security assurance case[13] is similar to a legal case, in that it presents arguments showing how a top-level claim (e.g., "The system is acceptably secure") is supported by objective evidence. Unlike a typical product certification, however, a security case considers people and processes as well as technology. A case is developed by showing how the top-level claim is supported by subclaims. For example, part of a security assurance case would typically address various sources of security vulnerabilities. The case would probably claim that a system has none of the common coding defects that lead to security vulnerabilities, including, for example, buffer overflow vulnerabilities.[14] A subclaim about the absence of buffer overflow vulnerabilities could be supported by showing that (1) developers received training on how to write code that minimizes the possibility of buffer overflow vulnerabilities; (2) experienced developers reviewed the code to see if any

---

13. Assurance cases were originally used to show that systems satisfied their safety-critical properties. In this usage, they were (and are) called safety cases. The notation and approach used in this chapter has been used for more than a decade in Europe to document why a system is sufficiently safe [Kelly 2004]. The application of the concept to reliability was documented in an SAE Standard [SAE 2004]. In this chapter, we extend the concept to cover system security claims.

14. Further information about the common coding defects that lead to security vulnerabilities can be found on the BSI Web site [BSI 04, 05, 06, 07] and in the computer security literature [Voas 1997; Viega 2001; Howard 2005; Howard 2006; Lipner 2005; McGraw 2006; Seacord 2005].

buffer overflow possibilities existed and found none; (3) a static analysis tool scanned the code and found no problems; and (4) the system and its components were tested with invalid arguments and all such inputs were rejected or properly handled as exceptions.

In this example, the "evidence" would consist of developer training credentials, the results of the code review, the output of the code scanner, and the results of the invalid-input tests. The "argument" is stated as follows: "Following best coding practice has value in *preventing* buffer overflow coding defects. Each of the other methods has value in *detecting* buffer overflow defects; none of them detected such defects (or these defects were corrected[15]), and so the existing evidence supports the claim that there are no buffer overflow vulnerabilities."[16] Further information could show that this claim is incorrect.

Our confidence in the argument (that is, in the soundness of the claim) depends on how convincing we find the argument and the evidence. Moreover, if we believe that the consequences of an invalid claim are sufficiently serious, we might require that further evidence or other subclaims be developed. The seriousness of a claim would depend on the potential impact of an attack (e.g., projected economic loss, injury, or death) related to that claim and on the significance of the threat of such an attack. Although an in-depth discussion of the relation of threat and impact to security cases is beyond the scope of this book, a comprehensive security case should include—or should at least be developed in the context of—analyses of the threats to a system and the projected outcomes of successful attacks.

2.4.2 A Security Assurance Case Example

The structure for a partially developed security assurance case focusing on buffer overflow coding defects appears in Figure 2–7. This case

---

15. The proper response to the detection of developer errors is not simply to correct the code but also to keep a record of the defects found and to use that information to improve the process that created the defect. For example, based on the nature of the defects detected, the training of developers in best coding practices might need to be improved. One might also search other products for similar defects and remind (or retrain) developers regarding these defects.

16. Of course, despite our best efforts, this claim might be invalid; the degree of confidence that we have in the argument supporting any given claim is an assertion about the case itself rather than an assertion about what is claimed. That is, when we say a system is "acceptably" secure or that it meets its security requirements, we provide an argument and evidence in support of these claims. The extent to which the case is convincing (or valid) is determined when the case is reviewed.

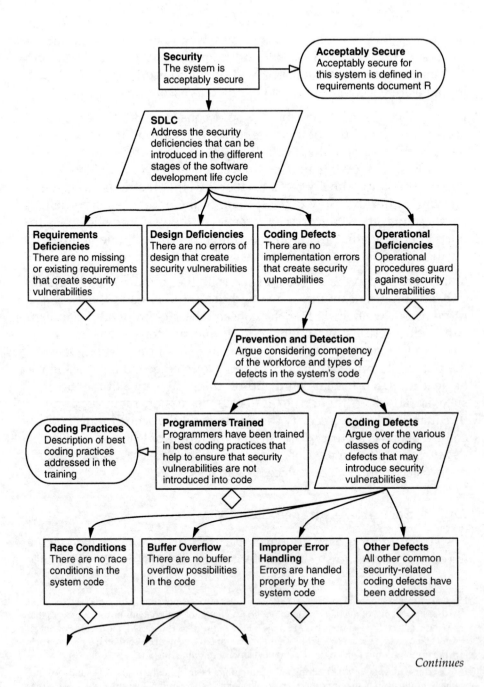

Continues

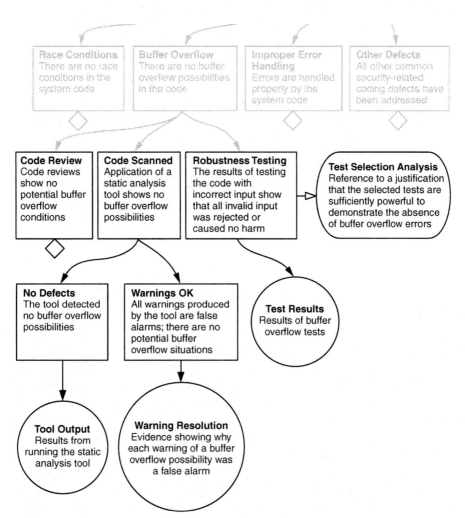

Figure 2–7: *Partially expanded security assurance case that focuses on buffer overflow*

is presented in a graphical notation called Goal Structuring Notation (GSN) [Kelly 2004].

The case starts with a claim (in the shape of a rectangle) that "The system is acceptably secure." To the right, a box with two rounded sides, labeled "Acceptably Secure," provides *context* for the claim. This element of the case provides additional information on what it means for the system to be "acceptably" secure. For example, the referenced document might cite Health Information Portability and Accountability

Act (HIPAA) requirements as they apply to a particular system, or it might classify the kinds of security breaches that would lead to different levels of loss (laying the basis for an expectation that more effort will be spent to prevent the more significant losses).

Under the top-level claim is a parallelogram labeled "SDLC." This element shows the *strategy* to be used in developing an argument supporting the top-level claim and provides helpful insight to anyone reviewing the case. In this example, the strategy is to address potential security vulnerabilities arising at the different stages of the SDLC—namely, requirements, design, implementation (coding), and operation.[17] One source of deficiencies is coding defects, which is the topic of one of the four subclaims. The other subclaims cover requirements, design, and operational deficiencies. (The diamond under a claim indicates that further expansion is required to fully elaborate the claim–argument–evidence substructure.) The structure of the argument implies that if these four subclaims are satisfied, the system is acceptably secure.

The strategy for arguing that there are no coding defects involves addressing actions taken both to *prevent* and to *detect* possible vulnerabilities caused by coding defects.[18] In Figure 2–7, only one possible coding defect—buffer overflow—is developed. Three types of evidence are developed to increase our confidence that no buffer overflow vulnerabilities are present, where each type of evidence is associated with each of three subclaims. The "Code Scanned" subclaim asserts that static analysis of the code has demonstrated the absence of buffer overflow defects. Below it are the subclaims that the tool definitively reported "No Defects" and that all warnings reported by the tool were subsequently verified as false alarms (that is, "Warnings OK"). Below these subclaims are two pieces of evidence: the tool output, which is the result of running the static analysis tool, and the resolution of each warning message, showing why each was a false alarm.

---

17. We omit validation and testing (as development activities) because these activities will be included within the security case itself.

18. The strategy might also consider actions taken to *mitigate* possible vulnerabilities caused by coding defects, although we don't illustrate this step in our example. Such actions could include the use of tools and techniques that provide runtime protection against buffer overflow exploits [BSI 08] in the event that some buffer overflow vulnerability was neither prevented nor detected prior to release of the code.

This is not a complete exposition of GSN. For instance, two other symbols, not shown in Figure 2–7, represent *justification* and *assumption*. As with the context element, they are used to provide additional information helpful in understanding the claim.

The claims in the example are primarily product focused and technical; that is, the claims address software engineering issues. An assurance case may also require taking into account legal, regulatory, economic (e.g., insurance), and other nontechnical issues [Lipson 2002]. For example, a more complete case might contain claims reflecting the importance of legal or regulatory requirements relating to the Sarbanes–Oxley Act or HIPAA. In addition, an analysis of the threat and consequences of security breaches will determine how much effort is put into developing certain claims or types of argument. If a security breach can lead to a major regulatory fine, the case may require a higher standard of evidence and argumentation than if a breach carries little economic penalty.

2.4.3 Incorporating Assurance Cases into the SDLC

Developing a security assurance case is not a trivial matter. In any real system, the number of claims involved and the amount of evidence required will be significant. The effort involved is offset by an expected decrease in effort required to find and fix security-related problems at the back end of product development and by a reduced level of security breaches and their attendant costs.

Creating and evolving the security case as the system is being developed is highly recommended. Developing even the preliminary outlines of an assurance case as early as possible in the SDLC can improve the development process by focusing attention on what needs to be assured and which evidence needs to be developed at each subsequent stage of the SDLC. Attempting to gather or generate the necessary security case evidence once development is complete may be not just much more costly, but simply impossible.

For maximum utility, a security assurance case should be a document that changes as the system it documents changes. That is, the case should take on a different character as a project moves through its life cycle. In the predevelopment stage, the case focuses on demonstrating the following points:

- The plan for a security case is appropriate for the security require-ments of the proposed system.
- The technical proposals are appropriate for achieving the security requirements of the proposed system.
- It will be possible to demonstrate that security has been achieved during the project.

At development time, the following steps are taken in relation to the security assurance case (which is derived from the predevelopment case):

- It is updated with the results of all activities that contribute to the security evaluation (including evidence and argumentation) so that, by the time of deployment, the case will be complete.
- It is presented at design (and other) reviews and the outcomes are included in the case.

Using a configuration control mechanism to manage the security case will ensure its integrity, as well as help the case remain relevant to the project's development status.

Security cases provide a structured framework for evaluating the impact of changes to the system and can help ensure that the changes do not adversely impact security. The case should continue to be maintained after deployment of the system, especially whenever the system is modified. Examining the current case can help determine whether modifications will invalidate or change arguments and claims and, if so, will help identify the appropriate parts of the case that need to be updated. In addition, if parts of the system prove inse-cure even in the face of a well-developed case, it is important to understand why this particular chain of evidence–argument–claim reasoning was insufficient.

2.4.4 Related Security Assurance and Compliance Efforts

Security-Privacy Laws and Regulations

Laws and regulations such as Sarbanes–Oxley and HIPAA mandate specific security and privacy requirements. Security assurance cases can be used to argue that a corporation is in compliance with a given law or regulation. One can envision the development of security case patterns for particular laws or regulations to assist in demonstrating such compliance.

Common Criteria

The Common Criteria (CC) is an internationally recognized standard for evaluating security products and systems [CCMB 2005a, 2005b]. *Protection profiles* represent sets of security requirements that products can be evaluated and certified against. The results of a CC evaluation include an Evaluation Assurance Level (EAL), which indicates the strength of assurance. Although a CC evaluation includes elements that are similar to those found in a security case, the security case is a more general framework into which the results of CC evaluations can be placed as evidence of assurance. Anyone creating a product or system meant to satisfy a protection profile needs a way to argue that it does, in fact, match the requirements of the profile. Unlike ad hoc approaches to arguing about the achievement of certain security levels, the security case method provides an organizing structure and a common "language" that can be used to make assurance arguments about satisfying the set of requirements in a protection profile (at a particular EAL), as well as providing a broader framework that can be used to place CC evaluations in the context of other available evidence of assurance.

The standard format of CC evaluations allows for reuse of some of the basic elements in an assurance argument and hence may be thought of as providing patterns of evaluation. For example, the Common Criteria provides catalogs of standard Security Functional Requirements and Security Assurance Requirements. In contrast, security case patterns allow for the reuse of entire claim–argument–evidence structures and are, therefore, patterns in a much more general sense. Unlike CC evaluations, a security case is well suited to be maintained over time as a system development artifact. Thus the assurance case could evolve along with the system, always reflecting the system's current state and configuration.

2.4.5 Maintaining and Benefitting from Assurance Cases

Assurance cases for security provide a structured and reviewable set of artifacts that make it possible to demonstrate to interested parties that the system's security requirements have been met to a reasonable degree of certainty.[19] Moreover, the creation of an assurance case can

---

19. We consider a "reasonable degree of certainty" to mean a "tolerable degree of uncertainty." What is reasonable and tolerable depends on the perceived threat, the consequences of a security breach, and the costs of security measures, including the costs associated with creating and maintaining a security case.

help in the planning and conduct of development. The process of maintaining an assurance case can help developers identify new security issues that may arise when changes are made to the system. Developing and maintaining security cases throughout the SDLC is an emerging area of best practice for systems with critical security requirements.

A key difference between arguments related to security and arguments related to other quality attributes of a system is the presence of an intelligent adversary. Intelligent adversaries do not follow predictable courses, but rather try to attack where you least expect. Having an intelligent adversary implies that security threats will evolve and adapt. As a consequence, a security case developed today may have its assumptions unexpectedly violated, or its strength may not be adequate to protect against the attack of tomorrow. This evolutionary nature of threats suggests that security assurance cases will need to be revisited more frequently than assurance cases for safety, reliability, or other dependability properties.

One should not think of the creation, use, sharing, and evolution of security cases as a method that is in competition with other security certification or evaluation methods, tools, or techniques. Security cases provide a general framework in which to incorporate and integrate existing and future certification and evaluation methods into a unified argument and evidentiary structure. The security case is particularly valuable as a supporting framework because it allows you to make meta-arguments about the methods, tools, and techniques being used to establish assurance. For example, a security case might argue that a certification method applied by a third-party certifier provides higher assurance than the same method applied by the vendor of the product being certified. This type of meta-argument is outside the scope of the certification method itself.

Although further research and tool development are certainly needed, you can take advantage of the assurance case method right now. There is much to be gained by integrating even rudimentary security cases and security case patterns into the development life cycle for any mission-critical system. Even a basic security case is a far cry above the typical ad hoc arguments and unfounded reassurances in its ability to provide a compelling argument that a desired security property has been built into a system from the outset and has continued to be maintained throughout the SDLC.

2.5 Summary

As a project manager looking for understanding and guidance on building better security into your software, it is first crucial that you understand which characteristics of software make it more or less secure.

Three areas of knowledge and practice were recommended in this chapter:

- A solid understanding of the core security properties (confidentiality, integrity, availability, accountability, and non-repudiation) and of the other properties that influence them (dependability, correctness, predictability, reliability, safety, size, complexity, and traceability) provides a solid foundation for communicating software security issues and for understanding and placing into context the various activities, resources, and suggestions discussed in this book.

- Understanding both the defensive and attacker's perspectives as well as activities (touchpoints) and resources (attack patterns and others) available to influence the security properties of software can enable you to place the various activities, resources, and suggestions described in this book into effective action and cause positive change.

- Assurance cases provide a powerful tool for planning, tracking, asserting, assessing, and otherwise communicating the claims, arguments, and evidence (in terms of security properties, perspectives, activities, and resources) for the security assurance of software.

Understanding the core properties that make software secure, the activities and knowledge available to influence them, and the mechanisms available to assert and specify them lays the foundation for the deeper discussion of software security practices and knowledge found in the following chapters. As you explore each life-cycle phase or concern and examine each discussed practice or knowledge resource, it may be beneficial for you to revisit this chapter, using the content here as a lens to understand and assess the practice or resource for value and applicability in your own unique context.

Chapter 3

Requirements Engineering for Secure Software

3.1 Introduction   Ⓔ Ⓜ Ⓛ

When security requirements are considered at all during the system life cycle, they tend to be general lists of security features such as password protection, firewalls, virus detection tools, and the like. These are, in fact, not security requirements at all, but rather implementation mechanisms that are intended to satisfy unstated requirements, such as authenticated access. As a result, security requirements that are specific to the system and that provide for protection of essential services and assets are often neglected. In addition, the attacker perspective is not considered, with the result being that security requirements—when they exist—are likely to be incomplete. We believe that a systematic approach to security requirements engineering will help avoid the problem of generic lists of features and take into account the attacker's perspective. Several approaches to security requirements engineering are described in this chapter, and references are provided to additional material that can help you ensure that your products effectively meet security requirements.

73

3.1.1 The Importance of Requirements Engineering

It comes as no surprise that requirements engineering is critical to the success of any major development project. Some studies have shown that requirements engineering defects cost 10 to 200 times as much to correct once the system has become operational than if they were detected during requirements development [Boehm 1988; McConnell 2001]. Other studies have shown that reworking requirements, design, and code defects on most software development projects accounts for 40 to 50 percent of the total project effort [Jones 1986a]; the percentage of defects originating during requirements engineering is estimated at more than 50 percent. The total percentage of project budget due to requirements defects ranges from 25 percent to 40 percent [Wiegers 2003]. Clearly, given these costs of poor security requirements, even a small improvement in this area would provide a high value. By the time that an application is installed in its operational environment, it is very difficult and expensive to significantly improve its security.

Requirements problems are among the top causes of the following undesirable phenomena [Charette 2005]:

- Projects are significantly over budget, go past schedule, have significantly reduced scope, or are cancelled
- Development teams deliver poor-quality applications
- Products are not significantly used once delivered

These days we have the further problem that the environment in which we do requirements engineering has changed, resulting in an added element of complexity. Today's software development takes place in a dynamic environment that changes while projects are still in development, with the result that requirements are constantly in a state of flux. Such changes can be inspired by a variety of causes—conflicts between stakeholder groups, rapidly evolving markets, the impact of tradeoff decisions, and so on.

In addition, requirements engineering on individual projects often suffers from the following problems:

- Requirements identification typically does not include all relevant stakeholders and does not use the most modern or efficient techniques.

- Requirements are often statements describing architectural constraints or implementation mechanisms rather than statements describing what the system must do.

- Requirements are often directly specified without any analysis or modeling. When analysis *is* done, it is usually restricted to functional end-user requirements, ignoring (1) quality requirements such as security, (2) other functional and nonfunctional requirements, and (3) architecture, design, implementation, and testing constraints.

- Requirements specification is typically haphazard, with specified requirements being ambiguous, incomplete (e.g., nonfunctional requirements are often missing), inconsistent, not cohesive, infeasible, obsolete, neither testable nor capable of being validated, and not usable by all of their intended audiences.

- Requirements management is typically weak, with ineffective forms of data capture (e.g., in one or more documents rather than in a database or tool) and missing attributes. It is often limited to tracing, scheduling, and prioritization, without change tracking or other configuration management. Alternatively, it may be limited to the capabilities provided by a specific tool, with little opportunity for improvement.

3.1.2 Quality Requirements

Even when organizations recognize the importance of functional end-user requirements, they often neglect *quality* requirements, such as performance, safety, security, reliability, and maintainability. Some quality requirements are nonfunctional requirements, but others describe system functionality, even though it may not contribute directly to end-user requirements.

As you might expect, developers of certain kinds of mission-critical systems and systems in which human life is involved, such as the space shuttle, have long recognized the importance of quality requirements and have accounted for them in software development. In many other systems, however, quality requirements are ignored altogether or treated in an inadequate way. Hence we see the failure of software associated with power systems, telephone systems, unmanned spacecraft, and so on. If quality requirements are not attended to in these types of systems, it is far less likely that they will be focused on in ordinary business systems.

This inattention to quality requirements is exacerbated by the desire to keep costs down and meet aggressive schedules. As a consequence, software development contracts often do not contain specific quality requirements, but rather offer up some vague generalities about quality, if they touch on this topic at all.

3.1.3 Security Requirements Engineering

If security requirements are not effectively defined, the resulting system cannot be evaluated for success or failure prior to its implementation [BSI 09]. When security requirements are considered, they are often developed independently of other requirements engineering activities. As a result, specific security requirements are often neglected, and functional requirements are specified in blissful ignorance of security aspects.

In reviewing requirements documents, we typically find that security requirements—when they exist—are in a section by themselves and have been copied from a generic list of security features. The requirements elicitation and analysis that are needed to produce a better set of security requirements seldom take place.

As noted previously, operational environments and business goals often change dynamically, with the result that security requirements development is not a one-time activity. Therefore the activities that we describe in this chapter should be planned as iterative activities, taking place as change occurs. Although we describe them as one-time activities for the sake of exposition, you can expect mini-life cycles to occur over the course of a project.

Much requirements engineering research and practice addresses the capabilities that the system will provide. As a consequence, a lot of attention is paid to the functionality of the system from the user's perspective, but little attention is devoted to what the system should *not* do [Bishop 2002]. Users have implicit assumptions for the software applications and systems that they use. They expect those products to be secure and are surprised when they are not. These user assumptions need to be translated into security requirements for the software systems when they are under development. Often the implicit assumptions of users are overlooked, and features are focused on instead.

Another important perspective is that of the attacker. An attacker is not particularly interested in functional features of the system, unless they provide an avenue for attack. Instead, the attacker typically looks for defects and other conditions outside the norm that will allow a successful intrusion to take place. For this reason, it is important for requirements engineers to think about the attacker's perspective and not just the functionality of the system from the end-user's perspective. The discussion of attack patterns in Chapter 2 provides a good place to start this analysis. Other techniques that can be used in defining the attacker's perspective are misuse and abuse cases [McGraw 2006], attack trees [Ellison 2003; Schneier 2000], and threat modeling [Howard 2002]. Some of these methodologies are discussed in later sections of this chapter.

For many projects, security requirements are stated as negative requirements. As a result, general security requirements, such as "The system shall not allow successful attacks," are usually not feasible, as there is no consensus on ways to validate them other than to apply formal methods to the entire system. We can, however, identify the essential services and assets that must be protected. Operational usage scenarios can be extremely helpful aids to understanding which services and assets are essential. By providing threads that trace through the system, such scenarios also help to highlight security requirements as well as other quality requirements such as safety and performance [Reifer 2003]. Once the essential services and assets are understood, we become able to validate that mechanisms such as access control, levels of security, backups, replication, and policy are implemented and enforced. We can also validate that the system properly handles specific threats identified by a threat model and correctly responds to intrusion scenarios.

As usable approaches to security requirements engineering continue to emerge and new mechanisms are identified to promote organizational use, project managers can do a better job of ensuring that the resulting product effectively meets security requirements. The following techniques are known to be useful in this regard:

- Comprehensive, Lightweight Application Security Process (CLASP) approach to security requirements engineering. CLASP is a life-cycle process that suggests a number of different activities across the development life cycle in an attempt to improve security. Among these is a specific approach for security requirements [BSI 12].
- Security Quality Requirements Engineering (SQUARE). This process is aimed specifically at security requirements engineering.

- Core security requirements artifacts [Moffett 2004]. This approach takes an artifact view and starts with the artifacts that are needed to achieve better security requirements. It provides a framework that includes both traditional requirements engineering approaches to functional requirements and an approach to security requirements engineering that focuses on assets and harm to those assets.

Other useful techniques include formal specification approaches to security requirements, such as Software Cost Reduction (SCR) [Heitmeyer 2002], and the higher levels of the Common Criteria [CCMB 2005a]. As an additional reference, the SOAR report *Software Security Assurance* [Goertzel 2007] contains a good discussion of SDLC processes and various approaches to security requirements engineering.

In this chapter we discuss several approaches to development of security requirements, including the use of misuse and abuse cases, security quality requirements engineering, security requirements elicitation, and security requirements prioritization. While the processes we discuss are similar to those used for requirements engineering in general, we have found that when we delve into the detailed steps of how to do security requirements engineering, certain techniques are particularly useful, and we highlight these where they occur.

3.2 Misuse and Abuse Cases[1]

To create secure and reliable software, we first must anticipate abnormal behavior. We don't normally describe non-normative behavior in use cases, nor do we describe it with UML, but we must have some way to talk about and prepare for it. *Misuse* (or *abuse*) cases can help you begin to see your software in the same light that attackers do. By thinking beyond normative features while simultaneously contemplating negative or unexpected events, you can better understand how to create secure and reliable software.[2]

---

1. [BSI 43] © 2004 IEEE. Reprinted, with permission, from "Misuse and Abuse Cases: Getting Past the Positive" by Paco Hope, Gary McGraw, and Annie I. Anton, *IEEE Security & Privacy* 2, 3 (May/June 2004): 90–92.

2. Since the original publication of this material, there have been a number of vendor efforts to improve security, such as the Microsoft effort described in [Howard 2007].

Guttorm Sindre and Andreas Opdahl extend use-case diagrams with misuse cases to represent the actions that systems should prevent in tandem with those that they should support for security and privacy requirements analysis [Sindre 2000]. Ian Alexander advocates using misuse and use cases together to conduct threat and hazard analysis during requirements analysis [Alexander 2003]. Here, we provide a nonacademic introduction to the software security best practice of misuse and abuse cases, showing you how to put the basic science to work.

3.2.1 Security Is Not a Set of Features

There is no convenient security pull-down menu that will let you select "security" and then sit back and watch magic things happen. Unfortunately, many software developers simply link functional security features and mechanisms somewhere into their software, mistakenly assuming that doing so addresses security needs throughout the system. Too often, product literature makes broad, feature-based claims about security, such as "built with SSL" or "128-bit encryption included," which represent the vendor's entire approach for securing its product.

Security is an emergent property of a system, not a feature. This is analogous to how "being dry" is an emergent property of being inside a tent in the rain. The tent will keep you dry only if the poles are stabilized, vertical, and able to support the weight of wet fabric; the tent also must have waterproof fabric (with no holes) and be large enough to protect everyone who wants to remain dry. Lastly, everyone must remain under the tent for the entire time it's raining. So, although having poles and fabric is important, it's not enough to say, "The tent has poles and fabric; thus it keeps you dry!" This sort of claim, however, is analogous to the claims that software vendors make when they highlight numbers of bits in cryptographic keys or the use of particular encryption algorithms. Cryptography of one kind or another is usually necessary to create a secure system, but security features alone are not sufficient for building secure software.

Because security is not a feature, it cannot be bolted on after other software features are codified, nor can it be patched in after attacks have occurred in the field. Instead, security must be built into the product from the ground up, as a critical part of the design from the very beginning (requirements specification) and included in every subsequent development phase, all the way through fielding a complete system.

Sometimes building security in at the beginning of the SDLC means making explicit tradeoffs when specifying system requirements. For example, ease of use might be paramount in a medical system designed for clerical personnel in doctors' offices, but complex authentication procedures, such as obtaining and using a cryptographic identity, can be hard to use [Whitten 1999]. Furthermore, regulatory pressures from HIPAA and California's privacy regulations (Senate Bill 1386) force designers to negotiate a reasonable tradeoff.

Technical approaches must go far beyond the obvious features, deep into the many-tiered heart of a software system, to provide enough security: Authentication and authorization can't stop at a program's front door. The best, most cost-effective approach to software security incorporates thinking beyond normative features and maintains that thinking throughout the development process. Every time a new requirement, feature, or use case is created, the developer or security specialist should spend some time thinking about how that feature might be unintentionally misused or intentionally abused. Professionals who know how features are attacked and how to protect software should play active roles in this kind of analysis.

3.2.2 Thinking About What You Can't Do

Attackers are not standard-issue customers. They're bad people with malicious intentions who want your software to act to their benefit. If the development process doesn't address unexpected or abnormal behavior, then an attacker usually has plenty of raw material with which to work [Hoglund 2004].

Although attackers are creative, they always probe well-known locations—boundary conditions, edges, intersystem communication, and system assumptions—in the course of their attacks. Clever attackers will try to undermine the assumptions on which a system was built. If a design assumes that connections from the Web server to the database server are always valid, for example, an attacker will try to make the Web server send inappropriate requests to access valuable data. If the software design assumes that the client never modifies its Web browser cookies before they are sent back to the requesting server (in an attempt to preserve some state), attackers will intentionally cause problems by modifying the cookies. *Building Secure Software* teaches us that we have to be on guard when we make any assumptions [Viega 2001].

When we design and analyze a system, we're in a great position to know our systems better than potential attackers do. We must leverage this knowledge to the benefit of security and reliability, which we can achieve by asking and answering the following critical questions: Which assumptions are implicit in our system? Which kinds of things make our assumptions false? Which kinds of attack patterns will an attacker bring to bear?

Unfortunately, a system's creators are not the best security analysts of that system. Consciously noting and considering all assumptions (especially in light of thinking like an attacker) is extremely difficult for those who have built up a set of implicit assumptions. Fortunately, these professionals make excellent subject matter experts (SMEs). Together, SMEs and security analysts can ferret out base assumptions in a system under analysis and think through the ways an attacker will approach the software.

3.2.3 Creating Useful Misuse Cases

One of the goals of misuse cases is to decide and document *a priori* how software should react to illegitimate use. The simplest, most practical method for creating misuse cases is usually through a process of informed brainstorming. Several theoretical methods require fully speci-fying a system with rigorous formal models and logics, but such activities are extremely time and resource intensive. A more practical approach teams security and reliability experts with SMEs. This approach relies heavily on expertise and covers a lot of ground quickly.

To guide brainstorming, software security experts ask many questions of a system's designers to help identify the places where the system is likely to have weaknesses. This activity mirrors the way attackers think. Such brainstorming involves a careful look at all user interfaces (including environmental factors) and considers events that develop-ers assume a person can't or won't do. These "can'ts" and "won'ts" take many forms: "Users can't enter more than 50 characters because the JavaScript code won't let them" or "Users don't understand the format of the cached data, so they can't modify it." Attackers, unfortu-nately, can make these can'ts and won'ts happen.

The process of specifying abuse cases makes a designer very clearly dif-ferentiate appropriate use from inappropriate use. To reach this point, however, the designer must ask the right questions: How can the system distinguish between good input and bad input? Can it tell whether a request is coming from a legitimate application or from a rogue application replaying traffic? All systems have more vulnerable places than the obvious front doors, so where might a bad guy be positioned? On the wire? At a workstation? In the back office? Any communication line between two endpoints or two components is a place where an attacker might try to interpose himself or herself, so what can this attacker do in the system? Watch communications traffic? Modify and replay such traffic? Read files stored on the workstation? Change registry keys or configuration files? Be the DLL? Be the "chip"?

Trying to answer such questions helps software designers explicitly question design and architecture assumptions, and it puts the designer squarely ahead of the attacker by identifying and fixing a problem before it's ever created.

3.2.4 An Abuse Case Example

This section describes a real-world example of a classic software security problem on a client/server application. The architecture had been set up so that the server relied on the client-side application, which manipulated a financially sensitive database, to manage all data-access permissions—no permissions were enforced on the server itself. In fact, only the client had any notion of permissions and access control. To make matters worse, a complete copy of the database (only parts of which were to be viewed by a given user with a particular client) was sent to the client program, which ran on a garden-variety desktop PC. As a consequence, a complete copy of the sensitive data (which was expressly *not* to be viewed by the user) was available on that user's PC in the clear. If the user looked in the application's cache on the hard disk and used a standard-issue unzip utility, he or she could see all sorts of sensitive information.

The client also enforced which messages were sent to the server, honoring these messages independent of the user's actual credentials. The server assumed that any messages coming from the client had passed the client software's access control system (and policy) and were, therefore, legitimate. By intercepting network traffic, corrupting values in the client software's cache, or building a hostile client, malicious users could inject data into the database that they were not even supposed to read (much less write to).

Determining the can'ts and won'ts in such a case is difficult for those who think only about positive features. Attack patterns can provide

Misuse/Abuse Case Templates

Templates for misuse and abuse cases appear in a number of references. They can be text or diagrams, and some are supported by tools. Some good sources for templates are in materials by Sindre and Opdahl [Sindre 2001] and Alexander [Alexander 2002]. Figure 3–1 is an example of a use/misuse-case diagram to elicit security requirements from Alexander's article. The high-level case is shown on the left; use cases are drawn in white and misuse cases are drawn in black.

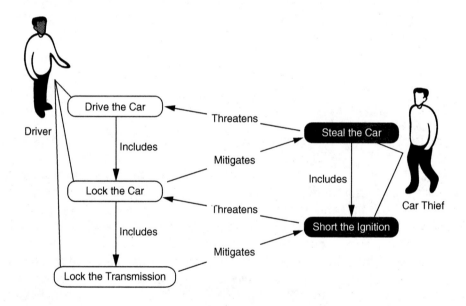

Use Cases for Car Security

Figure 3–1: *Misuse case example*

some guidance in this regard (see Section 2.3.2). Attack patterns are akin to patterns in sewing—that is, a blueprint for creating an attack. Everyone's favorite example, the buffer overflow, follows several different standard patterns, but patterns allow for a fair amount of variation on a theme. They can take into account many dimensions, including timing, resources required, techniques, and so forth [Hoglund 2004]. When we're trying to develop misuse and abuse cases, attack patterns can help.

It is possible for misuse cases to be overused (and generated forever with little impact on actual security). A solid approach to building them requires a combination of security know-how and subject matter expertise to prioritize misuse cases as they are generated and to strike the right balance between cost and value.

Although misuse and abuse cases can be used as a stand-alone activity, they are more effective when they are developed as part of an overall security requirements engineering process. As noted in Section 3.1.3, a number of processes can be used to address security requirements engineering. In the next section, we describe one such process, the SQUARE process model, in which misuse and abuse cases play important roles. Consult the reference material that we have provided to learn about other processes and select the process and methods that are best for your organization.

3.3 The SQUARE Process Model

Security Quality Requirements Engineering (SQUARE) is a process model that was developed at Carnegie Mellon University [Mead 2005].[3] It provides a means for eliciting, categorizing, and prioritizing security requirements for information technology systems and applications. (Note that this section and the following sections all discuss security requirements, regardless of whether the term "security" is specifically used as a qualifier.) The focus of the model is to build security concepts into the early stages of the SDLC. It can also be used for documenting and analyzing the security aspects of systems once they are implemented in the field and for steering future improvements and modifications to those systems.

After its initial development, SQUARE was applied in a series of client case studies [Chen 2004; Gordon 2005; Xie 2004]. Prototype tools were also developed to support the process. The draft process was revised and established as a baseline after the case studies were completed; the baselined process is shown in Table 3–1. In principle, Steps 1–4 are actually activities that precede security requirements engineering but are necessary to ensure that it is successful. Brief descriptions of each step follow; a detailed discussion of the method can be found in [Mead 2005].

---

3. The SQUARE work is supported by the Army Research Office through grant number DAAD19-02-1-0389 ("Perpetually Available and Secure Information Systems") to Carnegie Mellon University's CyLab.

Table 3–1: *The SQUARE Process*

Number	Step	Input	Techniques	Participants	Output
1	Agree on definitions	Candidate definitions from IEEE and other standards	Structured interviews, focus group	Stakeholders, requirements engineers	Agreed-to definitions
2	Identify security goals	Definitions, candidate goals, business drivers, policies and procedures, examples	Facilitated work session, surveys, interviews	Stakeholders, requirements engineers	Goals
3	Develop artifacts to support security requirements definition	Potential artifacts (e.g., scenarios, misuse cases, templates, forms)	Work session	Requirements engineers	Needed artifacts: scenarios, misuse cases, models, templates, forms
4	Perform (security) risk assessment	Misuse cases, scenarios, security goals	Risk assessment method, analysis of anticipated risk against organizational risk tolerance, including threat analysis	Requirements engineers, risk expert, stakeholders	Risk assessment results

Continues

Table 3–1: *The SQUARE Process (Continued)*

Number	Step	Input	Techniques	Participants	Output
5	Select elicitation techniques	Goals, definitions, candidate techniques, expertise of stakeholders, organizational style, culture, level of security needed, cost–benefit analysis	Work session	Requirements engineers	Selected elicitation techniques
6	Elicit security requirements	Artifacts, risk assessment results, selected techniques	Accelerated Requirements Method, Joint Application Development, interviews, surveys, model-based analysis, checklists, lists of reusable requirements types, document reviews	Stakeholders facilitated by requirements engineers	Initial cut at security requirements

Table 3–1: *The SQUARE Process (Continued)*

Number	Step	Input	Techniques	Participants	Output
7	Categorize requirements as to level (e.g., system, software) and whether they are requirements or other kinds of constraints	Initial requirements, architecture	Work session using a standard set of categories	Requirements engineers, other specialists as needed	Categorized requirements
8	Prioritize requirements	Categorized requirements and risk assessment results	Prioritization methods such as Analytical Hierarchy Process (AHP), triage, and win-win	Stakeholders facilitated by requirements engineers	Prioritized requirements
9	Inspect requirements	Prioritized requirements, candidate formal inspection technique	Inspection method such as Fagan and peer reviews	Inspection team	Initial selected requirements, documentation of decision-making process and rationale

3.3.1 A Brief Description of SQUARE

The SQUARE process is best applied by the project's requirements engineers and security experts in the context of supportive executive management and stakeholders. We have observed that this process works best when elicitation occurs after risk assessment (Step 4) has been done and when security requirements are specified before critical architecture and design decisions. Thus critical security risks to the business will be considered in the development of the security requirements.

Step 1, "Agree on definitions," is needed as a prerequisite to security requirements engineering. On a given project, team members tend to have definitions in mind, based on their prior experience, but those definitions often differ [Woody 2005]. For example, for some government organizations, security has to do with access based on security clearance levels, whereas for others security may have to do with physical security or cybersecurity. It is not necessary to invent definitions. Sources such as the Institute for Electrical and Electronics Engineers (IEEE) and the Software Engineering Body of Knowledge (SWEBOK) provide a range of definitions to select from or tailor. A focus group meeting with the interested parties will most likely enable the selection of a consistent set of definitions for the security requirements activity.

Step 2, "Identify security goals," should be done at the organizational level and is needed to support software development in the project at hand. This step provides a consistency check with the organization's policies and operational security environment. Different stakeholders usually have different goals. For example, a stakeholder in human resources may be concerned about maintaining the confidentiality of personnel records, whereas a stakeholder in a financial area may be concerned with ensuring that financial data is not accessed or modified without authorization. It is important to have a representative set of stakeholders, including those with operational expertise. Once the goals of the various stakeholders have been identified, they need to be prioritized. In the absence of consensus, an executive decision may be needed to prioritize them. It is expected that the goals identified in this step will link to the core properties discussed in Chapter 2.

Step 3, "Develop artifacts," is necessary to support all subsequent security requirements engineering activities. Organizations often do not have a documented concept of operations for a project, succinctly stated project goals, documented normal usage and threat scenarios, misuse or abuse cases, and other documents needed to support requirements definition. As a consequence, either the entire requirements process is built on unstated assumptions or a lot of time is spent backtracking to try to obtain such documentation.

Step 4, "Perform risk assessment," requires an expert in risk assessment methods, the support of the stakeholders, and the support of a security requirements engineer. A number of risk assessment methods are available (as discussed in detail in Section 3.4.1). The risk assessment expert can recommend a specific method based on the unique needs of the organization. The artifacts from Step 3 provide the input to the risk assessment process; the outcomes of the risk assessment, in turn, can help in identifying the high-priority security exposures (see also the discussion of the risk management framework in Section 7.4). Organizations that do not perform risk assessment typically do not have a logical approach to considering organizational risks when identifying security requirements, but rather tend to select specific solutions or technologies, such as encryption, without really understanding the problem that is being solved.

Step 5, "Select elicitation technique," becomes important when the project has diverse stakeholders. A more formal elicitation technique, such as the Accelerated Requirements Method [Hubbard 1999], Joint Application Design [Wood 1989], or structured interviews, can be effective in overcoming communication issues when stakeholders have variable cultural backgrounds. In other cases, elicitation may simply consist of sitting down with a primary stakeholder and trying to understand that stakeholder's security requirements needs.

Step 6, "Elicit security requirements," is the actual elicitation process using the selected technique. Most elicitation techniques provide detailed guidance on how to perform elicitation. This effort builds on the artifacts that were developed in earlier steps, such as misuse and abuse cases, attack trees, threats, and scenarios.

Step 7, "Categorize requirements," allows the security requirements engineer to distinguish among essential requirements, goals (desired requirements), and architectural constraints that may be present. Requirements that are actually constraints typically arise when a specific system architecture has been chosen prior to the requirements process. This is good, as it allows for assessment of the risks associated with these constraints. This categorization also helps in the prioritization activity that follows (Step 8).

Step 8, "Prioritize requirements," depends not only on the prior step, but may also involve performing a cost–benefit analysis to determine which security requirements have a high payoff relative to their cost. Prioritization may also depend on other consequences of security breaches, such as loss of life, loss of reputation, and loss of consumer confidence.

Step 9, "Requirements inspection," can be done at varying levels of formality, ranging from Fagan inspections (a highly structured and proven technique for requirements inspection) [Fagan 1999] to peer reviews. Once this inspection is complete, the project team should have an initial set of prioritized security requirements. It should also understand which areas are incomplete and must be revisited at a later time. Finally, the project team should understand which areas are dependent on specific architectures and implementations and should plan to revisit those areas as well.

3.3.2 Tools

A prototype tool has been developed to support SQUARE. It primarily provides an organizational framework for the artifact documents; in addition, it provides default content for some of the steps. The tool does not perform sophisticated functions such as requirements analysis. This prototype is undergoing further development so that it will provide better support to the SQUARE process and be more attractive to users. The current status of the SQUARE process and tool, as well as contact information, can be found at http://www.cert.org/nav/index_purple.html/square.html.

3.3.3 Expected Results

When you apply SQUARE, you can expect relevant security requirements to be identified and documented for the system or software that is being developed. SQUARE is better suited to use with a system under development than with a system that has already been fielded, although it has been used in both situations. Although quantitative measures do not exist, case study clients recognized the value of the new security requirements and have taken steps to incorporate them into their system specifications. You'll need to consider the resources required for this activity and for the implementation of the resulting requirements [Xie 2004].

Our experience with SQUARE suggests that the system and its elements must be considered within the context or environment in which it operates. For example, a system that operates on a single isolated workstation will have very different security requirements from a similar system that is Web based. Likewise, a medical information system will have different security requirements for workstations that are isolated in a physician's office than for those that are located in a public area in a hospital. These differences should be accounted for in the artifacts developed in Step 3—for example, in usage scenarios and misuse or abuse cases. When the context for a project changes, you should revisit the security requirements and reapply the SQUARE process. It may be that a subset of the SQUARE steps will be sufficient for this purpose, but we do not yet have enough experience with subsequent applications of SQUARE to the same system to make that determination.

3.4 SQUARE Sample Outputs

Several case studies have been conducted using the SQUARE process model [Chen 2004; Gordon 2005]. The goals of these case studies were to experiment with each step of the SQUARE process, make recommendations, and determine the feasibility of integrating the SQUARE methodology into standard software development practices. The case studies involved real-world clients that were developing large-scale IT projects, including an IT firm in Pittsburgh, Pennsylvania; a federal government research institute; and a department of the federal government.

Acme Corporation (an alias used to protect the identity of the client), a private IT firm headquartered in Pittsburgh, provides technical and management services to various public sectors and a number of diversified private sectors. Its product, the Asset Management System (AMS) version 2, provides a tool that enables companies to make strategic allocations and plans for their critical IT assets. This system provides specialized decision support capabilities via customized views. AMS provides a graphical interface to track and analyze the state of important assets. The security requirements surrounding the AMS are the subject of one of our case studies and the source of the sample outputs that follow.

3.4.1 Output from SQUARE Steps

We present a sample output for each step, all taken from the case studies, to provide concrete examples of the nine SQUARE steps. Given that these are actual results, they are not all that sophisticated or cutting edge, but they do reflect the typical state of affairs at present. Note, however, that these snippets leave out underlying assumptions and background information.

Step 1: Agree on Definitions

We worked with the client to agree on a common set of security definitions with which to create a common base of understanding. The following is a small subset of the definitions that were agreed to:

- *Access control:* Ensures that resources are granted only to those users who are entitled to them.
- *Access control list:* A table that tells a computer operating system which access rights or explicit denials each user has to a particular system object, such as a file directory or individual file.
- *Antivirus software:* A class of program that searches hard drives and memory for any known or potential viruses.

The full set of definitions was drawn from resources such as IEEE, Carnegie Mellon University, industry, and various dictionaries.

Step 2: Identify Security Goals

We worked with the client to flesh out security goals that mapped to the company's overall business goals. This is one example set of goals:

- *Business goal of AMS:* To provide an application that supports asset management and planning.
- *Security goals:* Three high-level security goals were derived for the system (it's not surprising that these are closely linked to the security properties of Chapter 2):

   a. Management shall exercise effective control over the system's configuration and use.

   b. The confidentiality, accuracy, and integrity of the AMS shall be maintained.

   c. The AMS shall be available for use when needed.

Step 3: Develop Artifacts

Architectural diagrams, use cases, misuse cases, abuse case diagrams, attack trees, and essential assets and services were documented in this step. As noted earlier, the attack patterns discussed in Chapter 2 provide a good starting point for developing artifacts that reflect the attacker's perspective. For instance, an attack scenario was documented in the following way:

System administrator accesses confidential information

1. by being recruited OR
    a. by being bribed OR
    b. by being threatened OR
    c. through social engineering OR
2. by purposefully abusing rights

An example abuse case diagram is shown in Figure 3–2.

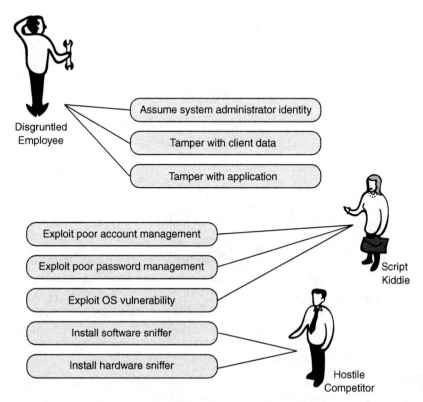

Figure 3–2: *Abuse case example*

This step creates needed documentation that serves as input for the following steps.

Step 4: Perform Risk Assessment

The risk assessment techniques that were field tested were selected after completing a literature review. This review examined the usefulness and applicability of eight risk assessment techniques:

1. General Accounting Office Model [GAO 1999]
2. National Institute of Standards and Technology (NIST) Model [Stoneburner 2002]
3. NSA's INFOSEC Assessment Methodology [NSA 2004]
4. Shawn Butler's Security Attribute Evaluation Method [Butler 2002]
5. Carnegie Mellon's Vendor Risk Assessment and Threat Evaluation [Lipson 2001]
6. Yacov Haimes's Risk Filtering, Ranking, and Management Model [Haimes 2004]
7. Carnegie Mellon's Survivable Systems Analysis Method [Mead 2002]
8. Martin Feather's Defect Detection and Prevention Model [Cornford 2004]

Each method was ranked in four categories:

1. Suitability for small companies
2. Feasibility of completion in the time allotted
3. Lack of dependence on historical threat data
4. Suitability in addressing requirements

The results of the ranking are shown in Table 3–2.

After averaging scores from the four categories, NIST's and Haimes's models were selected as useful techniques for the risk assessment step. Brainstorming, attack tree, and misuse case documentation were used to identify potential threat scenarios. The two independent risk assessment analyses produced a useful risk profile for the company's system, with two especially meaningful findings:

*   Insider threat poses the highest-impact risk to the AMS.
*   Because of weak controls, it is easy for an insider or unauthorized user to defeat authentication.

Table 3–2: *Ranking of Assessment Techniques*

Methodologies	Suitable for Small Companies	Feasible to Complete within Time Frame	Does Not Require Additional Data Collection	Suitable for Requirements	Average Score
GAO	2	4	2	2	2.50
NIST	2	2	1	1	1.50
NSA/IAM	3	3	2	2	2.50
SAEM	4	4	4	4	4.00
V-Rate	3	4	4	4	3.75
Haimes	2	2	2	2	2.00
SSA	2	2	2	4	2.50
DDP/Feather	3	4	2	4	3.25

In this particular case study, we also identified a set of essential services and assets as part of the artifact generation. This activity is not part of the standard SQUARE process but nevertheless can be a beneficial exercise if enough architectural information already exists to support it. All findings from the risk assessment, along with the findings from the essential services and asset identification process, were used to determine the priority level associated with each of the nine requirements.

We analyzed the importance of each of the major system services, outlined in the 11 use cases shown in Table 3–3, and made a determination as to which were essential.

Table 3–3: *Classification of Use Cases*

Use Case	Service	Status
UC-1	View floor plans	*Essential*
UC-2	Enter damage assessment	*Essential*
UC-3	Add/delete/edit Post-it notes	Nonessential
UC-4	Find specialized employees	*Important*
UC-5	Create journal entry	Nonessential
UC-6	Install the Asset Management System	Nonessential
UC-7	Create links to documents	Nonessential
UC-8	Archibus administration: Add user and assign privileges	Nonessential
UC-9	View contact information for maintenance tasks	*Important*
UC-10	Create open space report	*Essential*
UC-11	View incident command	*Essential*

There are two essential assets in this system. The first is the Windows Server computer, which houses the majority of the production system's intellectual assets (that is, the code that runs the system). This computer acts as a server that allows remote users to access the Asset Management System. The second essential asset is the information inside the Windows Server computer—specifically, the files stored in the Microsoft IIS server and the information stored in the Sybase database and MapGuide database are critical for making informed decisions. If this information is lost or compromised, the ability to make accurate decisions is lost.

Step 5: Select Elicitation Techniques

For this step, teams tested various elicitation techniques and models. It is often the case that multiple techniques will work for the same project. The difficulty lies in choosing a technique that can be adapted to the number and expertise of stakeholders, the size and scope of the client project, and the expertise of the requirements engineering team. It is extremely unlikely that any single technique will work for all projects under all circumstances, although our experience has shown that the Accelerated Requirements Method [Hubbard 2000] has been successful in eliciting security requirements. Selection of an elicitation technique is discussed in more detail in Section 3.5.

Steps 6 and 7: Elicit and Categorize Security Requirements

Nine security requirements were identified and then organized to map to the three high-level security goals (see Step 2). Examples include the following requirements:

- Requirement 1: The system is required to have strong authentication measures in place at all system gateways and entrance points (maps to Goals 1 and 2).

- Requirement 2: The system is required to have sufficient process-centric and logical means to govern which system elements (e.g., data, functionality) users can view, modify, and/or interact with (maps to Goals 1 and 2).

- Requirement 3: A continuity of operations plan (COOP) is required to assure system availability (maps to Goal 3).

- Requirement 6: It is required that the system's network communications be protected from unauthorized information gathering and/or eavesdropping (maps to Goals 1 and 2).

The nine security requirements were central to the security requirements document that was ultimately delivered to the client.

Step 8: Prioritize Requirements

In the first case study, the nine security requirements were prioritized based on the following qualitative rankings:

- *Essential:* The product will be unacceptable if this requirement is absent.
- *Conditional:* The requirement enhances security, but the product is acceptable if this requirement is absent.
- *Optional:* The requirement is clearly of lower priority than essential and conditional requirements.

Requirement 1 from Steps 6 and 7, which dealt with authentication at borders and gateways, was deemed essential because of its importance in protecting against the high-impact, authentication-related risks identified in the risk assessment. Requirement 3, dealing with continuity of operations planning, was still seen as an important element and worth considering, but it was found to be an optional requirement relative to the other eight requirements. That is, although COOP plans are valuable, the risk assessment phase found that greater threats to the system resulted from unauthorized disclosure of information than from availability attacks.

We also used the Analytical Hierarchy Process (AHP) methodology to prioritize requirements and found it to be successful both in client acceptance and in its ability to handle security requirements [Karlsson 1997; Saaty 1980]. Requirements prioritization is discussed in more detail in Section 3.6.

Step 9: Requirements Inspection

We experimented with different inspection techniques and had varying levels of success with each. None of the inspection techniques was sufficiently effective in identifying defects in the security requirements. Instead, we recommend experimenting with the Fagan inspection technique.

In one case study instance, each team member played a role in inspecting the quality of the team's work and deliverables. A peer review log was created to document what had been reviewed and was used to maintain a log of all problems, defects, and concerns. Each entry in the log was numbered and dated, and indicated the date, origin, defect type, description, severity, owner, reviewer, and status of the issue. Each entry was assigned to an owner, who was responsible for making sure that defects were fixed. This step was used as a sanity check to ensure that the system met quality goals and expectations.

3.4.2 SQUARE Final Results

The final output to the client was a security requirements document. The client could then use this document in the early stages of the SDLC to ensure that security requirements were built into project plans.

Once a system has been deployed, the organization can look back to its requirements documentation to analyze whether it met its requirements and, therefore, satisfied its security goals. As change occurs—be it a configuration concern in the system, the organization's risk profile, or a business goal—the SQUARE process can be revisited to determine how the change might affect the system's security requirements. In this way, SQUARE can be reapplied to a system as needed.

3.5 Requirements Elicitation

Using an elicitation method can help in producing a consistent and complete set of security requirements. However, brainstorming and elicitation methods used for ordinary functional (end-user) requirements usually are not oriented toward security requirements and, therefore, do not result in a consistent and complete set of security requirements. The resulting system is likely to have fewer security exposures when requirements are elicited in a systematic way.

In this section, we briefly discuss a number of elicitation methods and the kind of tradeoff analysis that can be done to select a suitable one. Companion case studies can be found in "Requirements Elicitation Case Studies" [BSI 10]. While results may vary from one organization to another, the discussion of our selection process and various methods should be of general utility. Requirements elicitation is an active research area, and we expect to see advances in this area in the future.

Eventually, studies will likely determine which methods are most effective for eliciting security requirements. At present, however, there is little if any data comparing the effectiveness of different methods for eliciting security requirements.

3.5.1 Overview of Several Elicitation Methods

The following list identifies several methods that could be considered for eliciting security requirements. Some have been developed specifically with security in mind (e.g., misuse cases), whereas others have been used for traditional requirements engineering and could potentially be extended to security requirements. In the future, we may have a better understanding of how the unique aspects of security requirements elicitation drive selection of a method. We also note recent work on requirements elicitation in general that could be considered in developing such a list [Hickey 2003, 2004; Zowghi 2005] and in doing the selection process [Hickey 2004]. We briefly describe each of the following elicitation methods:

- Misuse cases [Sindre 2000; McGraw 2006, pp. 205–222]
- Soft Systems Methodology [Checkland 1990]
- Quality Function Deployment [QFD 2005]
- Controlled Requirements Expression [Christel 1992; SDS 1985]
- Issue-based information systems [Kunz 1970]
- Joint Application Development [Wood 1995]
- Feature-oriented domain analysis [Kang 1990]
- Critical discourse analysis [Schiffrin 1994]
- Accelerated Requirements Method [Hubbard 2000]

Misuse Cases

As noted earlier, misuse/abuse cases apply the concept of a negative scenario—that is, a situation that the system's owner does *not* want to occur—in a use-case context. For example, business leaders, military planners, and game players are familiar with the strategy of analyzing their opponents' best moves as identifiable threats.

By contrast, a use case generally describes behavior that the system owner *wants* the system to show [Sindre 2000]. Use-case models and their associated diagrams (UCDs) have proven quite helpful for the specification of requirements [Jacobson 1992; Rumbaugh 1994]. However, a collection of use cases should not be used as a substitute for a requirements specification document, as this approach can result in overlooking significant requirements [Anton 2001]. As a result, it is controversial to use only use-case models for system and quality requirements elicitation.

Soft Systems Methodology (SSM)

SSM deals with problem situations in which there is a high social, political, and human activity component [Checkland 1990]. The SSM can deal with "soft problems" that are difficult to define, rather than "hard problems" that are more technology oriented. Examples of soft problems include how to deal with homelessness, how to manage disaster planning, and how to improve Medicare. Eventually technology-oriented problems may emerge from these soft problems, but much more analysis is needed to reach that point.

The primary benefit of SSM is that it provides structure to soft problem situations and enables their resolution in an organized manner. In addition, it compels the developer to discover a solution that goes beyond technology.

Quality Function Deployment (QFD)

QFD is "an overall concept that provides a means of translating customer requirements into the appropriate technical requirements for each stage of product development and production" [QFD 2005]. The distinguishing attribute of QFD is the focus on customer needs throughout all product development activities. By using QFD, organizations can promote teamwork, prioritize action items, define clear objectives, and reduce development time [QFD 2005].

Controlled Requirements Expression (CORE)

CORE is a requirements analysis and specification method that clarifies the user's view of the services to be supplied by the proposed system. In CORE, the requirements specification is created by both the user and the developer—not solely one or the other. The problem to be analyzed is defined and broken down into user and developer viewpoints. Information about the combined set of viewpoints is then analyzed. The last step of CORE deals with constraints analysis, such as the limitations imposed by the system's operational environment, in conjunction with some degree of performance and reliability investigation.

Issue-Based Information Systems (IBIS)

Developed by Horst Rittel, the IBIS method is based on the principle that the design process for complex problems, which Rittel terms *wicked* problems, is essentially an exchange among the stakeholders in which each stakeholder brings his or her personal expertise and perspective to the resolution of design issues [Kunz 1970]. Any problem, concern, or question can be an issue and may require discussion and resolution for the design to proceed.

Joint Application Development (JAD)

The JAD methodology [Wood 1995] is specifically designed for the development of large computer systems. Its goal is to involve all stakeholders in the design phase of the product via highly structured and focused meetings. In the preliminary phases of JAD, the requirements engineering team is charged with fact-finding and information-gathering tasks. Typically, the outputs of this phase, as applied to security requirements elicitation, are security goals and artifacts. The actual JAD session is then used to validate this information by establishing an agreed-on set of security requirements for the product.

Feature-Oriented Domain Analysis (FODA)

FODA is a domain analysis and engineering method that focuses on developing reusable assets [Kang 1990]. By examining related software systems and the underlying theory of the class of systems they represent, domain analysis can provide a generic description of the requirements of that class of systems in the form of a domain model and a set of approaches for their implementation.

The FODA method was founded on two modeling concepts: abstraction and refinement [Kean 1997]. Abstraction is used to create domain models from the specific applications in the domain. Specific applications in the domain are then developed as refinements of the domain models. The example domain used in the initial report on FODA [Kang 1990] is window management systems. The window management examples of that time are no longer in use, but include VMS, Sun, and Macintosh, among others.

Critical Discourse Analysis (CDA)

CDA uses sociolinguistic methods to analyze verbal and written discourse [Schiffrin 1994]. In particular, this technique can be used to analyze requirements elicitation interviews and to understand the narratives and "stories" that emerge during those interviews.

Accelerated Requirements Method (ARM)

The ARM process [Hubbard 2000] is a facilitated requirements elicitation and description activity. It includes three phases:

1. Preparation phase
2. Facilitated session phase
3. Deliverable closure phase

The ARM process is similar to JAD but has certain significant differences from the baseline JAD method, which contribute to its uniqueness. For example, in this process, the facilitators are content neutral, the group dynamic techniques used are different from those used in JAD, the brainstorming techniques used are different, and the requirements are recorded and organized using different conceptual models.

3.5.2 Elicitation Evaluation Criteria

Following are example evaluation criteria that may be useful in selecting an elicitation method, although you could certainly use other criteria. The main point is to select a set of criteria and to have a common understanding of what they mean.

- *Adaptability.* The method can be used to generate requirements in multiple environments. For example, the elicitation method works equally well with a software product that is near completion as it does with a project in the planning stages.
- *Computer-aided software engineering (CASE) tool.* The method includes a CASE tool.
- *Stakeholder acceptance.* The stakeholders are likely to agree to the elicitation method in analyzing their requirements. For example, the method isn't too invasive in a business environment.
- *Easy implementation.* The elicitation method isn't overly complex and can be properly executed easily.

- *Graphical output.* The method produces readily understandable visual artifacts.

- *Quick implementation.* The requirements engineers and stakeholders can fully execute the elicitation method in a reasonable length of time.

- *Shallow learning curve.* The requirements engineers and stakeholders can fully comprehend the elicitation method within a reasonable length of time.

- *High maturity.* The elicitation method has experienced considerable exposure and analysis with the requirements engineering community.

- *Scalability.* The method can be used to elicit the requirements of projects of different sizes, from enterprise-level systems to small-scale applications.

Note that this approach presumes that all criteria are equally important. If some criteria are more important than others, a weighted average can be used. For example, availability of a CASE tool might be more important than graphical output. A typical weighting scheme could consider criteria to be "essential" with weight 3, "desirable" with weight 2, and "optional" with weight 1. The elicitation methods can then be ranked using a tabular form, as shown in Table 3–4. The example in Table 3–4 is not intended to be an actual recommendation to use a specific method. You can develop your own comparison criteria and ratings.

In our case studies, we decided to use JAD, ARM, and IBIS on three different projects. These three methods were subjectively ranked to be the most suitable candidates for the case studies, given the time and effort constraints for the project. We considered not just the total score: The learning curve was an important factor, and the team attempted to select methods that were not too similar to one another, so as to have some variety. In our case studies, we had the most success using ARM to identify security requirements. Detailed results for all three methods can be found in the Requirements Engineering section of the Build Security In Web site [BSI 10].

Additional Considerations

It is possible that a combination of methods may work best. You should consider this option as part of the evaluation process, assuming that you have sufficient time and resources to assess how methods

Table 3–4: *Comparison of Elicitation Methods*

	Misuse Cases	SSM	QFD	CORE	IBIS	JAD	FODA	CDA	ARM
Adaptability	3[a]	1	3	2	2	3	2	1	2
CASE tool	1	2	1	1	3	2	1	1	1
Stakeholder acceptance	2	2	2	2	3	2	1	3	3
Easy implementation	2	2	1	2	3	2	1	1	2
Graphical output	2	2	1	1	2	1	2	2	3
Quick implementation	2	2	1	1	2	1	2	2	3
Shallow learning curve	3	1	2	1	3	2	1	1	1
High maturity	2	3	3	3	2	3	2	2	1
Scalability	1	3	3	3	2	3	2	1	2
Total Score	**18**	**18**	**17**	**16**	**22**	**19**	**14**	**14**	**18**

a. 3 = Very good; 2 = Fair; 1 = Poor.

may be combined and to actually combine them. You should also consider the time necessary to implement a particular elicitation method and the time needed to learn a new tool that supports a method. Selecting a requirements elicitation method that meets the needs of a diverse group of stakeholders aids in addressing a broader range of security requirements.

3.6 Requirements Prioritization

Once you have identified a set of security requirements, you will usually want to prioritize them. Given the existence of time and budget constraints, it can be difficult to implement all requirements that have been elicited for a system. Also, security requirements are often implemented in stages, and prioritization can help to determine which ones should be implemented first. Many organizations pick the lowest-cost requirements to implement first, without regard to importance. Others pick the requirements that are easiest to implement—for example, by purchasing a COTS solution. These ad hoc approaches are not likely to achieve the security goals of the organization or the project.

To prioritize security requirements in a more logical fashion, we recommend a systematic prioritization approach. This section discusses a tradeoff analysis that you can perform to select a suitable requirements prioritization method and briefly describes a number of methods. We also discuss a method of prioritizing requirements using AHP. More extensive coverage of this material is available elsewhere [Chung 2006].

While results may vary for your organization, the discussion of the various techniques should be of interest. Much work needs to be done before security requirements prioritization is considered a mature area, but it is one that we must start to address.

3.6.1 Identify Candidate Prioritization Methods

A number of prioritization methods have been found to be useful in traditional requirements engineering and could potentially be used for developing security requirements. We briefly mention here the binary search tree, numeral assignment technique, planning game, the 100-point method, Theory-W, requirements triage, Wiegers' method, requirements prioritization framework, and AHP. Further information can be found on the Build Security In Web site and in the references.

Binary Search Tree (BST)

A binary search tree is an algorithm that is typically used in a search for information and can easily be scaled to be used in prioritizing many requirements [Ahl 2005]. The basic approach for requirements is as follows, quoting from [Ahl 2005]:

1. Put all requirements in one pile.
2. Take one requirement and put it as the root node.
3. Take another requirement and compare it to the root node.
4. If the requirement is less important than the root node, compare it to the left child node. If the requirement is more important than the root node, compare it to the right child node. If the node does not have any appropriate child nodes, insert the new requirement as the new child node to the right or left, depending on whether the requirement is more or less important.
5. Repeat Steps 3 and 4 until all requirements have been compared and inserted into the BST.
6. For presentation purposes, traverse through the entire BST in order and put the requirements in a list, with the least important requirement at the end of the list and the most important requirement at the start of the list.

Numeral Assignment Technique

The numeral assignment technique provides a scale for each requirement. Brackett proposed dividing the requirements into three groups: mandatory, desirable, and unessential [Brackett 1990]. Participants assign each requirement a number on a scale of 1 to 5 to indicate its importance [Karlsson 1995]. The final ranking is the average of all participants' rankings for each requirement.

Planning Game

The planning game is a feature of extreme programming [Beck 2004] and is used with customers to prioritize features based on stories. It is a variation of the numeral assignment technique, where the customer distributes the requirements into three groups: "those without which the system will not function," "those that are less essential but provide significant business value," and "those that would be nice to have."

100-Point Method

The 100-point method [Leffingwell 2003] is basically a voting scheme of the type that is used in brainstorming exercises. Each stakeholder is given 100 points that he or she can use for voting in favor of the most important requirements. The 100 points can be distributed in any way that the stakeholder desires. For example, if there are four requirements that the stakeholder views as having equal priority, he or she can put 25 points on each. If there is one requirement that the stakeholder views as having overarching importance, he or she can put 100 points on that requirement. However, this type of scheme works only for an initial vote. If a second vote is taken, people are likely to redistribute their votes in an effort to move their favorites up in the priority scheme.

Theory-W

Theory-W (also known as "win-win") was initially developed at the University of Southern California in 1989 [Boehm 1989; Park 1999]. This method supports negotiation to solve disagreements about requirements, so that each stakeholder has a "win." It relies on two principles:

1. Plan the flight and fly the plan.
2. Identify and manage your risks.

The first principle seeks to build well-structured plans that meet predefined standards for easy development, classification, and query. "Fly the plan" ensures that the progress follows the original plan. The second principle, "Identify and manage your risks," involves risk assessment and risk handling. It is used to guard the stakeholders' "win-win" conditions from infringement. In win-win negotiations, each user should rank the requirements privately before negotiations start. In the individual ranking process, the user considers whether he or she is willing to give up on certain requirements, so that individual winning and losing conditions are fully understood.

Requirements Triage

Requirements triage [Davis 2003] is a multistep process that includes establishing relative priorities for requirements, estimating the resources needed to satisfy each requirement, and selecting a subset of requirements to optimize the probability of the product's success in the intended market. This technique is clearly aimed at developers of software products in the commercial marketplace. Davis's more recent book [Davis 2005a] expands on the synergy between software development and marketing; we recommend that you read it if you are considering this approach. Requirements triage is a unique approach that is worth reviewing, although it clearly goes beyond traditional requirements prioritization to consider business factors as well.

Wiegers' Method

Wiegers' method relates directly to the value of each requirement to a customer [Wiegers 2003]. The priority is calculated by dividing the value of a requirement by the sum of the costs and technical risks associated with its implementation [Wiegers 2003]. The value of a requirement is viewed as depending on both the value provided by the client to the customer and the penalty that occurs if the requirement is missing. Given this perspective, developers should evaluate the cost of the requirement and its implementation risks as well as the penalty incurred if the requirement is missing. Attributes are evaluated on a scale of 1 to 9.

Requirements Prioritization Framework

The requirements prioritization framework and its associated tool [Moisiadis 2000, 2001] includes both elicitation and prioritization activities. This framework is intended to address the following issues:

- Elicitation of stakeholders' business goals for the project
- Rating the stakeholders using stakeholder profile models
- Allowing the stakeholders to rate the importance of the requirements and the business goals using a fuzzy graphic rating scale
- Rating the requirements based on objective measures
- Finding the dependencies between the requirements and clustering requirements so as to prioritize them more effectively
- Using risk analysis techniques to detect cliques among the stakeholders, deviations among the stakeholders for the subjective ratings, and the association between the stakeholders' inputs and the final ratings

AHP

AHP is a method for decision making in situations where multiple objectives are present [Saaty 1980; Karlsson 1996, 1997]. This method uses a "pair-wise" comparison matrix to calculate the value and costs of individual security requirements relative to one another. By using AHP, the requirements engineer can confirm the consistency of the result. AHP can prevent subjective judgment errors and increase the likelihood that the results are reliable. It is supported by a stand-alone tool as well as by a computational aid within the SQUARE tool.

3.6.2 Prioritization Technique Comparison

We recommend comparing several candidate prioritization techniques to aid in selecting a suitable technique. Some example evaluation criteria are provided here:

- *Clear-cut steps:* There is clear definition between stages or steps within the prioritization method.
- *Quantitative measurement:* The prioritization method's numerical output clearly displays the client's priorities for all requirements.
- *High maturity:* The method has had considerable exposure and analysis by the requirements engineering community.
- *Low labor-intensity:* A reasonable number of hours are needed to properly execute the prioritization method.
- *Shallow learning curve:* The requirements engineers and stakeholders can fully comprehend the method within a reasonable length of time.

Note that this simple approach does not consider the importance of each criterion. It is also possible to construct a weighted average when comparing techniques. For example, maturity may be of greater importance than learning curve. This difference could be taken into account by weighting the results and ranking the various criteria as "essential" with weight 3, "desirable" with weight 2, and "optional" with weight 1. A comparison matrix used in a case study is shown in Table 3–5. This example is not intended to be an actual recommendation to use a specific technique; you can develop your own comparison criteria and ratings.

For one of our case studies, we considered the numeral assignment technique (NAT), Theory-W (TW), and AHP. The results of the comparison are summarized in Table 3–5.

Table 3–5: *Comparison of Prioritization Techniques for a Case Study*

Selection Criteria	NAT	TW	AHP
Clear-cut steps	3[a]	2	3
Quantitative measurement	3	1	3
Maturity	1	3	3
Labor-intensive	2	1	2
Learning curve	3	1	2
Total Score	**12**	**8**	**13**

a. 3 = Very good; 2 = Fair; 1 = Poor.

We decided to use AHP as a prioritizing method. This decision was made on the basis of the results shown in Table 3-5 comparison, recognizing that the rankings are subjective. Factoring into the rationale behind choosing AHP were the team members' familiarity with the method, its quantitative outputs, and its structure in providing definite steps for implementation. The detailed case study results are described in [BSI 11].

3.6.3 Recommendations for Requirements Prioritization

Prioritization of security requirements is an important activity. We recommend that stakeholders select candidate prioritization techniques, develop selection criteria to pick one, and apply that methodology to decide which security requirements to implement when. During the prioritization process, stakeholders can verify that everyone has the same understanding about the security requirements and further examine any ambiguous requirements. After everyone reaches consensus, the results of the prioritization exercise will be more reliable.

3.7 Summary Ⓔ Ⓜ Ⓛ

In this chapter, we initially focused on the role of misuse and abuse cases, which can motivate the identification and documentation of security requirements. The examination of SQUARE focused on the process to support security requirements engineering. We also explored a method for selecting a requirements elicitation process and provided experimental results for several candidate elicitation processes. We then focused on methods for prioritizing requirements and described the results of a case study in this area.

On the Build Security In Web site, we also discuss the Comprehensive, Lightweight Application Security Process (CLASP) approach to security requirements engineering, core security requirements artifacts, and the use of attack trees in security requirements engineering [BSI 12]. Formal specification approaches to security requirements, such as REVEAL and Software Cost Reduction (SCR), are also useful in this regard. The higher levels of the Common Criteria provide similar results [BSI 13]. Another article on BSI discusses the use of integer programming for optimizing investment in implementation of security requirements [BSI 14].

Although security requirements engineering is an area of active research, many promising techniques have already emerged that you can use to identify the requirements needed to improve your software products. It seems obvious that systematic and thorough identification of security requirements in the early stages of the SDLC will result in more secure software and reduced security costs later on.

Here are our recommendations for software project managers who wish to pay more attention to security requirements engineering:

- Review your existing development practices. Do you have development practices that are specific to requirements engineering? If not, put a standard requirements engineering practice in place.

- If you have an existing requirements engineering process, does it address security requirements? If not, use the material presented in this chapter and elsewhere to decide which steps need to be taken to produce good security requirements. If your process does address security requirements, have you considered the end-user's and attacker's perspectives, in addition to the perspectives of other stakeholders?

- There is no one-size-fits-all answer to security requirements engineering. You need to analyze your projects to figure out which ones need more attention to security requirements (such as mission-critical systems) and which ones are less critical (such as administrative systems that don't contain sensitive data). Note, however, that even unimportant systems can potentially provide an attacker with an indirect means to access more critical systems and sensitive data.

- Start small. Try out your new and improved practices on a couple of systems under development so that you can debug the process without making all of your projects part of a grand experiment. The case study results described on the BSI Web site give guidance on how to go about this [BSI 10, 11].

- Document your results—both positive and negative—and use them to improve your processes. As you know, development processes need to be revisited periodically, just like everything else we do in software and security engineering.

- Don't be a victim of NIH ("not invented here"). If someone else has an approach to security requirements engineering that could potentially be useful to you, give it a try. It's not necessary to reinvent the wheel every time.

Chapter 4

Secure Software Architecture and Design

4.1 Introduction

4.1.1 The Critical Role of Architecture and Design

Software architecture and design is where ambiguities and ideas are translated and transformed into reality, where the *what* and *why* of requirements become the *who*, *when*, *where*, and *how* of the software to be. From a functional perspective, this transition from desire to actual form is second only to the requirements phase in contributing to the overall quality and success of the eventual software deliverable. From a security perspective, architecture and design is considered by many experts as the single most critical phase of the SDLC. Good decisions made during this phase will not only yield an approach and structure that are more resilient and resistant to attack, but will often also help to prescribe and guide good decisions in later phases such as code and test. Bad decisions made during this phase can lead to design flaws that can never be overcome or resolved by even the most intelligent and disciplined code and test efforts.

General Objectives of Software Architecture and Design

- Completeness
  - Supports the full scope of the defined requirements
- Stability
  - Consistently performs as intended within its defined operational context
- Flexibility
  - Can adapt to changing conditions
  - Decomposable such that selected components can be replaced going forward with minimal impact to the software
- Extensibility
  - Leverages industry standards
  - Long-lived and resistant to obsolescence
- Scalability
  - Operates effectively at any size and load

Security-Specific Objectives of Software Architecture and Design

- Comprehensive functional security architecture
  - Security features and capabilities are fully enabled
- Attack resistance
  - Contains minimal security weaknesses that could be exploited
- Attack tolerance
  - While resisting attack, software function and capability are not unduly affected
- Attack resilience
  - In the face of successful attack, the effects on the software are minimized

While much of the fanfare of software security today focuses on buffer overflows, SQL injection, and other implementation bugs, the reality is that approximately half of the defects leading to security vulnerabilities found in today's software are actually attributable to flaws in architecture and design [McGraw 2006]. These flaws tend to have a much greater footprint in terms of their exploit and potential security impact within a single piece of software and potentially across multiple projects and systems. The goal of building security into the architecture and design phase of the SDLC is to significantly reduce the number of flaws as early as possible while also minimizing ambiguities and other weaknesses.

4.1.2 Issues and Challenges

Just as security software (e.g., application firewalls, encryption packages) is not the same thing as software security (the practice of making software more secure), so too security architecture (the architecture of security components) is not the same as secure architecture (architecture that is resilient and resistant to attack). Security is not simply about functionality. Rather, it is about the assurance both that the software will do what it is expected to do and that it will not do what it is not expected to do. The challenge to building security into the architecture and design portion of the SDLC is that not only must the architecture address currently understood security issues—both known weaknesses and attacks—but at its level of abstraction it must also be flexible and resilient under constantly changing security conditions.

This moving target of weakness and vulnerability, combined with the proactive and creative nature of the security attacker, means that no system can ever be perfectly secure. The best that can be achieved is a minimized risk profile accomplished through disciplined and continuous risk management. The practice of architectural risk analysis (involving threat modeling, risk analysis, and risk mitigation planning) performed during the architecture and design phase is one of the cornerstones of this risk management approach. (See Section 7.4.2 for a description of a high-level risk management framework within which to conduct architectural risk analysis.)

Because of their complex yet critical nature, both architectural risk analysis and the basic activities of secure architecture and design require the application of diverse, high-level knowledge. This knowledge is, for the most part, based on experience and historically has been very difficult to come by, leaving this field in the past to become the realm of a small number of experts and gurus. More recently, great strides have been made to capture, codify, and share this sort of knowledge among a much broader audience. With this foundation, every software development team, including architects and designers, can build on the knowledge of veteran experts. Some examples of these knowledge resources (security principles, security guidelines, and attack patterns) are described in Section 4.3.

This chapter introduces some of the resources available, in the form of practices and knowledge, for building security into the architecture and design phase of the SDLC. Although it is not a complete treatment of the topic, it does provide the more critical resources needed to address security as part of software development processes. Based on the context of your project, you can decide how best to integrate these practices and knowledge resources into your processes.

Specific Project Manager Concerns During Software Architecture and Design	
Concern	*Process/Knowledge*
Delivering what was specified • Deliverables must fulfill the objectives of the project	Architectural risk analysis
Getting it right the first time • Minimize rework	Architectural risk analysis
Effectively shoring up staff expertise shortfalls	Security principles Security guidelines Attack patterns

4.2 Software Security Practices for Architecture and Design: Architectural Risk Analysis[1, 2]

If you are looking to integrate security concerns into the software architecture and design phase of the SDLC, the practice of architectural risk analysis is of utmost importance. Architectural risk analysis is intended to provide assurance that architecture and design-level security concerns are identified and addressed as early as possible in the life cycle, yielding improved levels of attack resistance, tolerance, and resilience.[3] Without this kind of analysis, architectural flaws will remain unaddressed throughout the life cycle (though they often cause trouble during implementation and testing) and will likely result in serious security vulnerabilities in the deployed software. No other single action, practice, or resource applied during the architecture and design phase of the SDLC will have as much positive impact on the security risk profile of the software being developed.

While architectural risk analysis does not focus primarily on assets, it does depend on the accurate identification of the software's ultimate purpose and understanding of how that purpose ties into the business's activities to qualify and quantify the risks identified during this process. For this reason, a solid understanding of the assets that the software guards or uses should be considered a prerequisite to performing architectural risk analysis. Methodologies for asset identification are available from a wide variety of risk management sources.

During risk analysis, potential threats are identified and mapped to the risks they bring to bear. These risks are a function of the likelihood of a given threat exploiting a particular potential vulnerability and the resulting impact of that adverse event on the organization or on information assets. To determine the likelihood of an adverse event, threats to the software must be analyzed in conjunction with the potential vulnerabilities and the security controls in place for the software. The

---

1. The majority of the content in this section is adapted from the Architectural Risk Analysis content area of the Build Security In Web site authored by Paco Hope and Steve Lavenhar of Cigital, Inc., and Gunnar Peterson of Artec Group [BSI 15].

2. The Build Security In Web site contains a Software Risk Assessment Terminology description that provides further details on the terminology used in this section [BSI 16].

3. Attack resistance, tolerance, and resilience are defined in Section 2.3.

impact refers to the magnitude of harm that could be caused by realized risk. Its level is governed by the potential costs and losses to individuals or to the organization, its mission, or its assets and, in turn, leads to assignment of a relative value to the information assets and resources affected (e.g., the criticality and sensitivity of the software components and data). In the end, the results of the risk analysis help identify appropriate controls, revisions, or actions for reducing or eliminating risk during the risk mitigation process.

The risk analysis methodology consists of six activities:

- Software characterization
- Threat analysis
- Architectural vulnerability assessment
- Risk likelihood determination
- Risk impact determination
- Risk mitigation planning

These activities are described next.

4.2.1 Software Characterization

The first step required in analyzing any software, whether new or existing, for risk is to achieve a full understanding of what the software is and how it works. For architectural risk analysis, this understanding requires at least minimal description using high-level diagramming techniques. The exact format used may vary from organization to organization and is not critically important. What *is* important is coming up with a comprehensive, yet concise picture that unambiguously illustrates the true nature of the software.

One format that has proven itself particularly effective for this purpose is a simple whiteboard-type, high-level, one-page diagram that illustrates how the components are wired together, as well as how control and data flow are managed [McGraw 2006]. This "forest-level" view is crucial for identifying architecture and design-level flaws that just don't show up during code-level reviews. For more detailed analysis, this one-page diagram can be fleshed out as necessary with more detailed design descriptions.

Gathering information for this characterization of the software typically involves reviewing a broad spectrum of system artifacts and conducting in-depth interviews with key high-level stakeholders such as product/ program managers and software architects. Useful artifacts to review for software characterization include, but are not limited to, the following items:

- Software business case
- Functional and nonfunctional requirements
- Enterprise architecture requirements
- Use case documents
- Misuse/abuse case documents
- Software architecture documents describing logical, physical, and process views
- Data architecture documents
- Detailed design documents such as UML diagrams that show behavioral and structural aspects of the system
- Software development plan
- Transactions security architecture documents
- Identity services and management architecture documents
- Quality assurance plan
- Test plan
- Risk management plan
- Software acceptance plan
- Problem resolution plan
- Configuration and change management plan

In cases where the software is already in production or uses resources that are in production (e.g., databases, servers, identity systems), these systems may have already been audited and assessed. These assessments, when they exist, may provide a rich set of analysis information.

Although it is often not practical to model and depict all possible interrelationships, the goal of the software characterization activity is to produce one or more documents that depict the vital relationships between critical parts of the software. Using information gathered through asset identification, interviews, and artifact analysis, the diagrams and documents gradually take shape.

Figure 4–1 presents an example of a high-level, one-page system software architecture diagram. This diagram shows major system compo-

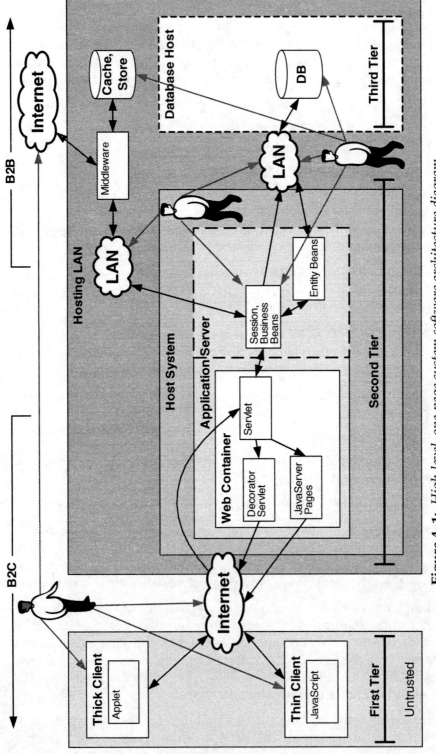

Figure 4–1: *High-level, one-page system software architecture diagram*

nents, their interactions, and various zones of trust.[4] Avatars and their associated arrows represent potential attackers and attack vectors against the system. These potential threats and attack vectors are further fleshed out and detailed during the following stages of architectural risk analysis.

4.2.2 Threat Analysis

Threats are agents that violate the protection of information assets and site security policy. Threat analysis identifies relevant threats for a specific architecture, functionality, and configuration. It may assume a given level of access and skill level that the attacker may possess. During this analysis, threats may be mapped to vulnerabilities to understand how the software may be exploited. A mitigation plan is composed of countermeasures that are considered to be effective against the identified vulnerabilities that these threats exploit.

Attackers who are not technologically sophisticated are increasingly performing attacks on software without really understanding what it is they are exploiting, because the weakness was discovered by someone else. These individuals, who are often referred to as "script kiddies," typically do not launch attacks in an effort to obtain specific information or target specific organizations. Instead, they use the knowledge of various vulnerabilities to broadly scan the entire Internet for systems that possess those vulnerabilities, and then attack whichever ones they come across. At the other end of the attacker spectrum, highly skilled threats targeting very specific organizations, systems, and assets have become increasing prevalent. Threat analysis should evaluate and identify threats across this spectrum.

Table 4–1, which was developed by NIST, summarizes a very generic set of potential threat sources [NIST 2002, p. 14].

An issue that greatly complicates the prevention of threat actions is that the attacker's underlying intention often cannot be determined. Both internal and external threat sources may exist, and an attack taxonomy should consider the motivation and capability of both types of threats. Internal attacks might be executed by individuals such as disgruntled employees and contractors. It is important to note that nonmalicious use by threat actors may also result in software vulnerabilities being

---

4. Zones of trust are areas of the system that share a common level and management mechanism of privilege (e.g., Internet, dmz, hosting LAN, host system, application server, database host).

Table 4–1: *NIST Threat Identification and Characterization*

Threat Source	Motivation	Threat Actions
Cracker	Challenge Ego Rebellion	• System profiling • Social engineering • System intrusion, break-ins • Unauthorized system access
Computer criminal	Destruction of information Illegal information disclosure Monetary gain Unauthorized data alteration	• Computer crime (e.g., cyberstalking) • Fraudulent act (e.g., replay, impersonation, interception) • Information bribery • Spoofing • System intrusion • Botnets • Malware: Trojan horse, virus, worm, spyware • Spam • Phishing
Terrorist	Blackmail Destruction Exploitation Revenge Monetary gain Political gain	• Bomb • Information warfare • System attack (e.g., distributed denial of service) • System penetration • System tampering

Table 4-1: *NIST Threat Identification and Characterization (Continued)*

Threat Source	Motivation	Threat Actions
Industrial espionage	Competitive advantage Economic espionage Blackmail	• Economic exploitation • Information theft • Intrusion on personal privacy • Social engineering • System penetration • Unauthorized system access (access to classified, proprietary, and/or technology-related information)
Insiders (poorly trained, disgruntled, malicious, negligent, dishonest, or terminated employees) [CERT 2007]	Curiosity Ego Intelligence Monetary gain Revenge Unintentional errors and omissions (e.g., data entry errors, programming errors) Wanting to help the company (victims of social engineering) Lack of procedures or training	• Assault on an employee • Blackmail • Browsing of proprietary information • Computer abuse • Fraud and theft • Information bribery • Input of falsified, corrupted data • Interception • Malicious code (e.g., virus, logic bomb, Trojan horse) • Sale of personal information • System bugs • System intrusion • System sabotage • Unauthorized system access

exploited. Internal threat actors may act either on their own or under the direction of an external threat source (for example, an employee might install a screensaver that contains a Trojan horse).

Some threat actors are external. These attackers could include structured external, transnational external, and unstructured external threats:

- Structured external threats are generated by a state-sponsored entity, such as a foreign intelligence service. The resources supporting the structured external threat are usually quite substantial and highly sophisticated.

- Transnational threats are generated by organized nonstate entities, such as drug cartels, crime syndicates, and terrorist organizations. Such threats generally do not have as many resources behind them as do structured threats (although some of the larger transnational threat organizations may have more resources than some smaller, structured threat organizations). The nature of the transnational external threat makes it more difficult to trace and provide a response, however. These kinds of threats can target members or staff of the Treasury, for example, by employing any or all of the techniques mentioned above.

- Unstructured external threats are usually generated by individuals such as crackers. Threats from this source typically lack the resources of either structured or transnational external threats but nonetheless may be very sophisticated. The motivation of such attackers is generally—but not always—less hostile than that underlying the other two classes of external threats. Unstructured threat sources generally limit their attacks to information system targets and employ computer attack techniques. New forms of loosely organized virtual hacker organizations (*hacktivists*—hackers and activists) are also emerging.

4.2.3 Architectural Vulnerability Assessment

Vulnerability assessment examines the preconditions that must be present for vulnerabilities to be exploited and assesses the states that the software might enter upon exploit. Three activities make up architectural vulnerability assessment: attack resistance analysis, ambiguity analysis, and dependency analysis. As with any quality assurance process, risk analysis testing can prove only the presence—not the absence—of flaws. Architectural risk analysis studies vulnerabilities and threats that might be malicious or nonmalicious in nature. Whether the vulnerabilities are exploited intentionally (malicious) or unintentionally (nonmalicious), the net result is that the desired security properties of the software may be affected.

One advantage when conducting vulnerability assessment at the architectural level is the ability to see the relationships and effects at a "forest-level" rather than "tree-level" view. As described earlier, this perspective takes the form of a one-page overview of the system created during software characterization. In practice, it means assessing vulnerabilities not just at a component or function level, but also at interaction points. Use-case models help to illustrate the various relationships among system components. In turn, the architecture risk analysis should factor these relationships into the vulnerabilities analysis and consider vulnerabilities that may emerge from these combinations.

Attack Resistance Analysis

Attack resistance analysis is the process of examining software architecture and design for common weaknesses that may lead to vulnerabilities and increase the system's susceptibility to common attack patterns.

Many known weaknesses are documented in the software security literature, ranging from the obvious (failure to authenticate) to the subtle (symmetric key management problems). Static code checkers, runtime code checkers, profiling tools, penetration testing tools, stress test tools, and application scanning tools can find some security bugs in code, but they do not as a rule address architectural flaws. For example, a static code checker can flag bugs such as buffer overflows, but it cannot identify security vulnerabilities such as transitive trust mistakes.[5] Architectural-level flaws can currently be found only through human analysis.

When performing attack resistance analysis, consider the architecture as it has been described in the artifacts that were reviewed for asset identification. Compare it against a body of known bad practices, such as those outlined in the Common Weakness Enumeration (CWE)

---

5. Transitive trust mistakes are improper assumptions of the form that because component A trusts component B, and component B trusts component C, component A should trust component C. When dealing with the complexities of security in software, these kinds of issues are rarely as straightforward as they appear and are fraught with risk owing to unvalidated assumptions.

[CWE 2007], or known good principles, such as those outlined in Section 4.3. For example, the *principle of least privilege* dictates that all software operations should be performed with the least possible privilege required to meet the need. To consider architecture in light of this principle, find all the areas in the software that operate at an elevated privilege level. To do so, you might perhaps diagram the system's major modules, classes, or subsystems and circle areas of high privilege versus areas of low privilege. Consider the boundaries between these areas and the kinds of communications that occur across those boundaries.

Once potential vulnerabilities have been identified, the architecture should be assessed for how well it would fare against common attack patterns such as those outlined in the Common Attack Pattern Enumeration and Classification (CAPEC) [CAPEC 2007]. CAPEC describes the following classes of attack, among others:

- Abuse of functionality
- Spoofing
- Probabilistic techniques
- Exploitation of privilege or trust
- Injection
- Resource manipulation
- Time and state attacks

Relevant attack patterns should be mapped against the architecture, with special consideration being given to areas of identified vulnerability. Any attack found to be viable against identified vulnerabilities should be captured and quantified as a risk to the software.

Ambiguity Analysis

Ambiguity is a rich source of vulnerabilities when it exists between requirements or specifications and development. A key role of architecture and design is to eliminate the potential misunderstandings between business requirements for software and the developers' implementation of the software's actions. All artifacts defining the software's function, structure, properties, and policies should be examined for any ambiguities in description that could potentially lead to multiple interpretations. Any such opportunities for multiple interpretations constitute a risk to the software.

A key consideration is to note places where the requirements or architecture are ambiguously defined or where the implementation and architecture either disagree or fail to resolve the ambiguity. For example, a requirement for a Web application might state that an administrator can lock an account, such that the user can no longer log in while the account remains locked. But what about sessions for that user that are actively in use when the administrator locks the account? Is the user suddenly and forcibly logged out, or does the active session remain valid until the user logs out? In an existing system, the authentication and authorization architecture must be compared to the actual implementation to learn the answer to this question. The security ramifications of logins that persist even after the account is locked should be balanced against the sensitivity of the information assets being guarded.

Dependency Analysis

An architectural risk assessment must include an analysis of the vulnerabilities associated with the software's execution environment. The issues addressed as part of this assessment will include operating system vulnerabilities, network vulnerabilities, platform vulnerabilities (popular platforms include WebLogic, WebSphere, PHP, ASP.net, and Jakarta), and interaction vulnerabilities resulting from the interaction of components. The goal of this analysis is to develop a list of software or system vulnerabilities that could be accidentally triggered or intentionally exploited, resulting in a security breach or a violation of the system's security policy. When credible threats can be combined with the vulnerabilities uncovered in this exercise, a risk exists that needs further analysis and mitigation.

The types of vulnerabilities that will exist and the methodology needed to determine whether the vulnerabilities are present can vary. At various times, the analysis might focus on the organization's security policies, planned security procedures, nonfunctional requirement definitions, use cases, misuse/abuse cases, architectural platforms/components/services, and software security features and security controls (both technical and procedural) used to protect the system, among other issues.

Independent of the life-cycle phase, online vulnerability references should be consulted. Numerous such resources are available, including the National Vulnerability Database (NVD) [NIST 2007], the Common Vulnerabilities and Exposures (CVE) database [CVE 2007], and the BugTraq email list [SecurityFocus 2007], among others. These sites and lists should be consulted regularly to keep the vulnerability list up-to-date for a given architecture.

Vulnerability Classification

Classifying vulnerabilities allows for pattern recognition of vulnerability types. This exercise, in turn, may enable the software development team to recognize and develop countermeasures to deal with classes of vulnerabilities by dealing with the vulnerabilities at a higher level of abstraction. The most comprehensive and mature example of such a classification taxonomy currently available is the Common Weakness Enumeration (CWE) [CWE 2007], which has been crafted as a normalized aggregation of dozens of the other such taxonomies recognized and respected by the industry. The CWE includes seven top-level categories for architecture and source code [Tsipenyuk 2005]:

- Data Handling
- API Abuse
- Security Features
- Time and State
- Error Handling
- Code Quality
- Encapsulation

Mapping Threats and Vulnerabilities

The combination of threats and vulnerabilities illustrates the risks to which the software is exposed. Several models exist to categorize the areas where these threats and vulnerabilities frequently intersect. One example is Microsoft's STRIDE [Howard 2002], which provides a model of risks to a computer system related to spoofing, tampering, repudiation, information disclosure, denial of service, and elevation of privilege.

Risk classification assists in communicating and documenting risk management decisions. Risk mitigation mechanisms should map to the risk category or categories of the threats and vulnerabilities that have been identified through this effort.

4.2.4 Risk Likelihood Determination

Having determined which threats are important and which vulnerabilities might exist to be exploited, it can be useful to estimate the likelihood of the various possible risks. In software security, "likelihood" is a qualitative estimate of how likely a successful attack will be, based on analysis and past experience. Because of the complexity of the software domain and the number of variables involved in risk analysis, this likelihood measure is not an actual mathematical *probability* of a successful attack. Nonetheless, the concept of likelihood can be useful when prioritizing risks and evaluating the effectiveness of potential mitigations.

Consider these factors, all of which are incorporated in the likelihood estimation:

- The threat's motivation and capability
- The vulnerability's impact (and therefore attractiveness to an attacker)
- The effectiveness of current controls

Threats' motivation and capability will vary widely. For instance, a college student who hacks for fun is less highly motivated than a paid hacker who has backing or the promise of a significant payment from an organized crime cabal. A former employee who has a specific grievance against a company will be more motivated and better informed than an outsider who has no special knowledge of the target software's internal workings.

The effectiveness of current controls characterizes how high the bar is set for an intentional attacker or how unlikely an accidental failure is. For example, simple user IDs and passwords can be compromised much more easily than most two-factor authentication systems. Adding a second authentication factor raises the bar for a would-be threat. However, if the second factor in the authentication is a biometric thumbprint reader that can be spoofed with latent image recovery techniques, then the system may be less secure than desired.

The likelihood estimation is a subjective combination of these three qualities—motivation, directness of vulnerability, and compensating controls—and is typically expressed as a rating of high, medium, or low. Table 4–2 describes one potential model for calculating likelihood from these three qualities. In most cases, such hard-and-fast rules cannot adequately cover all contingencies, so calculations must be tailored for each context and remain flexible to interpretation.

Table 4–2: *Model for Calculating Likelihood*

High	The three qualities are all weak. A threat is highly motivated and sufficiently capable, a vulnerability exists that is severe, and controls to prevent the vulnerability from being exploited are ineffective.
Medium	One of the three qualities is compensating, but the others are not. The threat is perhaps not very motivated or not sufficiently capable, the controls in place might be reasonably strong, or the vulnerability might be not very severe.
Low	Two or more of the three qualities are compensating. The threat might lack motivation or capability; strong controls might be in place to prevent, or at least significantly impede, the vulnerability from being exploited; and the vulnerability might have a very low impact.

4.2.5 Risk Impact Determination

Independent of the risk's likelihood and the system's controls against it, the risk's impact must be determined. That is, what consequences will the business face if the worst-case scenario in the risk description comes to pass? Furthermore, the risk analysis must account for other credible scenarios that are not the worst case, yet are bad enough to warrant attention. This section discusses three aspects of risk impact determination: identifying the threatened assets, identifying business impact, and determining impact locality.

Identify Threatened Assets

The assets threatened by realization of the risk, and the nature of what will happen to them, must be identified. Common impacts on information assets include loss of data, corruption of data, unauthorized or unaudited modification of data, unavailability of data, corruption of audit trails, and insertion of invalid data.

Identify Business Impact

The business will suffer some impact if an attack takes place. It is of paramount importance to characterize those effects in as specific terms as possible. Risk management efforts are almost always funded ultimately by management in the organization whose primary concern is monetary. Those managers' support and understanding can be assured only by quantifying software risks in terms of their fiscal implications. If the worst possible consequence of a software failure is the loss of $10,000 to the business, but it will take $20,000 in labor-hours and testing to fix the software, the return on the mitigation investment does not make financial sense. Furthermore, correct financial assessment of the risk's effects drives prioritization. It is usually more important to fix a flaw that can precipitate a $25 million drop in the company's market capitalization than to address a flaw that can expose the business to a regulatory penalty of $500,000. Unless software risks are tied to business impacts, however, such reasoning is not possible.

Examples of business impacts include loss of market share, loss of reputation, depreciation of stock value, fines, legal fees and judgments, costs of technical remediation, and theft. A good example of a case in which all of these impacts are relevant is the TJX data breach, where lax wireless security led to large quantities of customer data being accessed through exploitation of a vulnerability. TJX suffered severe brand damage and costs that some analysts predict may reach into the billions of dollars:

> IPLocks, a compliance and database security company, released a report earlier this month estimating that the TJX breach will eventually cost the company $100 per lost record, or a total of $4.5 billion. The company based the estimate on the accumulated costs of fines, legal fees, notification expenses, and brand impairment, according to Adrian Lane, the company's chief technology officer [Gaudin 2007].

Risk Exposure Statement

The risk exposure statement combines the likelihood of a risk with the impact of that risk. The product of these two analyses provides the overall summary of risk exposure for the organization for each risk. Table 4–3 describes a method of generating the risk exposure statement.

The risk exposure statement generalizes the overall exposure of the organization relative to the given risk and offers more granular visibility to both its impact and its likelihood. In this way, the risk exposure statement gives the organization finer-grained control over risk

Table 4–3: *Risk Exposure Calculation Matrix*

		Impact		
		Low	Medium	High
Likelihood	Low	Low	Low	Medium
	Medium	Low	Medium	High
	High	Medium	High	High

management but does not require all risks to be eliminated. As Alan Greenspan, Chairman of the Federal Reserve Board, said in 1994:

> There are some who would argue that the role of the bank supervisor is to minimize or even eliminate bank failure, but this view is mistaken in my judgment. The willingness to take risk is essential to the growth of the free market economy . . . [i]f all savers and their financial intermediaries invested in only risk-free assets, the potential for business growth would never be realized.[6]

4.2.6 Risk Mitigation Planning

Mitigation of a risk entails changing the architecture of the software or the business in one or more ways to reduce the likelihood or the impact of the risk. Formal and informal testing, such as penetration testing, may be used to test the effectiveness of these mitigation measures.[7]

Mitigations aimed at architectural flaws are often more complicated to implement than mitigations focusing on coding bugs, which tend to be more localized. Architectural mitigations often require changes to multiple modules, multiple systems, or at least multiple classes; and the affected entities may be managed and implemented by different teams. Thus, when a flaw is found, the fix often requires agreement across

6. Address to the Garn Institute of Finance, University of Utah, November 30, 1994.

7. Although changing how the business operates (e.g., insuring the business against impacts of risks) is a valid response to risk, it is outside the scope of architecture assessment, so this possibility will not be covered here.

multiple teams, testing of multiple integrated modules, and synchronization of release cycles that may not always be present in the different modules.

Measures intended to reduce the likelihood of a risk can take several forms. Raising the bar in terms of the skills necessary to exploit a vulnerability is often a first step in this direction. For example, changing authentication mechanisms from user IDs and passwords to pre-shared public key certificates can make it far more difficult to impersonate a user. Reducing the period of time when a vulnerability is available for exploit is another way to reduce the likelihood of a risk coming to fruition. For example, if sessions expire after 10 minutes of inactivity, then the window of opportunity for session hijacking is about 10 minutes long.

Measures intended to reduce the impact of a risk can also take several forms. Most developers immediately consider eliminating the vulnerability altogether or fixing the flaw so that the architecture cannot be exploited. Cryptography can help, for example, as long as it is applied correctly. It is easier to detect corruption in encrypted data than in unencrypted data, and encrypted data is more difficult for attackers to use if they collect it. Sometimes, from a business point of view, it makes more sense to focus on building functionality to detect and log successful exploits and providing enough related auditing information to effectively recover after the fact. Remediating a broken system might be too expensive, whereas adding enough functionality to allow recovery after an exploit might be sufficient.

Many mitigations can be described as either detection strategies or correction strategies. Depending on the cost of making failure impossible through correction, the organization may find it much more cost-effective to enable systems to detect and repair failure quickly and accurately. Imagine a software module that is very temperamental and tends to crash when provided with bad input and (for the sake of argument) cannot be modified or replaced. A focus on correction would add business logic to validate input and make sure that the software module never received input that it could not handle. In contrast, a focus on detection would add monitoring or other software to watch for a crash of the module and try to restart the module quickly with minimal impact.

Mitigation is never without cost. The fact that remediating a problem costs money makes it even more important to handle the risk impact determination step well. It is typically straightforward to characterize the cost of implementing mitigations—for example, in terms of hours of labor, cost of shipping new units with the improved software, or delay entering the market with new features because old ones must be fixed. This ability to characterize the mitigation's cost, however, is of little value unless the cost of the risk's business impact is known.

Of course, risk mitigation mechanisms themselves can introduce threats and vulnerabilities to the software. Designs also evolve and change over time. The risk analysis process is therefore iterative, accounting for and guarding against new risks that might have been introduced.

4.2.7 Recapping Architectural Risk Analysis

Architectural risk analysis is a critical activity in assuring the security of software. Current technologies cannot automate the detection process for architectural flaws, which often prove to be among the most damaging security defects found in software. Human-executed architectural risk analysis is the only way to effectively address these problems.

Risk management is an ongoing process, and architectural risk analysis follows suit. Architectural risk analysis is conducted at discrete points in time and performed iteratively as an ongoing process across the life cycle. As the software evolves, its architecture must be kept up-to-date. The body of known attack patterns (discussed in Chapter 2) is always growing, so continued success in attack resistance analysis depends on remaining current in software security trends. Ambiguity analysis is always necessary as conditions and the software evolve. Even with that focus, it is worthwhile to occasionally step back and reappraise the entire system for ambiguity. As platforms are upgraded and evolve in new directions, each subsequent release will fix older problems—and probably introduce new ones. Given this probability, dependency analysis must continue throughout the life of the product.

A master list of risks should be maintained during all stages of the architectural risk analysis. This list should be continually revisited to determine mitigation progress for the project at hand and to help improve processes for future projects. For example, the number of risks identified in various software artifacts and/or software life-cycle phases may be used to identify problematic areas in the software development process. Likewise, the number of risks mitigated over time may be used to show concrete progress as risk mitigation activities unfold. Ideally, the display and reporting of risk information should be aggregated in some automated way and displayed in a risk "dashboard" that enables the development team to make accurate and informed decisions.

4.3 Software Security Knowledge for Architecture and Design: Security Principles, Security Guidelines, and Attack Patterns

One of the significant challenges you may face when seeking to integrate security into the architecture and design of your software projects is the scarcity of experienced architects who have a solid grasp of security concerns. The problem here is the learning curve associated with security concerns: Most developers simply don't have the benefit of the years and years of lessons learned that an expert in software security can call on. To help address this issue, you can leverage codified knowledge resources—such as security principles, security guidelines, and attack patterns—to bolster your software architects' basic understanding of software security. These knowledge resources serve as the fuel that effectively drives the process of architectural risk analysis. They guide the architects and designers by suggesting which questions to ask, which issues to consider, and which mitigation measures to pursue. Although projects should still enlist the services of at least one truly experienced software security architect, knowledge resources such as security principles, security guidelines, and attack patterns can help organizations to more effectively distribute these scarce resources across projects.

4.3.1 Security Principles[8]

Security principles are a set of high-level practices derived from real-world experience that can help guide software developers (software architects and designers in particular) in building more secure soft-

---

8. The majority of the content provided in this section is adapted from the Principles content area of the Build Security In Web site authored by Sean Barnum and Michael Gegick of Cigital, Inc. [BSI 17].

ware. Jerome Saltzer and Michael Schroeder were the first researchers to correlate and aggregate high-level security principles in the context of protection mechanisms [Saltzer 1975]. Their work provides the foundation needed for designing and implementing secure software systems. Principles define effective practices that are applicable primarily to architectural-level software decisions and are recommended regardless of the platform or language of the software. As with many architectural decisions, principles, which do not necessarily guarantee security, at times may exist in opposition to each other, such that appropriate tradeoffs must be made. Software architects, whether they are crafting new software or evaluating and assessing existing software, should always apply these design principles as a guide and yardstick for making their software more secure.

Despite the broad misuse of the term "principle," the set of things that should be considered security principles is actually very limited. The Principles content area of the Build Security In (BSI) Web site [BSI 17] presents an aggregation of such principles, including many taken from Saltzer and Schroeder's original work and a few offered by other thought leaders such as Gary McGraw, Matt Bishop, Mike Howard, David LeBlanc, Bruce Schneier, John Viega, and NIST. The filter applied to decide what constitutes a principle and what does not is fairly narrow, recognizing that such lasting principles do not come along every day. The high-level and lasting nature of these principles leads to their widespread recognition, but also to a diversity of perspectives and interpretation.[9]

By leveraging security principles, a software development team can benefit from the guidance of the industry's leading practitioners and can learn to ask the right questions of their software architecture and design so as to avoid the most prevalent and serious flaws. Without these security principles, the team is reduced to relying on the individual security knowledge of its most experienced members.

The following list outlines a core set of security principles that every software development team member—from the people writing code on up to the project managers—should be aware of and familiar with. While this information is most actively put into play by software

---

9. Rather than instigating conflict by acting as self-appointed arbiters in defining the one true interpretation of each principle, the authors of the BSI content decided to present readers with the different points of view available and allow them to make their own interpretations based on their personal trust filters. In doing this, editorial comment and explanatory prose were kept to a minimum by design.

architects and designers, awareness of these foundational concerns across the team is a powerful force for reducing the risk to the software posed by security issues. Brief descriptions are given here for each principle; more detailed descriptions and examples are available on the Principles content area on the BSI Web site.

The Principles for Software Security

- Least privilege
- Failing securely
- Securing the weakest link
- Defense in depth
- Separation of privilege
- Economy of mechanism
- Least common mechanism
- Reluctance to trust
- Never assuming that your secrets are safe
- Complete mediation
- Psychological acceptability
- Promoting privacy

The Principle of Least Privilege

Only the minimum necessary rights should be assigned to a subject[10] that requests access to a resource and should be in effect for the shortest duration necessary (remember to relinquish privileges). Granting permissions to a user beyond the scope of the necessary rights of an action can allow that user to obtain or change information in unwanted ways. In short, careful delegation of access rights can limit attackers' ability to damage a system.

The Principle of Failing Securely

When a system fails, it should do so securely. This behavior typically includes several elements: secure defaults (the default is to deny access); on failure, undo changes and restore the system to a secure state; always check return values for failure; and in conditional code/ filters, make sure that a default case is present that does the right

---

10. The term *subject* used throughout the Principle descriptions is intended to denote a user, process, or other entity acting on the software system.

thing. The confidentiality and integrity of a system should remain unbreached even though availability has been lost. During a failure, attackers must not be permitted to gain access rights to privileged objects that are normally inaccessible. Upon failing, a system that reveals sensitive information about the failure to potential attackers could supply additional knowledge that threat actors could then use to create a subsequent attack. Determine what may occur when a system fails and be sure it does not threaten the system.

The Principle of Securing the Weakest Link

Attackers are more likely to attack a weak spot in a software system than to penetrate a heavily fortified component. For example, some cryptographic algorithms can take many years to break, so attackers are unlikely to attack encrypted information communicated in a network. Instead, the endpoints of communication (e.g., servers) may be much easier to attack. Knowing when the weak spots of a software application have been fortified can indicate to a software vendor whether the application is secure enough to be released.

The Principle of Defense in Depth

Layering security defenses in an application can reduce the chance of a successful attack. Incorporating redundant security mechanisms requires an attacker to circumvent each mechanism to gain access to a digital asset. For example, a software system with authentication checks may prevent intrusion by an attacker who has subverted a firewall. Defending an application with multiple layers can eliminate the existence of a single point of failure that compromises the security of the application.

The Principle of Separation of Privilege

A system should ensure that multiple conditions are met before it grants permissions to an object. Checking access on only one condition may not be adequate for enforcing strong security. If an attacker is able to obtain one privilege but not a second, the attacker may not be able to launch a successful attack. If a software system largely consists of one component, however, it will not be able to implement a scheme of having multiple checks to access different components. Compartmentalizing software into separate components that require multiple checks for access can inhibit an attack or potentially prevent an attacker from taking over an entire system.

The Principle of Economy of Mechanism

One factor in evaluating a system's security is its complexity. If the design, implementation, or security mechanisms are highly complex, then the likelihood that security vulnerabilities will exist within the system increases. Subtle problems in complex systems may be difficult to find, especially in copious amounts of code. For instance, analyzing the source code that is responsible for the normal execution of a functionality can be a difficult task, but checking for alternative behaviors in the remaining code that can achieve the same functionality may prove even more difficult. Simplifying design or code is not always easy, but developers should strive for implementing simpler systems when possible.

The Principle of Least Common Mechanism

Avoid having multiple subjects share those mechanisms that grant access to a resource. For example, serving an application on the Internet allows both attackers and users to gain access to the application. In this case, sensitive information might potentially be shared between the subjects via the same mechanism. A different mechanism (or instantiation of a mechanism) for each subject or class of subjects can provide flexibility of access control among various users and prevent potential security violations that would otherwise occur if only one mechanism were implemented.

The Principle of Reluctance to Trust

Developers should assume that the environment in which their system resides is insecure. Trust—whether it is extended to external systems, code, or people—should always be closely held and never loosely given. When building an application, software engineers should anticipate malformed input from unknown users. Even if users are known, they are susceptible to social engineering attacks, making them potential threats to a system. Also, no system is ever 100 percent secure, so the interface between two systems should be secured. Minimizing the trust in other systems can increase the security of your application.

The Principle of Never Assuming That Your Secrets Are Safe

Relying on an obscure design or implementation does not guarantee that a system is secure. You should always assume that an attacker can obtain enough information about your system to launch an attack. For example, tools such as decompilers and disassemblers may allow attackers to obtain sensitive information that may be stored in binary files. Also, insider attacks, which may be accidental or malicious, can lead to security exploits. Using real protection mechanisms to secure sensitive information should be the ultimate means of protecting your secrets.

The Principle of Complete Mediation

A software system that requires access checks to an object each time a subject requests access, especially for security-critical objects, decreases the chances that the system will mistakenly give elevated permissions to that subject. By contrast, a system that checks the subject's permissions to an object only once can invite attackers to exploit that system. If the access control rights of a subject are decreased after the first time the rights are granted and the system does not check the next access to that object, then a permissions violation can occur. Caching permissions can increase the performance of a system, albeit at the cost of allowing secured objects to be accessed.

The Principle of Psychological Acceptability

Accessibility to resources should not be inhibited by security mechanisms. If security mechanisms hinder the usability or accessibility of resources, then users may opt to turn off those mechanisms. Where possible, security mechanisms should be transparent to the users of the system or, at most, introduce minimal obstruction. Security mechanisms should be user friendly to facilitate their use and understanding in a software application.

The Principle of Promoting Privacy

Protecting software systems from attackers who may obtain private information is an important part of software security. If an attacker breaks into a software system and steals private information about a vendor's customers, then those customers may lose their confidence in the software system. Attackers may also target sensitive system information that can supply them with the details needed to attack that system. Preventing attackers from accessing private information or obscuring that information can alleviate the risk of information leakage.

Recapping Security Principles

Security principles are the foundational tenets of the software security domain. They are long-standing, universal statements of how to build software the right way if security is a concern (which it always is). These principles represent the experiential knowledge of the most respected thought leaders and practitioners in the field of software security. By leveraging them, your team gains access to the scalable wisdom necessary for assessing and mitigating the security risk posed by your software's architecture and design.

For a full understanding and treatment of the security principles discussed here, we recommend that you review the more detailed content available on the Build Security In Web site [BSI 17].

4.3.2 Security Guidelines[11]

Like security principles, security guidelines are an excellent resource to leverage in your projects. They represent experiential knowledge gained by experts over many years of dealing with software security concerns within more specific technology contexts than those covered by the broader security principles. Such guidelines can inform architectural decisions and analysis, but they also represent an excellent starting point and checklist for software designers who are charged with the task of integrating security concerns into their design efforts. You should ensure that resources such as security guidelines are readily available and frequently consulted by the software designers on your teams before, during, and after the actual execution of the architecture and design phase of the SDLC.

What Do Security Guidelines Look Like?

Numerous interpretations of what security guidelines are and what they look like have been put forth. The BSI Web site contains one interpretation. Gary McGraw's book *Software Security: Building Security In* [McGraw 2006] presents another.[12]

---

11. The majority of the content provided in this section is adapted from the Guidelines content area of the Build Security In Web site, which was authored by William L. Fithin of the Software Engineering Institute [BSI 06].

12. It would be far too lengthy to provide details for all interpretations in this book. An in-depth treatment of security guidelines would make an excellent book of its own targeted at software designers.

The full description for one of the security guidelines from the BSI Web site is included here as an example. This guideline is not necessarily any more important than any other guideline or interpretation; it was chosen at random to demonstrate the value of this resource.

Guideline: Follow the Rules Regarding Concurrency Management

Failure to follow proper concurrency management protocols can introduce serious vulnerabilities into a system. In particular, concurrent access to shared resources without using appropriate concurrency management mechanisms produces hard-to-find vulnerabilities. Many "functions" that are necessary to use can introduce "time of check/time of use" vulnerabilities [Viega 2001].

When multiple threads of control attempt to share the same resource but do not follow the appropriate concurrency protection protocol, then any of the following results are possible:

- Deadlock: One or more threads may become permanently blocked [Johansson 2005].
- Loss of information: Saved information is overwritten by another thread [Gong 2003; Pugh 1999; Manson 2001, 2005].
- Loss of integrity of information: Information written by multiple threads may be arbitrarily interlaced [Gong 2003; Pugh 1999; Manson 2001, 2005].
- Loss of liveness: Imbalance in access to shared resources by competing threads can cause performance problems [Gong 2003; Pugh 1999; Manson 2001, 2005].

Any of these outcomes can have security implications, which are sometimes manifested as apparent logic errors (decisions made based on corrupt data).

Competing "Systems" (Time of Check/Time of Use)

This is the most frequently encountered subclass of concurrency-related vulnerabilities. Many of the defects that produce these vulnerabilities are unavoidable owing to limitations of the execution environment (i.e., the absence of proper concurrency control mechanisms). A common mitigation tactic is to minimize the time interval between check and use. An even more effective tactic is to use a "check, use, check" pattern that can often detect concurrency violations, though not prevent them.

Applicable Context

All of the following must be true:

- Multiple "systems" must be operating concurrently.
- At least two of those systems must use a shared resource (e.g., file, device, database table row).
- At least one of those systems must use the shared resource in any of the following ways:
  - Without using any concurrency control mechanism. This includes the situation where no such mechanism exists, such as conventional UNIX file systems, causing corruption or confusion.
  - Using the right concurrency control mechanism incorrectly. This includes situations such as not using a consistent resource locking order across all systems (e.g., in databases), causing deadlocks.
  - Using the wrong concurrency control mechanism (even if it used correctly). This includes situations where a give resource may support multiple concurrency control mechanisms that are independent of one another [e.g., UNIX lockf() and flock()], causing corruption or confusion.

These defects are frequently referred to as time of check/time of use (or TOCTOU) defects because APIs providing access to the resource neither provide any concurrency control operations nor perform any implicit concurrency control. In this case, a particular condition (e.g., availability of resource, resource attributes) is checked at one point in time and later program actions are based on the result of that check, but the condition could change at any time, because no concurrency control mechanism guarantees that the condition did not change.

Competing Threads within a "System" (Races)

The second largest class of concurrency-related vulnerabilities is generated by defects in the sharing of resources such as memory, devices, or files. In such a case, the defect may be a design error associated with the concurrency control mechanisms or with an implementation error, such as not correctly using those mechanisms. Caching errors can be considered members of this class.

Strictly speaking, signal-handling defects are not concurrency defects. Signal handlers are invoked preemptively in the main thread of the process, so signal handlers are not really concurrently executed. However, from the developer's viewpoint, they "feel" like concurrent execution, so we classify them here, at least for now.

Applicable Context

All of the following must be true:

- A "system" must have multiple concurrently operating threads of control.
- Two or more of those threads must use a shared data object, device, or other resource.
- At least one thread must use the shared resource without using the appropriate concurrency control mechanism correctly (or at all).

Impact	Minimally	Maximally
1	None	Deadlock: One or more threads may become permanently blocked.
2	None	Loss of information: Saved information is overwritten by another thread.
3	None	Loss of integrity of information: Information written by multiple threads may be arbitrarily interlaced.
4	None	Loss of liveness: Imbalance in access to shared resources by competing threads can cause performance problems.

Security Policies to Be Preserved

1. Threads must not deadlock.
2. Information must not be lost.
3. Information must not be corrupted.
4. Acceptable performance must be maintained.

How to Recognize This Defect

Concurrency defects are extremely difficult to recognize. There is no general-purpose approach to finding them.

Efficacy	Mitigation
Low	Where no concurrency control mechanism is available, seek to minimize the interval between the time of check and the time of use. Technically this action does not correct the problem, but it can make the error much more difficult to exploit.
Infinite	The appropriate concurrency control mechanism must be used in the *conventional* way (assuming there is one).

Recapping Security Guidelines

Security guidelines represent prescriptive guidance for those software design-level concerns typically faced by the software development project team. They provide an effective complement to the more abstract and far-reaching security principles. When combined, these two resources provide the knowledge necessary to know what you *should* do when creating software architecture and design. When combined with representations of the attacker's perspective such as attack patterns (described in Section 4.3.3), they also can provide an effective checklist of what you may have failed to do to ensure that your software is both resistant and resilient to likely attack.

4.3.3 Attack Patterns

As discussed in Chapter 2, attack patterns are another knowledge resource available to the software project manager. They offer a formalized mechanism for representing and communicating the attacker's perspective by describing approaches commonly taken to attack software. This attacker's perspective, while important throughout the SDLC, has increased value during architecture and design phase. Attack patterns offer a valuable resource during three primary activities of architecture and design: design and security pattern selection, threat modeling, and attack resistance.

One of the key methods for improving the stability, performance, and security of a software architecture is the leveraging of proven patterns. Appropriate selection of design patterns and security patterns can offer significant architectural risk mitigation. Comprehensive attack patterns can facilitate this process through identification of prescribed and proscribed design and security patterns known to mitigate the risk of given attack patterns that have been determined to be applicable to the software under development.

During the asset identification and threat modeling (combining software characterization and threat analysis) portions of architectural risk analysis, the architects/analysts identify and characterize the assets of the software, the relevant potential threats they may face, and the topology and nature of the software's attack surface and trust boundaries. They combine these considerations into an integrated model that demonstrates likely vectors of attack against the attack surface by the identified threats and targeted at the identified assets. These attack vectors represent security risks. One of the more effective mechanisms for quickly identifying likely attack vectors, characterizing their nature, and identifying vetted mitigation approaches is the use of attack patterns as an integral part of the threat model.

Lastly, during the attack resistance analysis portion of the risk analysis process, in which the architectural security is vetted, attack patterns can be a valuable tool in identifying and characterizing contextually appropriate attacker perspectives to consider in a red teaming type of approach.

For further information about attack patterns, review Section 2.3.2 and see [Hoglund 2004].

4.4 Summary

The architecture and design phase of the SDLC represents a critical time for identifying and preventing security flaws before they become part of the software. As the connectivity, complexity, and extensibility of software increase, the importance of effectively addressing security concerns as an integral part of the architecture and design process will become even more critical. During this phase in the software development effort, architects, designers, and security analysts have an opportunity to ensure that requirements are interpreted appropriately through a security lens and that appropriate security knowledge is leveraged to give the software structure and form in a way that minimizes security risk. This can be accomplished through use of the following practices and knowledge resources:

- Beyond consistent application of good security common sense, one of the greatest opportunities for reducing the security risk of software early in the SDLC is through the practice of **architectural risk analysis**. By carrying out software characterization, threat analysis, architectural vulnerability assessment, risk likelihood determination, risk impact determination, and risk mitigation planning, project team members can identify, prioritize, and implement appropriate mitigating controls, revisions, or actions before security problems take root. These activities and their by-products not only yield more secure software, but also provide the software development team with a much richer understanding of how the software is expected to behave under various operating conditions and how its architecture and design support that behavior.

- The activities and processes that make up architectural risk analysis are enabled and fueled by a range of experiential security knowledge without which they would be meaningless. **Security principles** and **security guidelines** offer prescriptive guidance that serves as a positive benchmark against which to compare and assess software's architecture and design. The high-level abstraction, universal context, and lasting nature of security principles make the wisdom they bring to architectural-level decisions extremely valuable. The broad brush of security principles is enhanced and refined through the consideration of context-specific security guidelines that provide more concrete guidance down into the design level.

- Architectural risk analysis requires not only recognition of good defensive software practices, but also a solid understanding of the sort of threats and attacks that the software is likely to face. **Attack patterns,** describing common approaches to attacking software, provide one of the most effective resources for capturing this attacker's perspective. By developing the software's architecture and design to be resistant and resilient to the types of attack it is likely to face, the software development team lays a solid security foundation on which to build.

Project managers who can effectively leverage the practices (architectural risk analysis) and knowledge (security principles, security guidelines, and attack patterns) introduced in this chapter will gain a significant advantage in lowering the security risk profile of their software and will do so at a much lower cost than if they wait until later in the SDLC to act.

Chapter 5

Considerations for Secure Coding and Testing

5.1 Introduction

This chapter provides an overview of key security practices that project managers should include during software coding and testing. A number of excellent books and Web sites also provide detailed guidance on software security coding and software security testing. Thus the intent here is to summarize considerations for project managers and provide references for further reading.

Software security is first and foremost about identifying and managing risks. Assuming that appropriate requirements engineering, design, and architecture practices have been implemented, the next most effective way to identify and manage risks for a software application is to iteratively analyze and review its code throughout the course of the SDLC. In fact, many project managers start here because code analysis and review is better defined, more mature, and, therefore, more commonly used than some of the earlier life-cycle practices. This chapter identifies some of the more common software code vulnerabilities and effective practices for conducting source code review. It also briefly introduces the topic of practices for secure coding, and provides supporting references for further investigation.

The description of software security testing compares and contrasts software testing with testing software with security in mind. It describes two accepted approaches for software security testing: functional testing and risk-based testing. The chapter closes by describing practices and approaches to be considered when addressing security during unit test (including white-box testing), the testing of libraries and executable files, integration testing, and system testing (including black-box and penetration testing).

5.2 Code Analysis[1]

Developing robust software applications that are predictable in their execution and as vulnerability free as possible is a difficult task; making them completely secure is impossible. Too often software development organizations place functionality, schedules, and costs at the forefront of their concerns and make security and quality an afterthought. Nearly all attacks on software applications have one fundamental cause: The software is not secure owing to defects in its design, coding, testing, and operations.

A vulnerability is a software defect that an attacker can exploit. Defects typically fall into one of two categories: bugs and flaws.

A bug is a problem introduced during software implementation. Most bugs can be easily discovered and corrected. Examples include buffer overflows, race conditions, unsafe system calls, and incorrect input validation.

A flaw is a problem at a much deeper level. Flaws are more subtle, typically originating in the design and being instantiated in the code. Examples of flaws include compartmentalization problems in design, error-handling problems, and broken or illogical access control.

In practice, we find that software security problems are divided 50/50 between bugs and flaws [McGraw 2006]. Thus discovering and

---

1. This material is extracted and adapted from a more extensive article by Steven Lavenhar of Cigital, Inc. [BSI 19]. That article should be consulted for additional details and examples.

eliminating bugs during code analysis takes care of roughly half of the problem when tackling software security. Attack patterns, as discussed in Chapter 2, can also be used effectively during coding to help enumerate specific weaknesses targeted by relevant attacks, allowing developers to ensure that these weaknesses do not occur in their code.

This section focuses on implementation-level security bugs that can be addressed during source code analysis. Design-level flaws are discussed in Chapter 4, Secure Software Architecture and Design.

5.2.1 Common Software Code Vulnerabilities

The use of sound coding practices can help to substantially reduce software defects commonly introduced during implementation. The following types of security bugs are common. More details are available in [McGraw 2006] and [Tsipenyuk 2005] as well as the Common Vulnerabilities and Exposures Web site [CVE 2007], the Common Weakness Enumeration Web site [CWE 2007], and the National Vulnerability Database [NIST 2007].

Common Security Bugs and Attack Strategies with Known Solution Approaches

- Incorrect or incomplete input validation
- Poor or missing exception handling
- Buffer overflows
- SQL injection
- Race conditions

Input Validation

Trusting user and parameter input is a frequent source of security problems. Attacks that take advantage of little to no input validation include cross-site scripting, illegal pointer values, integer overflows, and DNS cache poisoning (refer to the glossary for definitions of these types of attacks). In addition, inadequate input validation can lead to buffer overflows and SQL defects as described below. All of these types of attacks can pose risks to confidentiality and integrity. One of the more effective approaches for input validation is to use a whitelist, which lists all known good inputs that a system is permitted to accept and excludes everything else (including characters used to perform each type of attack).

Exceptions

Exceptions are events that disrupt the normal flow of code. Programming languages may use a mechanism called an exception handler to deal with unexpected events such a divide-by-zero attempt, violation of memory protection, or a floating-point arithmetic error. Such exceptions could be handled by the code by checking for conditions that can lead to such violations. When such checks are not made, however, exception handling passes control from the function with that error to a higher execution context in an attempt to recover from that condition. Such exception handling disrupts the normal flow of the code. The security concerns that arise from exception handling are discussed in [McGraw 2006].

Buffer Overflows

Buffer overflows are a leading method used to exploit software by remotely injecting malicious code into a target application [Hoglund 2004; Viega 2001]. The root cause of buffer overflow problems is that commonly used programming languages such as C and C++ are inherently unsafe. No bounds checks on array and pointer references are carried out, meaning that a developer must check the bounds (an activity that is often overlooked) or risk encountering problems.

When writing to buffers, C/C++ programmers must take care not to store more data in the buffer than it can hold. When a program writes past the bounds of a buffer, a buffer overflow occurs and the next contiguous chunk of memory is overwritten. C and C++ allow programs to overflow buffers at will. No runtime checks are performed that might prevent writing past the end of a buffer, so developers have to perform the checks in their own code.

Reading or writing past the end of a buffer can cause a number of diverse (and often unanticipated) behaviors: (1) Programs can act in strange ways, (2) programs can fail completely, and (2) programs can proceed without any noticeable difference in execution. The side effects of overrunning a buffer depend on the following issues:

- How much data is written past the buffer bounds
- What data (if any) is overwritten when the buffer gets full and spills over
- Whether the program attempts to read data that is overwritten during the overflow
- Which data ends up replacing the memory that gets overwritten

The indeterminate behavior of programs that have overrun a buffer makes them particularly tricky to debug. In the worst cases, a program may overflow a buffer and not show any adverse side effects at all. As a result, buffer overflow problems often remain invisible during standard testing. The important thing to realize about buffer overflows is that any data that happens to be allocated near the buffer can potentially be modified when the overflow occurs.

Memory usage vulnerabilities will continue to be a fruitful resource for exploiting software until languages that incorporate memory management schemes enter into wider use.

SQL Injection

SQL injection is currently the principal technique used by attackers to take advantage of nonvalidated input defects to pass SQL commands through an application for execution by a database. The security model used by many applications assumes that a SQL query is a trusted command. In this case, the defect lies in the software's construction of a dynamic SQL statement based on user input.

Attackers take advantage of the fact that developers often chain together SQL commands with user-provided parameters, meaning that the attackers can, therefore, embed SQL commands inside these parameters. As a result, the attacker can execute arbitrary SQL queries and/or commands on the database server through the application. This ability enables attackers to exploit SQL queries to circumvent access controls, authentication, and authorization checks. In some instances, SQL queries may allow access to commands at the level of the host operating system. This can be done using stored procedures.

Race Conditions

Race conditions take on many forms but can be characterized as scheduling dependencies between multiple threads that are not properly synchronized, causing an undesirable timing of events. An example of a race condition that could have a negative outcome on security is when a specific sequence of events is required between Event A and Event B, but a race occurs and the proper sequence is not ensured by the software program. Developers can use a number of programming constructs to control the synchronization of threads, such as semaphores, mutexes, and critical sections. Race conditions fall into three main categories:

- Infinite loops, which cause a program to never terminate or never return from some flow of logic or control
- Deadlocks, which occur when the program is waiting on a resource without some mechanism for timeout or expiration and the resource or lock is never released
- Resource collisions, which represent failures to synchronize access to shared resources, often resulting in resource corruption or privilege escalations (see [Bishop 1996])

Additional security concerns that arise from these and other types of software vulnerabilities are discussed in [McGraw 2006].

5.2.2 Source Code Review

Source code review for security ranks high on the list of sound practices intended to enhance software security. Structured design and code inspections, as well as peer review of source code, can produce substantial improvements in software security. You can easily integrate these reviews into established software development processes. In this type of review, the reviewers meet one-on-one with developers and review code visually to determine whether it meets previously established secure code development criteria. Reviewers consider coding standards and use code review checklists (refer to Section 5.3.1) as they inspect code comments, documentation, the unit test plan, and the code's compliance with security requirements. Unit test plans detail how the code will be tested to demonstrate that it meets security requirements and design/coding standards intended to reduce design flaws and implementation bugs. The test plan includes a test procedure, inputs, and expected outputs [Viega 2001]. (See also Section 5.5.1.)

Manual inspection of code for security vulnerabilities can be time-consuming. To perform a manual analysis effectively, reviewers must know what security vulnerabilities look like before they can rigorously examine the code and identify those problems. The use of static analysis tools is preferred over manual analysis for this purpose because the former tools are faster, can be used to evaluate software programs much more frequently, and can encapsulate security knowledge in a way that does not require the tool operator to have the same level of security expertise as a human reviewer. Nevertheless, these tools cannot replace a human analyst; they can only speed up tasks that are easily automated.

Static Code Analysis Tools[2]

Static source code analysis is the process by which software developers check their code for problems and inconsistencies before compiling it. Developers can automate the analysis of source code by using static analysis tools. These tools scan the source code and automatically detect errors that typically pass through compilers and can cause problems later in the SDLC.

Many modern static analysis tools generate reports that graphically present the analysis results and recommend potential resolutions to identified problems.

Identifying security vulnerabilities is complicated by the fact that they often appear in hard-to-produce software states or crop up in unusual circumstances. Static analysis has the advantage of being performed before a program reaches a level of completion where dynamic analysis or other types of analysis can be meaningfully used. However, static code analyzers should not be viewed as a panacea to all potential problems. These tools can produce false positives and false negatives, so their results should be taken with the proverbial "grain of salt." That is, results indicating that zero security defects were found should not be taken to mean that your code is completely free of vulnerabilities or 100 percent secure; rather, these results simply mean that your code has none of the patterns found in the analysis tool's rulebase for security defects.

---

2. See [McGraw 2006, appendix A], [Chess 2004], [Chess 2007], and http://en.wikipedia.org/wiki/List_of_tools_for_static_code_analysis for further details and several examples.

What Static Analysis Tools Find

Static analysis tools look for a fixed set of patterns or rules in the code in a manner similar to virus-checking programs. While some of the more advanced tools allow new rules to be added to the rulebase, the tool will never find a problem if a rule has not been written for it.

Here are some examples of problems detected by static code analyzers:

- Syntax problems
- Unreachable code
- Unconditional branches into loops
- Undeclared variables
- Uninitialized variables
- Parameter type mismatches
- Uncalled functions and procedures
- Variables used before initialization
- Non-usage of function results
- Possible array bound errors
- Misuse of pointers

The greatest promise of static analysis tools derives from their ability to automatically identify many common coding problems. Unfortunately, implementation bugs created by developer errors are often only part of the problem. Static analysis tools cannot evaluate design and architectural flaws. They cannot identify poorly designed cryptographic libraries or improperly selected algorithms, and they cannot point out design problems that might cause confusion between authentication and authorization. They also cannot identify passwords or magic numbers embedded in code. One further drawback to automated code analysis is that the tools are prone to producing false positives when a potential vulnerability does not exist. This is especially true of older freeware tools, most of which are not actively supported; many analysts do not find these tools to be useful when analyzing real-world software systems.[3] Commercial tool vendors are actively addressing the problem of false positives and have made considerable progress in this realm, but much remains to be done.

Static code analysis can be used to discover subtle and elusive implementation errors before the software is tested or placed into operation. By correcting subtle errors in the code early, project managers can reduce testing efforts and minimize operations and maintenance costs. Static code analysis tools can be applied in a variety of ways, all of which lead to higher-quality software. This said, static analysis tools can identify only a subset of the vulnerabilities leading to security problems. These tools must always be used in conjunction with manual analysis and other software assurance methods to reduce vulnerabilities that cannot be identified based on patterns and rules.

Metric Analysis

Metric analysis produces a quantitative measure of the degree to which the analyzed code possesses a given attribute. An attribute is a characteristic or a property of the code. For example,

> When considered separately, "lines of code" and "number of security breaches" are two distinct measures that provide very little business meaning because there is no context for their values. A metric made up as "number of breaches/lines of code" provides a more interesting relative value. A comparative metric like this can be used to compare and contrast a given system's "security defect density" against a previous version or similar systems and thus provide management with useful data for decision making. [McGraw 2006, p. 247]

The process of using code metrics begins by deriving metrics that are appropriate for the code under review. Then data is collected, and metrics are computed and compared to preestablished guidelines and historical data (such as the number of defects per 1000 lines of code). The results of these comparisons are used to analyze the code with the intent of improving the measured qualities.

Two classes of quantitative software metrics are distinguished: absolute and relative. Absolute metrics are numerical values that represent

---

3. See Cigital's ITS4 software security tool (http://www.cigital.com/its4) and Fortify Software's RATS (Rough Auditing Tool for Security) (http://www.fortifysoftware.com/security-resources/rats.jsp).

a characteristic of the code, such as the probability of failure, the number of references to a particular variable in an application, or the number of lines of code. Absolute metrics do not involve uncertainty. There can be one and only one correct numerical representation of a given absolute metric. In contrast, relative metrics provide a numeric representation of an attribute that cannot be precisely measured, such as the degree of difficulty in testing for buffer overflows. There is no objective, absolute way to measure such an attribute. Multiple variables are factored into an estimation of the degree of testing difficulty, and any numeric representation is just an approximation.

Code Analysis Process Diagrams

The BSI Web site provides a number of code analysis process flow diagrams for source code review, static code analysis, and metric analysis, as well as for dynamic analysis, fault injection, cryptanalysis, and random-number generator analysis. We encourage you to consult the Web site [BSI 19] and [McGraw 2006] for further details.

5.3 Coding Practices[4]

Coding practices typically describe methods, techniques, processes, tools, and runtime libraries that can prevent or limit exploits against vulnerabilities. These measures may include the development and technology environment in which the coding practice is applied, as well as the risk of not following the practice and the type of attacks that could result.

Secure coding requires an understanding of programming errors that commonly lead to software vulnerabilities and the knowledge and use of alternative approaches that are less prone to error. Secure coding can benefit from the proper use of software development tools, including compilers. Compilers typically have options that allow increased or specific diagnostics to be performed on code during compilation. Resolving these warnings (by correcting the problem or determining that the warning is superfluous) can improve the security of the

---

4. This material is extracted and adapted from a more extensive article by Robert Seacord and Daniel Plakosh of Carnegie Mellon University [BSI 20]. That article should be consulted for additional details and examples.

deployed software system. In addition, compilers may provide options that influence runtime settings. Understanding available compiler options and making informed decisions about which options to use and which to omit can help eliminate vulnerabilities and mitigate against runtime exploitation of undiscovered or unresolved vulnerabilities.

As one example, CERT has observed through an analysis of thousands of vulnerability reports that most vulnerabilities stem from a relatively small and recurring number of common programming errors that could be easily avoided if developers learned to recognize them and understand their potential harm. In particular, the C and C++ programming languages have proved highly susceptible to these classes of errors. Easily avoided software defects are a primary cause of commonly exploited software vulnerabilities. By identifying insecure coding practices and developing secure alternatives, software project managers and developers can take practical steps to reduce or eliminate vulnerabilities before they are deployed in the field.

5.3.1 Sources of Additional Information on Secure Coding

We encourage readers to review the Coding Practices area of the BSI Web site for additional coding practices that can be used to mitigate common problems in C and C++ [BSI 20]. An example of the use of compiler checks to minimize integer vulnerabilities is described in the "Compiler Checks" section of the Web site. Examples of using other static and dynamic analysis tools to discover and mitigate vulnerabilities are described in "Runtime Analysis Tools" and "Heap Integrity Detection."

The CERT Secure Coding Initiative (http://www.cert.org/securecoding) works with software developers and software development organizations to reduce vulnerabilities resulting from coding errors before they are deployed in products. The initiative's work includes identifying common programming errors that lead to software vulnerabilities, establishing standard secure coding standards, educating software developers, and advancing the state of the practice in secure coding.

Table 5–1 provides a description of a number of recent and excellent books on the subject.

Table 5–1: *Books to Consult for Secure Coding Approaches and Practices*

Secure Programming with Static Analysis [Chess 2007]	Describes how static source code analysis can be used to uncover errors and the most common types of security defects that result in security vulnerabilities. The book describes how this method works, explains how to integrate it into your software development process, and explores how to conduct effective code reviews using the method.
Software Security: Building Security In [McGraw 2006]	Describes in detail how to put software security into practice. It presents the topic from the two sides of software security—attack and defense, exploiting and designing, breaking and building—including a description of seven essential "touchpoints" for software security. Excerpts and citations from *Software Security* are included throughout this chapter and on the BSI Web site.
The Secure Development Lifecycle [Howard 2006]	Describes Microsoft's Security Development Lifecycle (SDL) as one proven way to help reduce the number of software security defects during each phase of the development process. This process has been used effectively in many Microsoft products.
Secure Coding in C and C++ [Seacord 2005]	Provides a comprehensive description of common programming errors (for example, in string manipulation, integer operations, and dynamic memory management), the vulnerabilities that result from them, and mitigation strategies for minimizing their impact.
Exploiting Software: How to Break Code [Hoglund 2004]	Describes how to design software so that it is as resistant as possible to attack. This book describes how malicious hackers go about writing exploit scripts that can be used to cause software to fail; in this way, it provides software designers with an understanding of the types of attacks their software may be forced to deal with.

Table 5–1: *Books to Consult for Secure Coding Approaches and Practices (Continued)*

Secure Coding: Principles and Practices [Graff 2003]	Describes good and bad practices to consider during architecture, design, code, test, and operations, along with supporting case studies. Good practices for secure coding identified in this book include handling data with caution (perform bounds checking, set initial values for data), reusing good code whenever practicable, insisting on a sound review process (peer reviews, independent verification and validation), using checklists and standards, and removing obsolete code.
Writing Secure Code, second edition [Howard 2002]	Provides developers with detailed practices for designing secure applications, writing robust code that can withstand repeated attacks, and testing applications for security flaws. The book provides proven principles, strategies, and coding techniques.
Building Secure Software: How to Avoid Security Problems the Right Way [Viega 2001]	"Helps people involved in the software development process learn the principles necessary for building secure software. It is intended for anyone involved in software development, from managers to coders, although it contains the low-level detail that is most applicable to developers. Specific code examples and technical details are presented in the second part of the book. The first part is more general and is intended to set an appropriate context for building secure software by introducing security goals, security technologies, and the concept of software risk management" [Viega 2001, p. xxiii].

5.4 Software Security Testing[5]

Security test activities are primarily performed to demonstrate that a system meets its security requirements and to identify and minimize

---

5. This material is extracted and adapted from a more extensive article by C. C. Michael and Will Radosevich of Cigital, Inc. [BSI 21]. That article should be consulted for additional details.

the number of security vulnerabilities in the software before the system goes into production. Additionally, security test activities can aid in reducing overall project costs, protecting an organization's reputation or brand once a product is deployed, reducing litigation expenses, and complying with regulatory requirements.

The goal of security testing is to ensure that the software being tested is robust and continues to function in an acceptable manner even in the presence of a malicious attack. Security testing is motivated by probing undocumented assumptions and areas of particular complexity to determine how a software program can be broken. The designers and the specification might outline a secure design, and the developers might be diligent and write secure code, but ultimately the testing process determines whether the software will be adequately secure once it is fielded.

Testing is laborious, time-consuming, and expensive, so the choice of testing approaches should be based on the risks to the software and the system. Risk analysis provides the right context and information to make tradeoffs between time and effort to achieve test effectiveness (see Section 7.4.2). An effective testing approach balances efficiency and effectiveness to identify the greatest number of critical defects for the least cost.

This section is not intended to serve as a primer on software testing. Anyone responsible for security testing should be familiar with standard approaches to software testing such as those described in these books:

- *Testing Object-Oriented Systems: Models, Patterns, and Tools* [Binder 1999]
- *Automated Software Testing* [Dustin 1999]
- *Software Test Automation* [Fewster 1999]
- *The Craft of Software Testing: Subsystems Testing Including Object-Based and Object-Oriented Testing* [Marick 1994]
- *Black-Box Testing: Techniques for Functional Testing of Software and Systems* [Beizer 1995]
- *Managing the Testing Process: Practical Tools and Techniques for Managing Hardware and Software Testing, Second Edition* [Black 2002]
- *Testing Computer Software, Second Edition* [Kaner 1999]

5.4.1 Contrasting Software Testing and Software Security Testing

At one time, it was widely believed that security bugs in a software system were just like traditional programming bugs and that traditional quality assurance and testing techniques could be applied equally well to secure software development. Over time, however, developers have learned that security-related bugs can differ from traditional software bugs in a number of ways. These characteristics, in turn, influence the practices that you should use for software security testing [Hoglund 2004].

- Users do not normally try to search out software bugs. An enterprising user may occasionally derive satisfaction from making software break, but if the user succeeds, it affects only that user. Conversely, malicious attackers *do* search for security-related vulnerabilities in an intelligent and deliberate manner. One important difference between security testing and other testing activities is that the security test engineer needs to emulate an intelligent attacker. An adversary might do things that no ordinary user would do, such as entering a 1000-character surname or repeatedly trying to corrupt a temporary file. Test engineers must consider actions that are far outside the range of normal activity and might not even be regarded as legitimate tests under other circumstances. A security test engineer must think like the attacker and find the weak spots first.

- Malicious attackers are known to script successful attacks and distribute exploit scripts throughout their communities. In other words, a single, hard-to-find vulnerability can be exploited by a large number of malicious attackers using publicly available exploit scripts. This proliferation of attacker knowledge can cause problems for a large number of users, whereas a hard-to-find software bug typically causes problems for only a few users.

- Although most developers are not currently trained in secure programming practices, developers can (and do) learn from experience to avoid poor programming practices that can lead to software bugs in their code. However, the list of insecure programming practices is long and continues to grow, making it difficult for developers to keep current on the latest exploits and attack patterns (see also Section 2.3.2).

- Security testing differs from traditional software testing in that it emphasizes what an application should *not* do rather than what it *should* do. While it sometimes tests conformance to positive requirements such as "User accounts are disabled after three unsuccessful login attempts" and "Network traffic must be encrypted," more often it tests negative requirements [Fink 1997] such as "Outside attackers should not be able to modify the contents of the Web page" and "Unauthorized users should not be able to access data." This shift in emphasis from positive to negative requirements affects the way testing is performed (see Section 5.4.3). The standard way to test a positive requirement is to create the conditions in which the requirement is intended to hold true and verify that the requirement is satisfied by the software. By contrast, a negative requirement may state that something should never occur. To apply a standard testing approach to negative requirements, one would need to create every possible set of conditions, which is not feasible.

- Many security requirements, such as "An attacker should never be able to take control of the application," would be regarded as untestable in a traditional software development setting. It is considered a legitimate practice for testers to ask that such requirements be refined or perhaps dropped altogether. Many security requirements, however, can be neither refined nor dropped even if they are untestable. For example, one cannot reliably enumerate all of the ways in which an attacker might gain control of an application (which would be one way to make it more testable), and obviously one cannot drop the requirement either. Thus the challenge is to find both a way to specify these types of requirements and a way to adequately test them.

Project managers and security test engineers must ask which kinds of vulnerabilities can exist for the software being tested and which kinds of problems are likely to have been overlooked by the developers. Often the most important types of vulnerabilities to consider are the most common ones (described in Section 5.2.1), which are targeted by security scanners and reported in public forums.

Many traditional software bugs can have security implications. Buggy behavior is almost by definition unforeseen behavior, and as such it presents an attacker with the opportunity for a potential exploit. Indeed, many well-known vulnerabilities could cause software to crash if they were triggered. Crashing software can expose confidential information in the form of diagnostics or data dumps. Even if the software does not crash as the result of a bug, its internal state can become corrupted and lead to unexpected behavior at a later time. For this reason, error-handling software is a frequent target of malicious attacks. Attackers probing a new application often start by trying to crash it.

Ninety Percent Right

Finding 90 percent of a software program's vulnerabilities does not necessarily make the software less vulnerable; it merely reduces the cost of future fixes and increases the odds of finding the remaining problems before attackers do. The result is that secure software development is intrinsically more challenging than traditional software development. Given this fact, security testing needs to address these unique considerations and per-spectives to the extent possible and practical.

Security Testing Methods

Two common methods for testing whether software has met its security requirements are functional security testing and risk-based security testing [McGraw 2006]. Functional testing is meant to ensure that software behaves as specified and so is largely based on demonstrating that requirements defined in advance during requirements engineering (see Chapter 3) are satisfied at an acceptable level. Risk-based testing probes specific risks that have been identified through risk analysis. The next two sections discuss how functional and risk-based testing can be used to enhance confidence in the software's security.

5.4.2 Functional Testing

Functional testing usually means testing the system's adherence to its functional requirements. A functional requirement usually has the following form: "When a specific thing happens, then the software should respond in a certain way." This way of specifying a requirement is convenient for the tester, who can exercise the "if" part of the requirement and then confirm that the software behaves as it should.

Examples of functional security requirements are that a user's account is disabled after three unsuccessful login attempts and that only certain characters are permitted in a URL. These positive functional requirements can be tested in traditional ways, such as attempting three unsuccessful login attempts and verifying that the account is disabled, or by supplying a URL with illegal characters and making sure that those characters are stripped out before the URL is processed.

When risks are identified early in the SDLC, developers have adequate time to include *mitigations* for those risks (also known as countermeasures). Mitigations are meant to reduce the severity of the identified risks, and they lead to positive requirements. For example, the risk of password-cracking attacks can be mitigated by disabling an account after three unsuccessful login attempts or by enforcing long passphrases. Passphrases are largely immune to cracking and have the added benefit of often being easier to remember than complex passwords. The risk of SQL injection attacks from a Web interface can be mitigated by using an input validation whitelist (a list of all known good inputs that a system is permitted to accept) that excludes all other characters. These mitigations have to be tested not only to confirm that they are implemented correctly, but also to determine how well they actually safeguard the system against the risks they were designed to address.

A common software development practice is to ensure that every requirement can be mapped to a specific software artifact meant to implement that requirement. As a consequence, the tester who is probing a specific requirement knows exactly which code artifact to test. Generally, there is a clear mapping between functional requirements, code artifacts, and functional tests.

Some Caveats

Software engineers may not understand how to implement some security requirements. In one example, a Web application was found to be vulnerable to a directory traversal attack, where a URL containing the string ".." was used to access directories that were supposedly forbidden to remote clients. To counter this possibility, developers used a blacklist technique, in which a list is created and used to exclude or filter out bad input data and bad characters. URLs that contained this string were added to the blacklist and thus disallowed. However, blacklists are not infallible:

> [Blacklists] often fail because the enumeration is incomplete, or because the removal of bad characters from the input can result in the production of another bad input which is not caught (and so on recursively). Blacklists fail also because they are based on previous experience, and only enumerate known bad input. The recommended practice is the creation of whitelists that enumerate known good input. Everything else is rejected. [Meunier 2006]

Testing cannot demonstrate the absence of software problems; it can only demonstrate (sometimes) that problems are present [Dijkstra 1970]. The problem is that testers can try out only a limited number of test cases; the software might work correctly for those cases and fail for other cases. Therefore, testing a mitigation measure is not enough to guarantee that the corresponding risk has truly been eliminated, and this caveat is especially important to keep in mind when the risk in question is a severe one.

Also, when bugs are fixed, the fix is sometimes not subjected to the same scrutiny as those features that were part of the original software design. For example, a problem that should normally be detected in design reviews might slip through the cracks if it shows up as part of a bug fix. Sometimes software that has been repaired is retested simply by running the original test suite again—but that approach works poorly for the caveats described here.

Testing Beyond Requirements

Functional testing is meant to probe whether software behaves as it should, but so far we have focused only on requirements-based testing. A number of other functional testing techniques (as described in 170 on pages 170–171) do not rely on defined requirements. These techniques are described in more detail in [BSI 21].

5.4.3 Risk-Based Testing

Risk-based testing addresses negative requirements, which state what a software system should not do. Tests for negative requirements can be developed in a number of ways. They should be derived from a risk analysis, which should encompass not only the high-level risks identified during the design process but also low-level risks derived from the software itself.

Table 5–2: *Functional Testing Techniques*

Ad hoc testing (experience-based testing) and exploratory testing	Tests are based on the tester's skill, intuition, and experience with similar programs to identify tests not captured in more formal techniques.
Specification-based and model-based testing	Tests are derived automatically using a specification created in a formal language (rare) or through the use of a model of program interfaces.
Equivalence partitioning	Tests are derived by dividing the input domain into a collection of subsets or equivalence classes (such as output path or program structure) and then selecting representative tests for each class.
Boundary values analysis	Tests are selected on or near the boundaries of the input domain of variables, given that many defects tend to concentrate near the extreme values of inputs.
Robustness and fault-tolerance testing	Test cases are chosen outside the domain to test program robustness in the face of unexpected and erroneous inputs.
Decision table (also called logic-based) testing	Tests are derived by systematically considering every possible combination of conditions (such as inputs) and actions (such as outputs).
State-based testing	Tests are selected that cover states and transitions from a finite state machine model of the software.
Control-flow testing	Tests are selected to detect poor and incorrect program structures. Test criteria aim at covering all statements, classes, or blocks in a program (or some specified combinations).
Data-flow testing	This form of testing is often used to test interfaces between subsystems. It is accomplished by annotating a program-control flow graph with information about how variables are defined and used and then tracing paths from where the variable is defined to where it is used.

Table 5–2: *Functional Testing Techniques (Continued)*

Usage-based and use-case-based testing	Tests are derived by developing an operational scenario or set of use cases that describe how the software will be used in its operational environment. (See also Section 3.2.)
Code-based testing (also called white-box testing; see Section 5.5.1)	This approach is a superset of control-flow and data-flow testing. Tests are designed to cover the code by using the control structure, data-flow structure, decision control, and modularity.
Fault-based testing	Tests are designed to intentionally introduce faults to probe program robustness and reliability [Whittaker 2003].
Protocol conformance testing	Tests are designed to use a program's communication protocol as the test basis. In combination with boundary values testing and equivalence-based testing, this method is useful for Web-based programs and other Internet-based code.
Load and performance testing	Tests are designed to verify that the system meets its specified performance requirements (capacity and response time) by exercising the system to the maximum design load and beyond it.

When testing negative requirements, security test engineers typically look for common mistakes and test suspected weaknesses in the software. The emphasis is on finding vulnerabilities, often by executing abuse and misuse tests that attempt to exploit software weaknesses (see Section 3.2). In addition to demonstrating the actual presence of vulnerabilities, security tests can assist in uncovering symptoms that suggest potential vulnerabilities.

Requirements can be expected to contain mitigations for many risks. Mitigations generally result in positive requirements, but the fact that a risk has a mitigation does not imply that it should be ignored during risk-based testing. Even if a mitigation measure is correctly implemented, there is still a need to ask whether it really does safeguard against the risk it serves as a countermeasure for and to what extent. Each mitigation generates a positive requirement—the correct implementation of the mitigation strategy—but it also generates a negative requirement stating that the mitigation must not be circumventable. To put it another way, the mitigation might not be sufficient for avoiding the underlying risk, and this possibility constitutes a risk in and of itself.

Unfortunately, the process of deriving tests from risks is as much an art as a science, such that it depends a great deal on the skills and security knowledge of the test engineer. Many automated tools can be helpful during risk-based testing (for example, see the description of black-box testing in Section 5.5.4), but these tools can perform only simple tasks; the difficult tasks remain the responsibility of the test engineer. You might also consider the use of commercial tools for identifying vulnerabilities in Web applications such as those from SPI Dynamics and Watchfire.

Defining Tests for Negative Requirements

As a basis for defining test conditions, past experience comes into play in two ways. First, a mature test organization typically has a set of test templates that outline the test techniques to be used for testing against specific risks and requirements in specific types of software modules. Test templates are usually created during testing projects, and they accumulate over time to capture the organization's past experience. This book does not provide test templates, but attack patterns appropriate for this purpose are described in several other sources [Hoglund 2004; Whittaker 2002, 2003].

Another way to derive test scenarios from past experience is to use incident reports. Incident reports can simply be bug reports, but in the context of security testing they can also be forensic descriptions of successful intruder activity. Furthermore, vulnerability reports are often followed by proofs of concept to demonstrate how the reported vulnerability can be exploited. Sometimes these proofs of concept are actual exploits; at other times they simply show that a vulnerability is likely to be exploitable. For example, if a buffer overflow can be made to cause a crash, then it can usually be exploited by an attacker as well. Sometimes it is sufficient to find evidence of vulnerabilities as opposed to actual exploits, so that the resulting proofs of concept can be used as the basis for test scenarios. When devising risk-based tests, it can be useful to consult IT security personnel, as their jobs involve keeping up-to-date on vulnerabilities, incident reports, and security threats.

Attack patterns (as discussed in Chapter 2) can be used effectively during software security testing to craft test cases that reflect attacker behavior and to help identify test cases that validate secure behavior.

Finally, threat modeling can be leveraged to help create risk-based tests. For example, if inexperienced intruders (e.g., script kiddies) are expected to pose a major threat, then it might be appropriate to probe the software under test with automated tools; intruders often use the same tools (see the description of black-box testing in Section 5.5.4).

Additional thought processes that might be helpful in creating new tests for negative requirements include (1) understanding a software component and its environment, (2) understanding the assumptions of the developers, and (3) building a fault model (hypotheses about what might go wrong). Consult [BSI 21] for further details.

5.5 Security Testing Considerations Throughout the SDLC[6]

Activities related to testing take place throughout the software life cycle, not just after coding is complete. Preparations for security testing can begin even before the planned software system has definite requirements and before a risk analysis has been conducted. For example, past experience with similar systems can provide a wealth of information about relevant attacker activity.

As part of a preliminary risk analysis, you might consider which environment factors the software will be subjected to, what its security needs are, and what kinds of effects a breach of security might have. This information provides useful and early inputs for test planning. If risk analysis starts early in the SDLC, it becomes possible to take a security-oriented approach when defining requirements.

During the requirements phase, test planning focuses on outlining how each requirement can and will be tested. Some requirements may initially appear to be untestable. If test planning is already under way, then those requirements can be identified and possibly revised to make them more testable. Testing is driven by both risks and requirements, and

---

6. This material is extracted and adapted from a more extensive article by C. C. Michael and Will Radosevich of Cigital, Inc. [BSI 21]. That article should be consulted for additional details.

risks are especially important to consider in security testing. While traditional non-security-related risks are linked to what can go wrong if a requirement is not satisfied, security analysis often uncovers severe security risks that were not anticipated in the requirements phase. In fact, a security risk analysis (as discussed in Chapters 4 and 7) is an integral part of secure software development, and it should drive requirements derivation and system design as well as security testing.

Risks identified during this phase may inspire additional requirements that call for features to mitigate those risks. The software development process can be expected to go more smoothly if these security measures are defined early in the SDLC, when they can be more easily implemented. If the development team faces intense time pressure, it is often a legitimate strategy to spend less time testing against a risk that has a known countermeasure, on the assumption that a mitigated risk is less severe.

Functional security testing generally begins as soon as software is available to test. Given this timeline, a test plan should be established at the beginning of the coding phase and the necessary infrastructure and personnel should be determined before testing starts.

Software is tested at many levels in a typical development process. This section cannot hope to catalog every possible software test activity. Instead, it describes several broader activities that are common to most test processes, some of which are repeated at different times for software artifacts at different levels of complexity. We discuss the role of security testing in each of these activities:

- Unit testing, where individual classes, methods, functions, or other relatively small components are tested
- Testing libraries and executable files
- Functional testing, where software is tested for adherence to requirements (as described in Section 5.4.2)
- Integration testing, where the goal is to test whether software components work together as they should
- System testing, where the entire system is under test

5.5.1 Unit Testing

Unit testing is usually the first stage of testing that a software artifact goes through. This type of testing involves exercising individual functions, methods, classes, or stubs. As a functional-based approach to unit testing, white-box testing is typically very effective in validating design decisions and assumptions and in finding programming errors and implementation errors. It focuses on analyzing data flows, control flows, information flows, coding practices, and exception and error handling within the system, with the goal of testing both intended and unintended software behavior. White-box testing can be performed to validate whether code implementation follows the intended design, to validate implemented security functionality, and to uncover exploitable vulnerabilities.

White-box testing requires knowing what makes software secure or insecure, how to think like an attacker, and how to use different testing tools and techniques. The first step in such testing is to comprehend and analyze the source code (see Section 5.2.2), so knowing what makes software secure is a fundamental requirement. In addition, to create tests that exploit software, a tester must think like an attacker. Finally, to perform testing effectively, testers need to know what kinds of tools and techniques are available for white-box testing. The three requirements do not work in isolation, but together.

Further details on how to conduct white-box testing and what sorts of benefits it confers are available at [BSI 22].

5.5.2 Testing Libraries and Executable Files

In many development projects, unit testing is closely followed by a test effort that focuses on libraries and executable files. Usually test engineers who are experienced in testing security—rather than software developers—perform testing at this level. As part of this testing, there may be a need for specialized technology that crafts customized network traffic, simulates fault and stress conditions, allows observation of anomalous program behavior, and so on.

Coverage analysis (which measures the degree to which the source code has been fully tested, including all statements, conditions, paths, and entry/exit conditions) can be especially important in security testing [Hoglund 2004]. Because a determined attacker will probe the software system thoroughly, security testers must do so as well. Error-handling routines are difficult to cover during testing, and they are also notorious for introducing vulnerabilities. Good coding practices can help reduce the risks posed by error handlers, but it may still be useful to have test tools that simulate error conditions during testing so as to exercise the error handlers in a dynamic environment.

Libraries need special attention in security testing, because components found in a library might eventually be reused in ways that are not anticipated in the current system design. For example, a buffer overflow in a particular library function might seem to pose little risk because attackers cannot control any of the data processed by that function; in the future, however, this function might be reused in a way that makes it accessible to outside attackers. Furthermore, libraries may be reused in future software development projects even if such reuse was not planned during the design of the current system.

5.5.3 Integration Testing

Integration testing focuses on a collection of subsystems, which may contain many executable components. Numerous software bugs are known to appear only because of the way components interact, and the same is true for security bugs as well.

Integration errors often arise when one subsystem makes unjustified assumptions about other subsystems. For example, an integration error can occur if the calling function and the called function each assume that the other is responsible for bounds checking and neither one actually does the check. The failure to properly check input values is one of the most common sources of software vulnerabilities. In turn, integration errors are one of the most common sources of unchecked input values, because each component might assume that the inputs are being checked elsewhere. (Components should validate their own data, but in many systems this ideal is sacrificed for reasons of efficiency.) During security testing, it is especially important to determine which data flows and controls flows can and cannot be influenced by a potential attacker.

5.5.4 System Testing

Certain activities relevant to software security, such as stress testing, are often carried out at the system level.[7] Penetration testing is also carried out at the system level, and when a vulnerability is found in this way, it provides tangible proof that the vulnerability is real: A vulnerability that

---

7. See also Chapter 6, Security and Complexity: System Assembly Challenges.

can be exploited during system testing will be exploitable by attackers. In the face of schedule, budget, and staff constraints, these problems are the most important vulnerabilities to fix.

Stress Testing for Security

Stress testing is relevant to security because software performs differently when it is under stress. For example, when one component is disabled because of insufficient resources, other components may compensate in insecure ways. An executable that crashes may leave sensitive information in places that are accessible to attackers. Attackers might be able to spoof subsystems that are slow or disabled, and race conditions (see Section 5.2.1) might become easier to exploit. Stress testing may also exercise error handlers, which are often fraught with vulnerabilities. Security testers should look for unusual behavior during stress testing that might signal the presence of unsuspected vulnerabilities.

Black-Box Testing

One popular approach to system testing is black-box testing. Black-box testing uses methods that do not require access to source code. Either the test engineer does not have access or the details of the source code are irrelevant to the properties being tested. As a consequence, black-box testing focuses on the externally visible behavior of the software, such as requirements, protocol specifications, APIs, or even attempted attacks. Within the security test arena, black-box testing is normally associated with activities that occur during the pre-deployment test phase (system test) or on a periodic basis after the system has been deployed.

Black-box test activities almost universally involve the use of tools, which typically focus on specific areas such as network security, database security, security subsystems, and Web application security. For example, network security tools include port scanners to identify all active devices connected to the network, services operating on systems connected to the network, and applications running for each identified service. Vulnerability scanning tools identify specific security vulnerabilities associated with the scanned system based on information contained within a vulnerability database. Potential vulnerabilities include those related to open ports that allow access to insecure services, protocol-based vulnerabilities, and vulnerabilities resulting from poor implementation or configuration of an operating system or application.

For more information on black-box testing and test tools, refer to [BSI 23].

Penetration Testing

Another common approach for conducting certain aspects of system security testing is penetration testing, which allows project managers to assess how an attacker is likely to try to subvert a system. At a basic level, the term "penetration testing" refers to testing the security of a computer system and/or software application by attempting to compromise its security—in particular, the security of the underlying operating system and network component configurations.

Conventional penetration testing tools come in a variety of forms, depending on which sort of testing they can perform. A key distinguishing factor is the perspective from which each type of tool operates—that is, whether a testing tool evaluates its target from afar or from relatively close up (i.e., at least within the same computer system). Popular classes of tools used in penetration testing today include host-based, network-based, and application scanning [Fyodor 2006].

For example, most organizations, when doing network-based penetration testing, follow a process that looks something like this (Steps 1–3 constitute the vulnerability scanning approach mentioned earlier):

1. *Target acquisition.* The test engineer identifies legitimate test targets. This step is most often performed using a combination of manual and automated approaches in which the person responsible for the system under test provides a starting list of network addresses and the test engineer uses software tools to look for additional computers in the network vicinity.

2. *Inventory.* The test engineer uses a set of tools to conduct an inventory of available network services to be tested.

3. *Probe.* The test engineer probes the available targets to determine whether they are susceptible to compromise.

4. *Penetrate.* Each identified vulnerability (or potential vulnerability) is exploited in an attempt to penetrate the target system. The level

of invasiveness involved in exploiting a vulnerability can influence this step dramatically. For example, if a vulnerability can result in the attacker (in this case, the test engineer) having the ability to overwrite an arbitrary file on the target system, great care should be taken in how the vulnerability is exploited.

5. *Host-based assessment.* This step is typically carried out for any system that is successfully penetrated. It enables the test engineer to identify vulnerabilities that provide additional vectors of attack, including those that provide the ability to escalate privileges once the system is compromised.

6. *Continue.* The test engineer obtains access on any of the systems where identified vulnerabilities were exploited and continues the testing process from the network location(s) of each compromised system.

For more information on penetration testing and pitfalls to avoid, refer to [BSI 24]. For more information on penetration testing tools, refer to [BSI 25].

5.5.5 Sources of Additional Information on Software Security Testing

Articles in the *IEEE Security & Privacy* "Building Security In" series provide excellent guidance on software security testing. Articles titled "Software Penetration Testing," "Static Analysis for Security," and "Software Security Testing" are available on the BSI Web site under Additional Resources [BSI 26].

The Art of Software Security Testing [Wysopal 2006] reviews software design and code vulnerabilities and provides guidelines for how to avoid them. This book describes ways to customize software debugging tools to test the unique aspects of any software program and then analyze the results to identify exploitable vulnerabilities. Coverage includes the following topics:

* Thinking the way attackers think
* Integrating security testing into the SDLC
* Using threat modeling to prioritize testing based on risk
* Building test labs for conducting white-, gray-, and black-box testing
* Choosing and using the right tools

- Executing today's leading attacks, from fault injection to buffer overflows
- Determining which flaws are most likely to be exploited

Exploiting Software: How to Break Code [Hoglund 2004] provides examples of real attacks, attack patterns, tools, and techniques used by attackers to break software. It discusses reverse engineering, classic attacks against server software, surprising attacks against client software, techniques for crafting malicious input, buffer overflows, and rootkits.

How to Break Software Security: A Practical Guide to Testing [Whittaker 2003] defines prescriptive techniques (attacks that software test engineers can use on their own software) that are designed to reveal security vulnerabilities in software programs. The book's chapters discuss fault models for software security testing, the creation of unanticipated user input scenarios, and ways to attack software designs and code that focus on the most common places where software vulnerabilities occur (e.g., user interfaces, software dependencies, software design, and process and memory).

5.6 Summary

It is no secret that common, everyday software defects cause the majority of software vulnerabilities. The most widely used operating systems and most application software contain at least one or two defects per thousand lines of code and, therefore, may include hundreds to thousands of defects. While not every software defect is a security defect, if only 1 or 2 percent lead to security vulnerabilities, the risk is still substantial. Understanding the sources of vulnerabilities and learning to program securely are essential for protecting the Internet, your software, and your systems from attack. Reducing security defects, and thereby security vulnerabilities, requires a disciplined engineering approach based on sound coding practices [Howard 2006; McGraw 2006; Seacord 2005].

The key secure coding practices highlighted in this chapter include these approaches:

- Using sound and proven secure coding practices to aid in reducing software defects introduced during implementation

- Performing source code review using static code analysis tools, metric analysis, and manual review to minimize implementation-level security bugs

Security testing relies on human expertise to an even greater extent than does ordinary testing, so full automation of the test process is even less feasible when focusing on security issues than in a traditional testing environment. Although tools are available that automate certain types of tests, organizations using these tools should not be lulled into a false sense of security, because they cover only a small part of the spectrum of potential vulnerabilities. Instead, test tools should be viewed as aides for human testers, automating many tasks that are time-consuming or repetitive.

Creating security tests other than ones that directly map to security requirements is challenging, especially tests that intend to exercise the non-normative behavior of the system. When creating such tests, it is helpful to view the software under test from multiple angles, including the data the system will handle, the environment in which the system will operate, the users of the software (including software components), the options available to configure the system, and the error-handling behavior of the system. There is an obvious interaction and overlap between the different views; however, treating each one individually and specifically provides unique perspectives that are very helpful in developing effective tests.

This chapter has highlighted the following key software security testing practices:

- Understanding the differences between software security testing and traditional software testing, and planning how best to address these (including thinking like an attacker and emphasizing how to exercise what the software should not do)
- Constructing meaningful functional test cases (using a range of techniques) that demonstrate the software's adherence to its functional requirements, including its security requirements (positive requirements)
- Developing risk-based test cases (using, for example, misuse/abuse cases, attack patterns, and threat modeling) that exercise common mistakes, suspected software weaknesses, and mitigations intended to reduce or eliminate risks to ensure they cannot be circumvented (negative requirements)

- Using a complement of testing strategies, including white-box testing (based on deep knowledge of the source code), black-box testing (focusing on the software's externally visible behavior), and penetration testing (identifying and targeting specific vulnerabilities at the system level)

An organization should not rely exclusively on security test activities to build security into a system. This said, security testing—when it is coupled with other security activities performed throughout the SDLC—can be very effective in validating design assumptions, discovering vulnerabilities associated with the software environment, and identifying implementation issues that may lead to security vulnerabilities.

Chapter 6

Security and Complexity: System Assembly Challenges

6.1 Introduction   ⒺⓂ‌Ⓛ

The primary theme of this chapter is how aspects of complexity due to technical difficulty, size, and conflicting objectives affect security as systems expand to support multiple processes within and across organizations.[1] Mitigation strategies and project management approaches are suggested for each area, including examples of "planning for failure" in the context of Web services and identity management.

System development has always encountered new and often complex problems that were not represented in project plans. Often, the hard-to-solve problems are not new. Not many years ago, for example, the Common Object Request Broker Architecture (CORBA) received considerable

---

1. Robert Ferguson at the SEI has been studying the effects of systems engineering complexity on project management. The discussion of complexity factors in this chapter reflects discussions with him and was also influenced by the Incremental Commitment Model (ICM) [Boehm 2007].

attention as an approach for integrating distributed systems; now much of that attention has shifted to Web services. The sequence of solutions over multiple decades is not just a measure of the difficulty of the challenges, but also an indicator of the progress that is made in overcoming them. For example, Web services protocols have significantly eased the mechanics of connecting systems and offer the opportunity to address a number of business requirements.

The improved capability to assemble systems does not by itself address the problem of the failures observed in complex systems, but rather may increase the risk of deploying systems whose behavior is not predictable. The theme of a 2007 *New York Times* article is captured in a quote by Peter Neumann: "We don't need hackers to break the systems because they're falling apart by themselves" [Schwartz 2007]. For example, 17,000 international travelers flying into Los Angeles International Airport were stranded on planes for hours one day in August 2007 after U.S. Customs and Border Protection Agency computers went down and stayed down for nine hours. The Northeastern power grid failure in the summer of 2003 is another recent example of the effects of a system failure. Voting machine failures continue to be publicized. Customers for Skype, the Internet-based telephone company, encountered a 48-hour failure in August 2007.

The Los Angles airport failure was traced to a malfunctioning network card on a desktop computer that slowed the network and set off a domino effect of failures on the customs network. The power grid failure was not caused by a single event but rather by a cascading set of failures with multiple causes. Avi Rubin, a professor of computer science at Johns Hopkins University, noted that for voting machines the focus might have been too much on hackers and not on accidental events that sometimes can cause the worst problems. The Skype failure was initiated by a deluge of login attempts by computers that had restarted after downloading a security update. The logins overloaded the Skype network and revealed a bug in the Skype program that allocated computer resources that normally would have mitigated the excessive network load [Schwartz 2007].

The individuals interviewed for the *New York Times* article include a number of well-known experts in computer security, but the general observations focused more on reliability and complexity than on security:

- Most of the problems we have today have nothing to do with malice. Things break. Complex systems break in complex ways. (Steve Bellovin, Columbia University)

- We have gone from fairly simple computing architectures to massively distributed, massively interconnected and interdependent networks. As a result, flaws have become increasingly hard to predict or spot. Simpler systems could be understood and their behavior characterized, but greater complexity brings unintended consequences. (Andreas M. Antonopoulos, Nemertes Research)

- Change is the fuel of business, but it also introduces complexity, whether by bringing together incompatible computer networks or simply by growing beyond the network's ability to keep up. (Andreas M. Antonopoulos)

- Complexity was at the heart of the problem at the Los Angeles airport. Problems are increasingly difficult to identify and correct as we move from stovepipes to interdependent systems. (Kenneth M. Ritchhart, the chief information officer for the U.S. Customs and Border Protection Agency)

This chapter considers how some of those observations relate to security analysis. One perspective is that insufficient effort has been made to analyze potential failures and to apply known methods and technology. If a system is designed correctly in the first place, it can be made reliable, secure, fault tolerant, and human safe. The focus of this perspective, then, is developing and using best practices and better integrating security into the overall SDLC. Security analysis should be able to take advantage of an increased emphasis on managing failures. Attackers create events that take advantage of errors that are ignored or poorly managed by the system. Section 6.2 provides an introduction to categories of errors that are associated with security failures. Security analysis involves considering both functional and attacker perspectives of a system. In Section 6.3, those perspectives are applied to the examples of Web services and identity management.

Unfortunately, existing best practices do not fully address the security challenges caused by increased system complexity and distributed operational environments. The wider spectrum of failures, changing and conflicting goals, and incremental development challenge some of the traditional security assumptions. For instance, risk assessments are affected by reduced visibility for distributed systems and the wider spectrum of failures. Large systems are developed incrementally and must deal with changing and sometimes conflicting stakeholder objectives. As a consequence, security now needs to consider general system failures that usually have been associated with reliability. The security research world is constantly evolving, and assumptions about certain vulnerability classes can change overnight [Howard 2007]. Howard emphasizes a critical lesson that most vendors have learned the hard way: Today's denial of service is tomorrow's exploit. An attacker could, for example, exploit any of a variety of failures [Schwartz 2007] to create a denial of service. The security challenges created by increased system complexity may prove to be difficult-to-mitigate problems that do not have known solutions. The effects of multisystem complexity on security are discussed in Section 6.4, and Section 6.5 provides an overview of approaches for managing deep technical problems.

6.2 Security Failures

A failure—an externally observable event—occurs when a system does not deliver its expected service (as specified or desired). An error is an internal state that may lead to failure if the system does not handle the situation correctly; a fault is the cause of an error. For example, in a buffer overflow, the error might be in a functional component that does not check the size of user input. An attacker could exploit that error by sending an input stream that is larger than available storage and that includes executable code: This is the fault. The program logic that accepts the bad input actually overwrites another part of program logic. The attacker then executes the added code, which enables him or her to bypass authentication controls. In this way, the functional error can be leveraged into a security failure.

A number of errors have been demonstrated to lead to exploitable failures. Historically, a significant number of security vulnerabilities have been associated with errors in functional components rather than in security functions, such as those employed for authentication and authorization. An attacker may, for example, try to put a system into a state that was not anticipated during development. Such a situation might lead to a system crash and hence a denial of service, or it might let the attacker bypass the authentication and authorization controls and access normally protected information. Attacks have also exploited errors in parts of the system that were not fully analyzed during development or that were poorly configured during deployment because that effort concentrated on primary usage. Attacks can also create an unlikely collection of circumstances that were not considered in the design and exploit aspects of an interface that developers have left exposed.

Software engineers should be aware of the ever-lengthening list of exploitable errors (although even an expert can find it difficult to navigate through all of them). Specific weaknesses or underlying issues that that may cause vulnerabilities are described in the Common Weakness Enumeration [CWE 2007]. Several systematic, in-depth, and lengthy discussions have examined the difficulties associated with building trustworthy systems [Anderson 2001; Neumann 2004; Schneider 1999] and can provide a solid foundation of awareness. Although these sources concentrate on software and system errors, be aware that a design may also need to mitigate exploitable operator and user errors.

6.2.1 Categories of Errors

To aid in the analysis of security failures, errors can be categorized according to their occurrence in these five system elements:

1. *Specific interface.* An interface controls access to a service or component. Interfaces that fail to validate input often crop up on published vulnerability lists.

2. *Component-specific integration.* Assembly problems often arise because of conflicts in the design assumptions for the components. Project constraints may require using components, COTS software, or legacy systems that were not designed for the proposed usage, which raises the likelihood of mismatches. The increasing importance of business integration requirements compounds the problems associated with component integration and serves as the motivation for designs based on a service-oriented architecture.

3. *Architecture integration mechanisms.* Commercial software tool vendors often provide a built-in capability for purchasers to integrate a tool into their systems and tailor its functionality for their specific needs. Unfortunately, the capability to reconfigure a system rapidly is typically accompanied by an increased probability of component inconsistencies generated by the more frequently changing component base, as well as the increased risk that the dynamic integration mechanisms could be misused or exploited. These mechanisms represent another interface that must be properly constrained [Hoglund 2004].

4. *System behavior: component interactions.* The behavior of a system is not the simple sum of the behaviors of its individual components. System behavior is strongly influenced by the interactions of its components. Components may individually meet all specifications, but when they are aggregated into a system, the unanticipated interactions among components can lead to unacceptable system behavior. Components that are not secure as stand-alone components in an operating environment may be secure when used in a system that controls access to those components. The technical problems for this category of errors can be significantly more challenging to solve than the corresponding problems for the first three categories.

5. *Operations and usage.* Operational errors are also a frequent source of system failures, as noted in *Trust in Cyberspace* [Schneider 1999]:

> Errors made in the operation of a system also can lead to system-wide disruption. NISs are complex, and human operators err: An operator installing a corrupted top-level domain name server (DNS) database at Network Solutions effectively wiped out access to roughly a million sites on the Internet in July 1997 [Wayner 1997]; an employee's uploading of an incorrect set of translations into a Signaling System 7 (SS7) processor led to a 90-minute network outage for AT&T toll-free telephone service in September 1997 [Perillo 1997]. Automating the human operator's job is not necessarily a solution, for it simply exchanges one vulnerability (human operator error) for another (design and implementation errors in the control automation).

6.2.2 Attacker Behavior

Modeling attacker behavior presents significant challenges in software failure analysis. The analysis for quality attributes such as performance and hardware reliability is based on well-established failure rates, but security analysis does not have as solid a foundation. We may be able to model the work processes so as to generate authentication and authorization requirements, but we also have to model an active agent—the attacker—who can change the details of an attack in response to defensive actions.

The buffer overflow exploit described earlier in this chapter is a good example of the complexity of security analysis in terms of the interaction of models. Whereas the architect may have modeled the authentication and authorization mechanisms and demonstrated that they satisfy the design requirements, the new code that the exploit allowed to be executed enables the attacker to move outside the implemented software controls and hence outside the model. As a consequence, the validity of the authorization model becomes dependent on a security analysis of the data flow.

Social engineering exploits are other examples of external events that put a system in a state that may not be accounted for by the usage models. In these exploits, an attacker typically tries to convince users or administrators to take an action that lets the attacker circumvent a security control. For example, the attacker might try to impersonate a user and convince help-desk personnel that they should change an account password so that a customer order could be submitted.

Attack patterns, which are discussed in Chapter 2, are a good way to describe known attacker perspectives of a system.

6.3 Functional and Attacker Perspectives for Security Analysis: Two Examples

Security analysis must take both a functional perspective and the attacker's perspective. The functional perspective identifies the importance of an issue to the business functionality of the system and hence is a component of a risk assessment. The attacker's perspective considers the opportunities that business usage and the specifics of a technology create. For example, a capability to easily configure Web services could also be used by attackers to configure those services to support their objectives. Central services that consolidate authentication and authorization are also highly prized targets for attackers, because any vulnerabilities in those services can provide access to desired targets such as business information assets.

These two perspectives capture the fact that distributed decision making across both physical and organizational boundaries is a necessity for software-intensive systems that support human interactions. As work processes extend beyond the corporate IT perimeter and encompass services and data provided by external systems and organizations, the concept of a perimeter becomes even more elusive. Frequently each interface must be monitored to reflect the dynamically changing assurance associated with it. The interfaces among systems may depend on organizational relationships. Thus the central control represented by a firewall-protected perimeter has increasingly been replaced by multiple, and potentially conflicting, control points.

The next two sections introduce some of the security issues associated with Web services and identity management. Web services are often deployed to support business requirements for the integration of geographically distributed systems. Identity management concentrates on one aspect of system interoperability: authentication and authorization across multiple systems. We take both a functional perspective and attacker's perspective with each example.

By "functional," we mean the added value from the organizational perspective. For Web services, the functional perspective includes the capability of dynamically exchanging information without having to hard-wire the mechanics of that exchange into each system. Thus a change in business requirements may be implemented by changing the Web service interfaces rather than changing the functional business logic. For identity management, the functional perspective is represented by two objectives:

- Interoperability across systems to enable sharing of identity information
- Consolidation and, where desired, centralization of the security services of authentication and authorization across multiple systems

6.3.1 Web Services: Functional Perspective

To support greater business efficiency and agility, information systems and their operations have become increasingly decentralized and heterogeneous. Business processes are distributed among far-flung business divisions, suppliers, partners, and customers, with each participant having its own special needs for technology and automation. As a consequence, the demand for a high degree of interoperability among disparate information systems has never been greater. Moreover, this high degree of interoperability must be sustained as participants continually modify their systems in response to new or changing business requirements.

Traditional assembly and integration methods (and the resulting integration software market stimulated by these methods) are not particularly well suited to this new business environment. These methods rely on a tight coupling between cooperating systems, which requires either the universal deployment of homogeneous systems (unlikely, considering the diversity and broad scale of modern business services) or extraordinarily close coordination among participating development organizations during initial development and sustainment (e.g., to ensure that any changes to APIs or protocols are simultaneously reflected in all of the deployed systems). Such tight coordination is often impractical (e.g., prohibitively expensive), and rapid evolution in response to a new business opportunity is typically out of the question.

In contrast to traditional assembly and integration methods, Web services technology uses messages (in the form of XML documents) that are passed among diverse, loosely coupled systems as the focal point for integration. These systems are no longer viewed solely as components within a larger system of systems, but rather as providers of services that are applied to the messages. Web services are a special case of the more general notion of service-oriented architecture (SOA). Service-oriented architectures represent interconnected systems or components as collections of cooperating services. The goal of Web services technology is to dramatically reduce the interoperability issues that would otherwise arise when integrating disparate systems using traditional means.

The distributed aspects of a business transaction also affect how we manage identities. A Web services message, for example, might contain an order for materials and be submitted by an organization to a supplier. For infrequent transactions, an employee from the purchasing organization could log into a supplier's online application and submit the request. That employee would be authenticated by the supplier's identity management system. This type of online purchasing system is synchronous—that is, the supplier's system requests information and waits for a response. Such a synchronous communication protocol can tie up computing resources waiting for responses. In contrast, for high-volume transactions (and particularly those associated with just-in-time delivery), the transactions are system generated and the communication protocols are asynchronous—that is, the sending system does *not* wait for a reply. With an asynchronous interface, a business purchasing transaction might start with a message from the purchaser to the supplier that describes the details of the order. Later, the supplier would send another message—an acknowledgment of the order or confirmation of shipment—to the purchaser. Each of these messages updates the transaction state that is maintained independently by both organizations. In such a communication process, messages can be thought of as events, and an application architecture that processes messages is often described as an event-driven architecture.

In an event-driven architecture, the system that processes a message needs the equivalent to the user login for the synchronous online application to authenticate the purchaser and, in some instances, to verify that the purchaser is authorized by the purchasing organization to submit the order. The purchaser does not directly log into the supplier's system; rather, the purchaser's user authentication and authorization information is incorporated into the order sent to the supplier. Although this purchase order may contain business-sensitive information that should require authentication and authorization to access, the purchaser cannot directly observe or monitor the processing of that order by the supplier. As a consequence, the purchasing organization may require assurance that the order was accepted by the supplier.

A Web services message not only contains the ordering data, but also provides mechanisms for the necessary authentication and authorization. Encryption might be used by the sender to restrict access to this information. Signing can be used to confirm data integrity or as a means to identify the author of specific components of the message. Security Assertion Markup Language (SAML) can be used to share user identities and attributes.

6.3.2 Web Services: Attacker's Perspective

We next look at the attack risks associated with Web services. Our analysis assumes that Web services have been implemented using the Simple Object Access Protocol (SOAP). SOAP is an XML-based protocol that lets applications exchange information. The information exchanged might consist of business data (such as a purchasing order) or instructions on how the business process should be done.

This section describes illustrative—not canonical—threats and vulnerabilities that Web services applications face. To do so, it uses Shirey's model [Shirey 1994], which categorizes threats in terms of their impact as disclosure, deception, disruption, and usurpation. The threats are further categorized by the service-level threats that are common to most distributed systems and the message-level threats that affect Web services XML messages. A more detailed description of the threats and mitigations appears in [BSI 27].

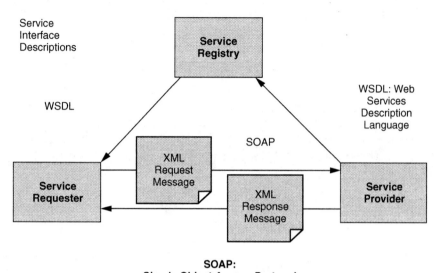

Figure 6–1: *Web services*

Figure 6–1 depicts an exchange based on Web services. Web services are designed to support interchanges among diverse systems. The initial step of an interchange is for the purchasing organization to acquire a description of the data transaction and the protocols used for encryption and signing. The eventual objective is for the initial exchanges to establish security policies that are acceptable to both parties. A service registry contains the message exchange pattern, types, values, methods, and parameters that are available to the service requester. It could be controlled by the service provider or could be a more widely accessible site operated by a third party.

Two main risk factors are associated with Web services:

- *Distributed systems risks*—that is, risks to the service providers themselves that are similar to risks that exist in Web applications and component applications. For example, malicious input attacks such as SQL injection fit this description. These risks arise simply because the system is distributed on a network. Note that standard IT security controls such as network firewalls are largely blind to Web services risks, because Web services are deployed on commonly available open ports. Nevertheless, some types of application firewalls have the ability to examine content, such as XML message bodies, and can use application-specific knowledge to thwart some attacks. Unfortunately, they are by no means a panacea for all distributed systems risks [BSI 28].

- *Message risks*—that is, risks to the document and data that are exchanged among participants. The document may participate in a multisystem transaction or be subject to inspection by a variety of intermediaries, each operating in different security zones, including separate policy, geographic, technical, and organizational domains. The message's content may also, of course, contain sensitive data.

Using Shirey's threat categories based on impact, Tables 6–1 through 6–4 describe general threats for Web services, the tactics that an attacker might use, and the ways that a developer might mitigate those threats. Studying attack patterns that use those tactics can assist in analyzing the possible mitigation options.

Table 6–1: *Disclosure of Information*

Attack tactics	The XML-based messages may be passed without encryption (in the clear) and may contain valuable business information, but an attacker may be more interested in gaining knowledge about the system to craft attacks against the service directly and the system in general. A security vulnerability in the service registry (like that shown in Figure 6–1) might let the attacker identify the system's data types and operations. That same information could be extracted from messages sent in the clear. Messages may also contain valuable information such as audit logs and may lead to identity spoofing and replay attacks, which use message contents to create a new message that might be accepted.
Mitigations	Authentication and authorization mechanisms may be used to control access to the registry. There are no centralized access control mechanisms that can protect the XML messages, but message-level mechanisms such as encryption and digital signatures can be used.

Table 6–2: *Deception*

Attack tactics	An attack can try to spoof the identity of the service requester by sending a well-formed message to the service provider. The identity of the service provider could also be spoofed. XML messages are passed without integrity protection by default. Without integrity protection, an attacker could tamper with the XML message to execute code or gain privileges and information on service requesters and providers.
Mitigations	Web services provide a number of integrity and authentication mechanisms that can mitigate deception. For example, WS-Security defines how to include X.509, Kerberos, and username and password security information in the XML message to support end-to-end authentication. Message integrity is supported through digital signatures and message origin authentication.

Table 6–3: *Disruption*

Attack tactics	An attacker could execute a denial of service at the network level against a Web service. Messages could also be used for a denial-of-service attack. For example, an attacker could send a specially formed XML message that forces the application into an infinite loop that consumes all available computing resources. The receipt of a large volume of malformed XML messages may exceed logging capabilities.
Mitigations	A network-level denial of service is mitigated in a similar fashion to a Web application denial of service—that is, by using routers, bandwidth monitoring, and other hardware to identify and protect against service disruption. Mitigation of message-level disruptions depends on validating the messages, but that mitigation can be tricky, because the target of such attacks is that mitigation component. One tactic would be to encapsulate message validation in a service that is applied before messages are passed to applications.

Table 6–4: *Usurpation*

Attack tactics	An attacker may usurp command of a system by elevating his or her privileges. One way to do so is to exploit the service registry to redirect service requests, change security policy, and perform other privileged operations. XML messages may be used to propagate viruses that contain malicious code to steal data, usurp privileges, drop and alter tables, edit user privileges, and alter schema information.
Mitigations	When service registries are used in Web services, they become a central organizing point for a large amount of sensitive information about services. The service registry (and communication to and from the service registry) should be hardened to the highest degree of assurance that is feasible in the system. Vulnerability analysis of source code pays particular attention to system calls to privileged modules in the operating system. The service registry can affect policy, runtime, and locale for other services and hence is analogous in importance to the operating system. Therefore particular attention must be paid to how service requesters access the service registry. At the message level, vendors are beginning to realize the significant threat that viruses, when attached and posted with XML documents, may pose to the environment. For systems that may have XML or binary attachments, virus protection services should be deployed to scan XML and binary messages for viruses in a similar fashion to email messages—that is, before the messages are executed for normal business operations.

6.3.3 Identity Management: Functional Perspective[2]

Information systems are increasingly interconnected, such as when companies' intranet sites provide single sign-on capabilities to other companies that provide 401(k) and health benefit services. These parties—that is, the financial and health benefits services organizations—may rely on their customers' systems to provide information about the identities of the users who are connecting to their services. However, the two systems may not have consistent security policy, enforcement, audit, or privacy requirements.

---

2. This material is extracted from "Identity in Assembly and Integration" by Gunnar Peterson [BSI 27].

Identity management (IM) is an administrative system that deals with the creation, maintenance, and use of digital identities. The use of a digital identity is controlled by the authorizations associated with it. IM includes the business processes associated with organization governance, as well as the supporting computing infrastructure. Operating systems, specific applications, and database management systems have each defined their own digital identity and implemented access control mechanisms. The initial technical challenge associated with implementing organizational governance policies is whether those policies can be implemented consistently across that diverse collection of identities and access control mechanisms. Even more difficult technical challenges arise from the following trends:

- Identity must be consistently managed across multiple and often geographically distributed systems. In some instances, identities can pass between organizations. A number of technical issues have to be resolved before such management is possible, however:

  - **Access control.** Identity is a foundation-level component for many access control mechanisms. Identity information about a digital subject is bound to a principal, which is typically an end user. Access control mechanisms consume identity data from the principal to make and enforce access control decisions. Weaknesses in identity systems affect the overall viability of access control, security, and privacy mechanisms.

  - **Audit and reporting.** These systems can be used to record, track, and trace identity information throughout systems. Audit logs and usage reports may be used for regulatory, compliance, and security purposes. Depending on their implementation, however, they may create privacy issues for individuals when that information is reported. Some techniques allow for system reporting and monitoring without disclosing identity information.

  - **Identity mapping services.** Distributed systems may have different implementations of identities. Identity mapping services can transform identities in a variety of ways so that a principal on one system can be mapped to a principal on another system.

  - **Domain provisioning services.** In this context, a domain is a system in which computing subsystems have common definitions for security objects such as identities and authorizations.

A domain could, for example, consist of a collection of Windows workstations or be a database management system deployed on a single server. The organizational identity and authorization information must be mapped to each domain. Provisioning services perform that function.

- Identities are associated with more than just employees. Some organizations may have to manage customer, contractor, and business partner identities as well.

- Increasingly, legislation and regulation have begun to recognize the value of identity data. Countries and industries have specific points that must be addressed to ensure that identity is protected. For applications that have an international user base, additional regulatory and legal concerns may span legal boundaries.

- Privacy concerns relate to identity information that is linked at some level to an individual. They center on which personal data is disclosed and may manifest themselves in the system design through privacy legislation, liability, and/or psychological acceptability and success of the solution. Systems may implement privacy mechanisms using pseudonyms or anonymous mechanisms.

- Information relating to digital subjects is used by a wide array of applications from Internet portals (e.g., business Web sites, loyalty programs, customer relationship management services, personalization engines, and content management servers) to enhance the customer experience and provide convenience and targeted services on behalf of businesses and consumers. Personal data, when stored by organizations, may also be shared and correlated for a variety of reasons, including data mining and target marketing; these uses of personal data may directly conflict with goals related to pseudonymous protection of data subject information.

6.3.4 Identity Management: Attacker's Perspective

Given that identity information is so central to so many security decisions and to so much application functionality, it represents a highly prized target for attackers. From a cultural viewpoint, identity information is understood to require extra due diligence by government, regulatory bodies, and individual users. This kind of information and its related architectural constituents, therefore, may be held to a higher standard for both security and privacy elements, and additional security analysis, design, implementation, operations, and auditing may be

---

Security Versus Privacy

An inherent tension exists between security and privacy that plays out most directly in the identity space. This tension revolves around the extent to which the user and the relying party have control and visibility of personal data. To be effective, the identity architecture must resolve these concerns in a manner that is congruent with each party's requirements.

---

required. Throughout all phases of the SDLC, you should examine the security model of the identity services and identity stores in the context of your overall system security to ensure that those services and stores are among the strongest links in the system. The more identity information is centralized logically or physically, the more risk to identity information is aggregated.

Identity information leakage can occur when identity providers supply more information than is necessary to perform the functional task and do not protect the identity information when it is transmitted across the domains' boundaries. A classic example would be a service that requires authorized users to be 21 years of age or older. In this case, the relying party asks the identity provider for the age information. If the identity provider gives the relying party the user's birth date so that the relying party can calculate the age of the user, then the user's birth date has been propagated to a separate service that now can retain (or disclose or otherwise lose) a valuable piece of personal information that the service does not absolutely require to perform its functions. A more appropriate response could be that the relying party queries the identity provider or the data subject if the user is more than 21 years old and receives a Boolean yes/no response. Some information has been revealed to the service provider in this instance, but it is far less critical.

Emerging technologies such as Web services and federated identity have direct implications on identity information leakage. An objective for federated identity is to enable a portable identity by sharing identity information among normally autonomous security domains. With federated identity, a traveler could, for example, log into a hotel system and then reserve a rental car or reconfirm an air reservation without explicitly logging into the car rental or airline systems. Those systems would accept the user's identity as authenticated by the hotel. Early efforts related to portable identity for Web usage, such as Microsoft Passport, suffered from disclosure of identity information to parties that did not have a justifiable place in the transaction [Cameron 2005]. Directory services that replicate identity information at the data level can also create exposure by replicating more identity information than is required for dependent systems.

General mitigations for identity management risks are listed in Table 6–5.

Table 6–5: *Identity Management Risk Mitigations*

Availability	Identity services provide an interface to information about subjects stored in the identity stores in a system. They also can provide a single point of failure that attackers may target to bring application systems down, without the need for the attackers to target the application itself. In fact, because identity services and stores are often reused in organizations serving identity information to multiple applications, an attacker who successfully executes a denial-of-service or other availability attack against identity services and stores can have a large adverse impact on the availability of the system. Incorporating redundancy and automatic failover for identity services can be used to combat availability threats. Services are often consolidated to reduce costs, but consolidation of identity services can expand the consequences of a successful exploit. Decentralizing the deployment and management of identity services may be an appropriate tradeoff for this risk, albeit with increased operational costs.
Hardened servers and services	Given the critical nature of the data that identity servers host and the access they vouch for in the system, identity servers should be hardened to the highest level of surety that is practical. The goal of identity servers to is provide and verify identity information for applications—not to run Web servers, database servers, and so on. Standard server-hardening techniques that limit privileges and services available only to those strictly necessary apply in this instance. Hardening special-purpose identity servers such as directory services servers

Table 6–5: *Identity Management Risk Mitigations (Continued)*

	is a relatively more straightforward task than hardening identity servers; the latter are more general-purpose tools in the organization and may contain both identity and line of business or domain information. Host integrity monitoring, network- and host-based intrusion detection systems, network security monitoring, and secure exception management practices enable more robust detection when protection mechanisms fail.
Incident response	Many attacks against identity—and particularly identity theft attempts—rely in large part on the victim remaining ignorant that theft has occurred for some period of time. The damage an attacker can cause can be partially mitigated by an effective, rapid, and targeted response to identity data theft. An effective program could include clear communication lines and response patterns, along with a set of guidelines that the victimized users can implement to deal with the aftermath of an identity theft.
Usability: endpoint attacks	At runtime, the endpoint for identity data is frequently the user session and user desktop. Therefore, securing identity information often boils down to a battle between usability and security. The work done in protecting an identity across dozens of hops across servers and nodes can be defeated by attackers who target the desktop layer or the user. Robust identity systems must ensure that the usability of identity is factored in so that users understand their roles and responsibilities in using their identity in the system. Individual users are typically not able to discern when it is appropriate and safe to disclose personal information.

6.3.5 Identity Management and Software Development

Software development teams may lack agreed-upon plans for adoption of standard representation and consumption patterns for authentication, attribute query or update, and authorization of identity information across technological and organizational domains. The current state of identity may consist of numerous identity silos that are directly bound to domain-specific technologies, policies, and organizational domains, each with its own interpretation of how to issue, encapsulate, and negotiate identity data and services. This potential lack of consistency creates issues for distributed systems that are required to traverse multiple identity silos and domains and has the overall effect of stimulating numerous one-off solutions for identity, each of which contains its own arcane, tightly coupled, and technology-specific ways of dealing with identity. There is a well-understood best practice in software development that developers should not attempt to write their own cryptographic algorithms because of the complexity, lack of peer review, and value of that which the cryptographic functions are protecting. Developers, in contrast, routinely write one-off identity solutions that are never peer reviewed by a wider audience. This identity information is then propagated and integrated throughout software systems and used as a basis for making security decisions about access control to critical resources and the confidentiality of personal and business data.

In many systems, these one-off solutions are further integrated with other identity silos, creating a mishmash of identity solutions with varying limitations, and in the worst case generating a lowest common denominator effect. Exacerbating this problem further is the fact that many identity solutions are already in place as legacy systems while software is being developed, such that the projects inherit the standard issues found in legacy integrations with identity, including brittleness and lack of support for robust protocols and current standards. Why is this proliferation of solutions an especially serious problem for identity management? As noted by Matt Bishop, "Every access control mechanism is based on an identity of some sort." Bishop goes on to state that all decisions of access and resource allocation assume that the binding of an identity to the principal is correct [Bishop 2002]. Hence, identity is a foundation-level element for security and accountability decisions, and breakage at this level in design has profound implications for the system's security as a whole. Transactions may employ multiple identity contexts throughout their life cycles, broadening the scope of identity's usage for access.

Piling on to the previously mentioned system-level problems are users' lack of awareness, ability, and tools for managing and propagating their own digital identity information and their lack of ability and technical tools to use in determining the veracity of requests for their personal information. The net result: The emergence of phishing and other attacks targeting these vulnerabilities at the directory, user desktop, and client levels.

To protect identity on the client and server and throughout the system as a whole, software development teams require an overarching understanding of identity's architectural elements and approaches to integrating identity into software systems. Such an understanding will enable them to bridge the chasm that exists between the assumptions made about identities and the actual state that exists in the system with which they are attempting to integrate. The acquisition of knowledge regarding the union of identity elements, behaviors, and constraints and the software user's knowledge and abilities related to the desktop and clients will give software development teams the tools they need to build more robust software based on secure usage of identity.

6.4 System Complexity Drivers and Security Ⓜ Ⓛ ⌷2

Satisfying business requirements increasingly depends on integrating and extending existing systems. In particular, new development must often be integrated with an existing operational environment. The analysis described in Section 6.3 concentrated on how an attacker might exploit the Web services interfaces that support a desired integration. Such analysis is representative of current security analysis techniques. Nevertheless, characteristics of the resulting operational environment can not only generate additional security risks, but also constrain the mitigation of those risks.

Some consequences of this tradeoff for security analysis of the distributed operational environments are described in Table 6–6. Security risk assessments are affected by unanticipated risks, reduced visibility, and the wider spectrum of failures possible. A number of these factors affect the software development process. The wider spectrum of errors, for example, may require that more attention be devoted to fault tolerance. Other factors may dictate which risk mitigation options can be applied. Factors such as less development freedom, changing goals, and the importance of incremental development all affect how security is incorporated into the software development process.

Table 6–6: *Consequences of Expanded Scope for Security*

Unanticipated risks	The dynamic nature of the operational environment raises software risks that are typically not addressed in current systems. Interoperability across multiple systems may involve resolving conflicting risk profiles and associated risk mitigations among those systems. As work processes cross business units and multiple organizations, change becomes increasingly difficult to control, and any changes might invalidate the existing security analysis.
Reduced visibility	Work processes often involve external, COTS, or legacy systems that cannot be observed or whose behavior cannot be thoroughly analyzed. Testing the subsets of such systems is not sufficient to establish confidence in the fully networked system. That is particularly true when some of the subsystems are uncontrollable or unobservable [Schneider 1999]. In these circumstances, it is much more difficult to distinguish an attacker-induced error from a nonmalicious event. Business requirements may increase the need for interoperability with less than fully trusted systems. Under such circumstances, the security architect cannot have the in-depth knowledge that existing techniques often assume.
Wider spectrum of failures	As noted by Leveson for safety [Leveson 2004], the cause of a system security failure may be not a single event, but rather a combination of events that individually would be considered insignificant. The probability of a single combination of events is typically quite small, but the probability of some adverse combination of events occurring can increase as system size increases. One of the more challenging problems for security analysis involves establishing priorities for identified risks. Increasingly, security risks are associated with high-impact, low-probability events. The relationship frequently applied in risk analysis, Expected Cost = Probability of Event × Impact is not valid for such events.

Table 6–6: *Consequences of Expanded Scope for Security (Continued)*

Less development freedom	Architectural principles provide guidance on how to decompose a system so that the components can later be assembled into a system that meets the security requirements. The decomposition guidance assists in addressing issues associated with component and system interactions. When we integrate existing subsystems or incrementally add functionality to an existing system, most aspects of the decomposition have already been defined. We no longer have the ability to specify a decomposition that best supports the desired system characteristics. At some point, the stress between what we have and what we should have becomes great enough that the only option is reengineering.
Incremental and evolutionary development	Large systems typically emerge from a smaller system by incremental additions of new functionality. A successfully deployed system may encourage new usages that were not anticipated in the original design. While the knowledge that supported the initial design might have been considered sufficient for that context, it may be incomplete for the new functionality and usage.
Conflicting or changing goals	Business usage and underlying technology are typically changing faster than our capability to change the software. Computing systems can be friction points for organizational change.

6.4.1 Wider Spectrum of Failures

Software failure analysis in this context may require a different model of accidents than that used for hardware. Hardware failure analysis typically relies on event-based models of accidents. Such models, with their relatively simple cause-and-effect links, were created in an era of mechanical systems and then adapted for electromechanical systems. The use of software in engineered systems has removed many of the physical constraints that limit complexity and has allowed engineers to incorporate greatly increased complexity and coupling in systems containing large numbers of dynamically interacting components. In the simpler systems of the past, where all the interactions between components could be predicted and handled, component failure was the primary cause of accidents. In today's highly complex systems, this is no longer the case.

While vulnerabilities are often associated with just a single component, the more challenging classes of vulnerability derive from interactions among multiple system components. Such vulnerabilities are difficult to locate and predict, because it may not be possible to model the behavior of multiple systems under all conditions. An unexpected pattern of usage might overload a shared resource and lead to a denial of service, for example. In addition, multiple factors may contribute to the vulnerability and prove difficult to identify. For example, a vulnerability could arise from a software design that increases the possibility of errors by human operators.

Bellovin observed (in [Schwartz 2007]) that the power grid failure in August 2003 was not caused by a single failure but rather by a cascading set of events. Certainly, a race condition that disabled the subsystem that alerted the power grid controllers to potential failure conditions was a significant factor, but that failure by itself likely could have been managed. After that subsystem failure, a combination of operator and management missteps led to a significant time period during which the power grid controllers were not aware of serious transmission line problems. The operators saw no system-generated alerts and had not been told of the alert system failure. During that same period, a second monitoring system managed by an independent organization also suffered a series of failures.

The combination of system, management, and operational errors delayed mitigating the transmission line problems until recovery was impossible. The combination of such events does not have to be concurrent to produce a failure of the system. In this case, the lack of staff mitigation training had existed for some time, which had reduced the capability to mitigate system or operator failures.

Discrepancies between the expected and the actual arise frequently in the normal course of business processes. Discrepancies can be thought of as stresses that may drive a business process into an unacceptable state. Stress types include interactions, resources, and people. Missing, inconsistent, or unexpected data are examples of interaction stresses, whereas resource stresses may include excessive network latency, insufficient capacity, and unavailable services. People stresses can consist of information overload that slows analysis, distraction (too much browsing) and a "Not my job" attitude, which can inhibit effective responses to problems.

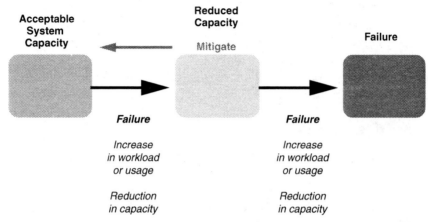

Figure 6–2: *System failures*

Figure 6–2 depicts one way to represent system behavior when the cause of a failure is a combination of events. Think of system capacity as a collective measure of the resources available, both computing and human. A system might be thought of as in a healthy state when sufficient resources are available to manage temporary increases in usage, even with some discrepancies. Over time, however, changes in usage may increase resource loading so that an internal fault that previously could be mitigated now leads to system failure. In the case of the power grid failure, the lack of training reduced the capacity of the system and increased the probability of a mitigation failure.

As we integrate multiple systems, we should expect technical discrepancies. Systems developed at different times will inevitably have variances in technology and expected usage. In addition, technical stresses can arise because large distributed systems are constructed incrementally. The functionality of the initial deployment of a system may suggest other applications that were not anticipated in the initial design. Finally, users frequently exploit system functionality in unanticipated ways that may improve the business processes, but their efforts may also stress the operation of components that were not designed for the new usage.

The overall success of a business process depends on how the staff and supporting computing systems handle those discrepancies. Changes in business processes and systems, for example, can introduce new discrepancies. In addition, dealing with discrepancies becomes much more difficult as the number of participants—people and systems—increases. Each participant must cope with multiple sources of discrepancies, and a single discrepancy can affect multiple participants. In this situation, the likelihood that a discrepancy will not be properly managed by some participant increases, with that failure then affecting other participants.

Partitioning Security Analysis

The system complexity associated with business system integration requirements expands the spectrum of development, user, and system management failures that security analysis has to consider. One way to partition that effort is to consider two perspectives for the analysis of work processes that span multiple systems.

The first perspective focuses on the global work process. The compositions of the functions associated with the individual systems certainly must meet the functional requirements for the work process, but the challenge is most likely meeting quality requirements such as those for security, performance, and reliability. How do individual system failures affect the work process? The individual system risks and chosen mitigations may not be compatible with the risk profile desired for the work process, particularly when the individual systems are independently managed or provide services to multiple work processes.

The second perspective is that of a service provider. An essential requirement is to provide the specified functionality, but as with the work process perspective, the quality requirements pose the greater challenge. An individual system has to meet the quality requirements associated with a request, yet there are also risks associated with servicing a request. A requesting system may have been compromised, for example, but system resources must remain protected. Unexpected patterns of usage by a single or multiple requesters may adversely affect the capability to provide a service. Whereas a global work process has limited knowledge about individual systems, a service provider is in an equivalent position with the requesting systems and about the effects that a system action might have on external work process.

Mitigations

- Concentrate first on the first three categories of security failures described in Section 6.2.1. With more interfaces to less trusted systems, it is critical to first deal with known interface vulnerabilities. Pay particular attention to network-based interfaces such as those included in Web services. Web services provide mechanisms to manage security across geographically and even independently operated systems, but the use of those protocols could also be exploited by an attacker. Some of the vulnerabilities associated with Web services are described in Section 6.3.2.

The remaining mitigations apply to the general problem of integrating multiple systems.

- One approach to simplifying security across multiple systems is to share essential security services such as user authentication and authorization. Interoperability among multiple systems often results in security problems raised by multiple access control and authentication control points. For example, an operating system supports user authentication and controls access to operating system objects such as files and processes; a database server supports independent user authentication and access control mechanisms for database objects such as tables or individual data items. Identity management refers to an approach to integrating those multiple authentication and authorization mechanisms so that some aspects of identity can be shared among systems. Identity management represents an essential aspect of security functionality. A successful attack on identity management services can enable the attacker to gain enhanced privileges and thereby access confidential information. Security issues for identity management are discussed in Section 6.3.4.

- An essential design task for a large system is delegating the responsibilities for meeting security requirements. Delegation of responsibilities goes beyond system components and includes users and system management. For example, a password or private key used for authentication can be compromised by a careless user, so in this sense the authentication responsibilities are shared by users and the system. The user responsibilities might be reduced by using a one-time password mechanism or a biometric device such as a fingerprint scanner.

The delegation of responsibilities can purposely introduce redundancy to support a "defense in depth" strategy. A simple form of defense in depth is to always check the validity of inputs to a component even though the design calls for those checks to occur in advance of the call to the component.

Poor delegation of responsibilities is often reflected by a "Not my job" response and inaction when problems arise. Causal analysis for engineered systems usually concentrates on component failures that are mitigated by prevention or redundancy. That focus does not account for (1) social and organizational factors in accidents, (2) system accidents and software errors, (3) human error, (4) system interactions, (5) tradeoffs among system properties such as performance and reliability, and (6) adaptation over time [Leveson 2004]. A risk for security is that it is typically treated as a separate concern, with responsibility being assigned to different parts of the organization that often function independently. That isolation becomes even more problematic as the scope and scale of systems expand.

Business integration requirements and the use of technologies such as Web services to support the integration of distributed systems can affect the delegation of responsibilities. It is not unusual to find that an organization's development, operational, and business groups are tackling common problems with little coordination or that some security problems have been ignored.[3]

- [BSI 30] and [BSI 31] provide guidance on risk assessment and security concerns for COTS and legacy systems.

A number of organizations are exploring approaches to better manage the risks associated with system complexity. Such practices are on the leading edge of security initiatives and certainly have not been proven. The following suggestions are drawn from those experiences:

- *Operational monitoring.* Failures of some sort are a given for a complex system. A system design usually identifies some set of potentially adverse events and corresponding mitigations, but that set of adverse events is never truly complete. Given this fact of life, it is critical to monitor any unexpected events that fall outside that set. Potential security failures may change because of the appearance

---

3. A more detailed discussion of the affects of operations on development appears in [Woody 2007].

of new attack patterns, and changes in usage or system configurations may generate unexpected activity. It can be helpful to analyze system failures that have affected other organizations, because they may identify a similar internal weakness. The monitoring strategy is similar to that applied to deal with hard-to-solve problems. With this approach, the analysis serves as a learning experience for the staff and increases their capability to respond to future failures and to incorporate that knowledge into system enhancements.

- *Consolidation of failure analysis and mitigations.* The multiplicity of systems and increasing number of possible error states arising from the interactions can overwhelm analysis. The risk in this case is having too many point solutions that mitigate narrowly specified events. Changes in usage could then generate a significant reengineering effort. Failure analysis is done for security, reliability, and safety if applicable. How much of that effort can be consolidated?

Given system complexity and dynamics of usage, it is not realistic to assume that a system is entirely free of vulnerabilities. Instead, error management must be perceived as an ongoing activity for any large system. When an error occurs, there is rarely sufficient information to immediately identify a specific cause, let alone characterize that cause as malicious. The runtime choice of an appropriate mitigation might be based simply on the impact of the failure. If the identified error involves data integrity, the general strategy independent of the cause may be to contain the damage and enable recovery. A recovery from a security breach may be able to take advantage of the general failure mitigations.

An attacker may be able to exploit how a system manages failures—particularly failures in the interfaces with normally trusted components. As an example, one of the causes of the 2003 electric power grid blackout was a race condition in a subsystem that monitored sensor data. While there were no malicious events for that blackout, could an attacker crash such control systems by targeting trusted sensors?

- *Generalization of the problem.* Some organizations are revisiting how they treat availability. Is it a security requirement or a business requirement? Should those two perspectives be consolidated? As a business requirement, availability supports business continuity, which is based on the dependability of the computing infrastructure, service providers, the technology deployed, operations, information processing, and communications. Security, reliability, and compliance are all part of business continuity.

Aspects of such guidance could be applied to enterprise architectures that are not geographically distributed. One tactic for supporting business continuity for a system of systems could be to maintain sufficient independence among the systems so that essential aspects of business processing can be restored with a subset of the systems rather than the full system of systems or so that processing can continue asynchronously with an eventual synchronization.

6.4.2 Incremental and Evolutionary Development

Incremental system development affects the design of the software architecture for most of the quality attributes, not just security. A software architecture can realistically support only a limited number of anticipated changes. The consequences of change can be greater for security than the other quality attributes, however, if incremental development introduces vulnerabilities.

The authors of the 2007 National Research Council (NRC) report *Towards a Safe and More Secure Cyberspace* observed the lack of adoption of known techniques for improving system security [Goodman 2007]. Section 4.3.1 describes a number of architectural principles used to enhance software security, such as least privilege, defense in depth, and securing the weakest link. Researchers have found that the use of such architectural principles by system designers and architects correlates highly with the security and reliability of a system [Goodman 2007]. Unfortunately, these principles have not been widely adopted. The NRC committee proposed that the primary reasons for that lack of use included the following issues:

- A mismatch between the principles and current development methodologies
- The short-term costs associated with serious adherence to those principles
- Potential conflicts with performance

As stated in the report, an examination of the architectural principles suggests that a serious application of them depends on designers and architects knowing very well and in considerable detail exactly what the software component is supposed to do and under which conditions. All too frequently, however, system requirements and specifications are incomplete. In addition, user requirements may change during development. Likewise, architectural tradeoff analysis among quality attributes such as reliability, security, and performance can lead to revisions of requirements. While incremental development, simulation, and prototyping can enable users to better specify their needs and provide the developer with a better knowledge of how to implement the desired behavior, the use of legacy systems, COTS components, or systems developed and operated by external organizations means that our system knowledge will always be incomplete. Perhaps not surprisingly, the NRC report listed the ability to incorporate security into an incremental development process as an important research topic.

Increasingly, system development depends on integrating existing systems, as reflected in both the Web services and identity management examples. Size complexity can be mitigated by the use of commercial products, the sharing of software-based services among multiple systems, and the reuse of existing software components or systems (i.e., legacy systems). The support for multisystem work processes—particularly those that involve multiple organizations—depends on the ability to create a system of systems. The security issues raised by the design of computing support for a multisystem work process are similar to those associated with the design of a large system in the typical IT environment that uses a significant number of commercially supplied products and legacy systems. In both cases, a new or updated component must merge with an existing operational environment to form a satisfactory operational whole. And in both cases, the systems have not necessarily been designed for the new use or for any additional threats associated with the new use or operating environment.

6.4.3 Conflicting or Changing Goals Complexity

Conflicting goals occur when desired product quality attributes or customer values conflict with one another. There may be conflicts between portability and performance requirements. In addition, conflicts frequently arise between security and ease-of-use requirements. Meeting the cost requirements for implementing the desired features may increase operational costs and create a conflict between development costs and operational goals. Conflicting goals affect both the developer and the project manager, and there is a learning component for addressing these problems. What are the important interactions among those goals? Which aspects of the software architecture might be affected by a resolution of these conflicts? Do requirements for future needs adversely affect current cost and schedule constraints?

Web services protocols provide mechanisms that describe at runtime which security policy is associated with a transaction. That security policy could describe how authentications are done, how data is encrypted, or which data fields must be signed. This adaptability comes at a cost, however: An application might need to support multiple security protocols, and a number of the security threats described in Section 6.3.4 could potentially exploit that adaptability.

Changes in goals can generate equivalent problems. The implementation of a new objective may conflict with earlier design tradeoffs. Often changes in goals arise from changes in business requirements, changes in usage of existing functionality, or customers gaining new understanding of their own needs. The tendency is to add but rarely remove functionality for an existing system. Over time, that feature creep and any interaction among features can be source of vulnerabilities.

Changes or conflicts can require some form of experimentation on the part of the user and/or the developer in the form of simulation, scenario analysis, or prototypes. Such problems must be resolved before the final design is attempted. In practice, incremental development methods are often used to address ambiguous or vague functional requirements; such methods can delay decisions about troublesome requirements.

The existence of unanticipated hard-to-solve problems and conflicts and changes in requirements are often just a recognition that our understanding of the problem domain and the tradeoffs among requirements or design options is incomplete when a development project is initiated.

Mitigations

- *Assurance cases.* Changes in requirements or threats and the evolution of usage all require that the security aspects of a system be regularly reviewed. For a large system, that kind of analysis could be daunting, but an assurance case can simplify and improve that task (see Section 2.4). An assurance case describes the arguments and evidence that support the security claims for a system. It can be analyzed when changes are made to identify any arguments or evidence that may no longer be valid and hence those claims and associated components that may require a more detailed analysis.

- *Operational monitoring.* Our information is always incomplete for complex systems. The reality of ongoing changes increases the importance of operational monitoring, as described in Section 6.4.1.

- *Continuous risk assessments.* Existing risk assessments and security testing procedures should be reviewed and updated if necessary.

- *Flexibility and support for change.* The ability to easily change systems is a general problem. A number of efforts—for example, the Object Management Group's Model-Driven Architecture, Microsoft's Software Factory, and service-oriented architecture (SOA)—have sought to address certain aspects of that problem. Aspect-oriented programming proposes techniques that make it easier to change the behavior of the system as described by the quality attributes. At this point, we are still dependent on good software engineering to anticipate the most likely changes or to find ways to adapt existing components to meet the new requirements. As we noted earlier, at some point the gap between what we have and what we should have will become great enough that the only option is reengineering.

6.5 Deep Technical Problem Complexity

Deep technical problems appear to arise more frequently when the software development team focuses on meeting the quality measures for reliability, performance, and security rather than satisfying a functional requirement. Grady Booch commented on this phenomenon in his Web log on March 22, 2005:

> Most enterprise systems are architecturally very simple, yet quite complex in manifestation: simple because most of the relevant architectural patterns have been refined over decades of use in many tens of thousands of systems and then codified in middleware; complex because of the plethora of details regarding vocabulary, rules, and nonfunctional requirements such as performance and security. [Booch 2005]

Because security can be a source of hard-to-solve technical problems for the implementation of a single system, it should come as no surprise that it becomes a rich source of deep problems as we deploy more complex systems and systems of systems. All of the items listed in Table 6–6 can lead to hard-to-solve security problems. Both usage and potential threats are dynamic factors. Complexity affects both the functional and attacker's security perspectives. The functional perspective captures the obvious requirements for authentication and authorization and hence is likely to be considered early in the development cycle. The attacker's perspective may not receive equivalent attention, yet may be a source of problems that require reengineering for their resolution when identified later in development.

Mitigations

Some general guidelines are applicable for managing hard-to-solve problems.

- The hard-to-solve problems should be tackled first. A deep technical problem can generate extraordinary delays if the solution is postponed, but schedule pressures often lead project teams to work on easy-to-solve problems so they can demonstrate rapid progress. The following quotations from [BSI 29], which refer to the Correctness by Construction (CbyC) method, are a good summary of the justifications for this recommendation:

  > When faced with a complex task, the natural tendency is to start with the parts you understand with the hope that the less obvious parts will become clearer with time. CbyC consciously reverses this. As risk and potential bugs hide in the most complex and least understood areas, these areas should be tackled first. Another reason for tackling uncertainty early is that freedom for maneuver tends to decrease as the project progresses; we don't want to address the hardest part of a problem at the point with the smallest range of design options. Of course, one could take the fashionable approach and refactor the design; however, designing, building, and incrementally validating a system only to change it because risky areas were not proactively considered is hardly efficient and is not CbyC.

  > Managing risk must be done on a case-by-case basis. Common examples are prototyping of a user interface to ensure its acceptability, performance modeling to ensure the selected high-level design can provide adequate throughput, and early integration of complex external hardware devices.

- Enable the technical staff to concentrate on such problems. When the highly skilled staff that is addressing a deep problem attempts to achieve multitasking, this approach typically delays a solution and affects its quality. The analysis and solution of deep technical problems take time but not many people. A solution for the developer may require both learning and experimentation. That is, a developer needs to identify which techniques might work, where a technique might be an algorithm, an architecture design pattern, or hardware. Under what conditions does the specific technique work? How might it be used for the current problem? Does the technique introduce constraints that adversely affect satisfying other system requirements?

- The existence of hard-to-solve problems can affect the feasibility, risks, and costs associated with specific requirements and hence can influence stakeholder commitments to those requirements. The Incremental Commitment Model explores the effects of hard problems on requirements, project management, and acquisition [Boehm 2007].

- The project manager needs to consider risk mitigations such as alternative implementations at least for the interim, but must recognize that such alternatives may not fully meet quality attribute objectives.

6.6 Summary

The technologies and dynamic nature of the operational environment raise software risks that are typically not addressed in current practice. Security assessments are often done for a point in time, and the techniques are not easily adapted to the more dynamic environment that software now has to address. Vulnerability analysis, for example, evaluates an operationally ready network, system, or software set against previously identified and analyzed defects and failures at a given point in time for a specified configuration. Such techniques have only limited value, however, when the system can be dynamically configured to meet changing operational and business needs.

While security analysis is rarely complete, such completeness is often tacitly assumed. The increasing complexity of deployed systems certainly invalidates such an assumption now. Business requirements increasingly lead to the need to integrate multiple systems to support business processes. The design objective to better support rapidly evolving business requirements or to deal with conflicting or ambiguous functional requirements has led to increased use of incremental development methods. For the project manager, such techniques often translate into hard-to-solve technical problems for meeting the security requirements. General guidance for dealing with these kinds of complex problems should be part of any project plan. System complexity leads to a growing need to explicitly incorporate learning into the project schedule that builds the necessary knowledge base about the operational environment, the dependencies and potential interactions among systems, and the risks that may be associated with proposed designs.

General recommendations include the following:

1. Tackle known interface vulnerabilities first. With systems having more interfaces to less trusted systems, developers should concentrate first on known interface vulnerabilities, such as those found in Web services.

2. Conduct end-to-end analysis of cross-system work processes. With increasing complexity, vulnerability analysis of individual systems is not sufficient. The security analysis of work processes that cross multiple systems has to consider the risks for those processes (including end-to-end analysis) as well as the risks that each work process creates for the systems that support it. In short, security analysis has to account for a wider spectrum of errors.

3. Recognize the unavoidable risk that, with the reduced visibility and control of multiple systems, security analysis will be incomplete. One approach to this situation is to focus first on mitigating the possible impacts of an attack and not on the vulnerabilities that were exploited.

   a. Attend to containing and recovering from failures. Assume the existence of discrepancies of some form, whether in systems, operations, or users, during the execution of work processes, particularly as usage evolves. Give increased attention to containment and recovery from failures. These issues should be considered in the context of business continuity analysis.

   b. Explore failure analysis and mitigation to deal with complexity. The multiplicity of systems and increasing number of possible error states arising from interactions can overwhelm analysis or generate too many point solutions that mitigate narrowly specified events. Explore how security could take advantage of a consolidated failure analysis and mitigation effort.

4. Coordinate security efforts across organizational groups. Security is typically treated as a separate concern, with responsibility often being assigned to independent parts of the organization (such as development and operations). It is not unusual to find that an organization's development, operational, and business groups are tackling common problems with little coordination or that some security problems have fallen through the cracks. This separation becomes even more problematic as the scope and scale of systems expand. Vulnerability analysis and mitigations should be integrated across organization units, users, technology, systems, and operations.

Chapter 7

Governance, and Managing for More Secure Software

7.1 Introduction

The objective of this chapter is to help software project managers (1) more effectively engage their leaders and executives in security governance and management by understanding how to place security in a business context and (2) better understand how to enhance their current management practices and thereby produce more secure software. Armed with this material, managers can become attentive, security-conscious leaders who are in a better position to make well-informed security investment decisions. With this support, managers can then take actionable steps to implement effective security governance and management practices across the software and system development life cycle.

Governance and management of security are most effective when they are systemic—that is, woven into the culture and fabric of organizational behaviors and actions. In this regard, culture is defined as the predominating shared attitudes, values, goals, behaviors, and practices that characterize the functioning of a group or organization. Culture creates and sustains connections among principles, policies, procedures, processes, products, people, and performance. Effective security should be thought of as an attribute or characteristic of an organization. It becomes evident when all members of the organization proactively carry out their roles and responsibilities, creating a culture of security that displaces ignorance and apathy.

To achieve this outcome, security must come off the technical sidelines, abandoning its traditional identity of "activities and responsibilities solely relegated to software development and IT departments." Today, boards of directors, senior executives, and managers all must work to establish and reinforce a relentless, ongoing drive toward effective enterprise, information, system, and software security. If the responsibility for these tasks is assigned to roles that lack the authority, accountability, and resources to implement and enforce them, the desired level of security will not be articulated, achieved, or sustained.

Contrary to the popular belief that security is a technical issue, even the best efforts to buy secure software and build security into developed software and operational systems encounter "considerable resistance because the problem is mostly organizational and cultural, not technical" [Steven 2006]. Software and information security are about spending money where the definition of success is "nothing bad happens." As time goes on, this kind of effort can become a tough sell to business leaders as the "We haven't been attacked lately, so we can cut back on spending" mentality sets in.

Project managers need to elevate software security from a stand-alone, technical concern to an enterprise issue. Because security is a business problem,[1] the organization must activate, coordinate, deploy, and direct many of its core resources and competencies to manage security risks in concert with the entity's strategic goals, operational criteria, compliance requirements, and technical system architecture. To *sustain* enterprise security, the organization must move toward a security management process that is strategic, systematic, and repeatable, with efficient use of resources and effective, consistent achievement of goals [Caralli 2004b].

---

1. See also "Governing for Enterprise Security" [Allen 2005], "Security Is Not Just a Technical Issue" [BSI 32], and *Governing for Enterprise Security Implementation Guide* [Westby 2007].

7.2 Governance and Security

Governance entails setting clear expectations for business conduct and then following through to ensure the organization fulfills those expectations. Governance action flows from the top of the organization to all of its business units and projects. Done right, governance facilitates an organization's approach to nearly any business problem, including security. National and international regulations call for organizations—and their leaders—to demonstrate due care with respect to security. This is where governance can help.

7.2.1 Definitions of Security Governance

The term *governance* applied to any subject can have a wide range of interpretations and definitions. For the purpose of this chapter, we define governing for enterprise security[2] as follows:

> Directing and controlling an organization to establish and sustain a culture of security in the organization's conduct (beliefs, behaviors, capabilities, and actions)
>
> Treating adequate security as a non-negotiable requirement of being in business [Allen 2005]

In its publication *Information Security Handbook: A Guide for Managers* [Bowen 2006], NIST defines information security governance as:

> The process of establishing and maintaining a framework and supporting management structure and processes to provide assurance that information security strategies
>
> – are aligned with and support business objectives,
> – are consistent with applicable laws and regulations through adherence to policies and internal controls, and
> – provide assignment of responsibility,
>
> all in an effort to manage risk.

---

* L4 for information security; L3 for software security.

2. The term "security," as used here, includes software security, information security, application security, cybersecurity, network security, and information assurance. It does not include disciplines typically considered to reside within the domain of physical security, such as facilities, executive protection, and criminal investigations.

In his article "Adopting an Enterprise Software Security Framework," John Steven, a Principal at Cigital, states

> In the context of an Enterprise Software Security Framework, governance is competency in measuring software-induced risk and supporting an objective decision-making process for remediation and software release. This competency involves creating a seat at the project management table for software risk alongside budget and scheduling concerns [Steven 2006].

(See also Section 7.5.)

In the context of security, governance incorporates a strong focus on risk management. Governance is an expression of responsible risk management, and effective risk management requires efficient governance. One way governance manages risk is to specify a framework for decision making. It makes clear who is authorized to make decisions, what the decision making rights are, and who is accountable for decisions. Consistency in decision making across an enterprise boosts confidence and reduces risk.

7.2.2 Characteristics of Effective Security Governance and Management

One of the best measures that an organization is addressing security as a governance and management concern is a consistent and reinforcing set of beliefs, behaviors, capabilities, and actions that match up with security best practices and standards. These measures aid in building a security-conscious culture. They can be expressed as statements about the organization's current behavior and condition:[3]

- Security is managed as an enterprise issue, horizontally, vertically, and cross-functionally throughout the organization. Executive leaders understand their accountability and responsibility with respect to security for the organization; for their stakeholders; for the communities they serve, including the Internet community; and for the protection of critical national infrastructures and economic and national security interests.

---

3. See also "Characteristics of Effective Security Governance" for a table of 11 characteristics that compares and contrasts an organization with effective governance practices and an organization in which these practices are missing [Allen 2007].

- Security is treated as a business requirement. It is considered a cost of doing business and perceived as an investment rather than an expense or a discretionary budget-line item. Security policy is set at the top of the organization with input from key stakeholders. Business units and staff are not allowed to decide unilaterally how much security they want. Adequate and sustained funding and allocation of adequate security resources are a given.

- Security is considered an integral part of normal strategic, capital, project, and operational planning cycles. Security has achievable, measurable objectives that are integrated into strategic and project plans and implemented with effective controls and metrics. Reviews and audits of plans identify security weaknesses and deficiencies and requirements for the continuity of operations and measure progress against plans of action and milestones.

- Security is addressed as part of any new project initiation, acquisition, or relationship and as part of ongoing project management. Security requirements are addressed throughout all system/software development life-cycle phases, including acquisition, initiation, requirements engineering, system architecture and design, development, testing, operations, maintenance, and retirement.

- Managers across the organization understand how security serves as a business enabler. They view security as one of their responsibilities and understand that their team's performance with respect to security is measured as part of their overall performance.

- All personnel who have access to digital assets and enterprise networks understand their individual responsibilities to protect and preserve the organization's security, including the systems and software that it uses and develops. Awareness, motivation, and compliance are the accepted, expected cultural norm. Rewards, recognition, and consequences with respect to security policy compliance are consistently applied and reinforced.

Leaders who are committed to dealing with security at a governance level can use this checklist to determine the extent to which a security-conscious culture is present (or needs to be present) in their organizations. The relative importance of each statement depends on the organization's culture and business context.

In the next section, which was originally published as an article in *IEEE Security & Privacy,* John Steven explains which governance and management actions to take to address software security at the enterprise level.

Example: Bank of America

Rhonda MacLean, (former) chief information security officer at Bank of America, describes the bank's approach to enterprise security at both a governance and management level:

> On a structural level, Bank of America has established a security compliance framework that includes commitment and account-ability, policies and procedures, controls and supervision, regulatory oversight, monitoring, training and awareness, and reporting. Bank of America has also established a four-level information security governance model that maps out the responsibilities of board directors, business executives, chief information officers, corporate audit, the security department, legal, corporate and line-of-business, privacy, and supply chain management.
>
> The board of directors is responsible for reviewing the corporate information security program and policy, while senior management is accountable for ensuring compliance with applicable laws, regulations, and guidelines and for establishing compliance roles, accountabilities, performance expectations, and metrics. It's up to the auditors to ensure the commitment and accountability for information security controls.
>
> Bank of America's corporate information security department focuses on people, technology, and processes using a protect/detect/respond–recover model and measures its progress based on the Six Sigma quality methodology. Bank of America measures security based on failed customer interactions rather than on downtime, performance, or the number of infections or attacks. Achieving 99 percent uptime isn't important if the 1 percent downtime impacts 30 million customers [McCollum 2004].

7.3 Adopting an Enterprise Software Security Framework[4]

Most organizations no longer take for granted that their deployed applications are secure. But even after conducting penetration tests, network

---

4. [BSI 44] © 2006 IEEE. Reprinted, with permission, from "Adopting an Enterprise Software Security Framework" by John Steven, *IEEE Security & Privacy* 4, 2 (March/April 2006): 84–87.

and hosting security personnel spend considerable time chasing incidents. Your organization might be one of the many that have realized the "secure the perimeter" approach doesn't stem the tide of incidents because the software it's building and buying doesn't resist attack.

Painfully aware of the problem, savvy organizations have grappled with how to build security into their software applications for a few years now. Even the best efforts have met considerable resistance because the problem is mostly organizational and cultural, not technical—although plenty of technical hurdles exist as well.

Unfortunately, software security might be new to your organization's appointed "application security" czar—if one even exists. Even knowing where to start often proves a serious challenge. The first step toward establishing an enterprise-wide software security initiative is to assess the organization's current software development and security strengths and weaknesses. Yes, this applies to software built in-house, outsourced, purchased off-the-shelf, or integrated as part of a vendor "solution."

As an exercise, ask yourself the first question in my imaginary software security assessment: "How much software does my organization purchase compared to how much it builds in-house?" If the overwhelming majority of deployed software is outsourced, software security looks a lot more like outsourced assurance than it does building security in! Most organizations do quite a bit of both, so we'll have to solve both problems.

7.3.1 Common Pitfalls

Whether tackling the problem formally or informally, top-down or bottom-up, organizations hit the same roadblocks as they prepare to build and buy more secure applications. How each organization overcomes these roadblocks depends a great deal on its strengths and weaknesses: No one-size-fits-all approach exists. Just knowing some of the landmines might help you avoid them, though. Let's look at some of the most common ones.

Lack of Software Security Goals and Vision

It bears repeating: The first hurdle for software security is cultural. It's about how software resists attack, not how well you protect the environment in which the software is deployed. Organizations are beginning to absorb this concept, but they don't know exactly what to do about it. Their first reaction is usually to throw money and one of their go-getters at it. He or she might make some progress initially by defining some application security guidelines or even buying a static analysis tool—essentially, picking the low-hanging fruit.

Although it sounds compelling, avoid charging off to win this easy battle. If your organization is large, you don't need to be reminded of what role politics plays. At the director level, headcount, budget, and timelines are the system of currency, and demanding that development teams adhere to guidelines requiring development they haven't budgeted for, or imposing a tool that spits out vulnerabilities for them to fix prior to release, can quickly send software security efforts into political deficit.

To use a war analogy, each of the chief information officer's majors must understand their role in software security prior to going into battle. To win, each major will have to take on at least a small amount of responsibility for software security, but the most crucial aspect of success is for each of them to know his or her responsibility and when to collaborate.

Put simply, without executive sponsorship, a unified understanding of roles, responsibilities, and a vision for software security, the effort will sink quickly into political struggle or inaction.

Creating a New Group

Some organizations respond to the software security problem by creating a group to address it. Headcount and attention are necessary, but it's a mistake to place this headcount on an island by itself. It's an even bigger mistake to use network security folks to create a software security capability—they just don't understand software well enough.

Software security resources must be placed into development teams and seen as advocates for security, integration, and overcoming development roadblocks.

Software Security Best Practices Nonexistent

Security analysts won't be much more effective than penetration testing tools if they don't know what to look for when they analyze software architecture and code. Likewise, levying unpublished security demands on developers is nonproductive and breeds an us-versus-them conflict between developers and security.

Instead, build technology-specific prescriptive guidance for developers. If the guidance doesn't explain exactly what to do and how to do it, it's not specific enough. Specific guidance removes the guesswork from the developer's mind and solves the problem of consistency between security analysts.

Software Risk Doesn't Support Decision Making

Although most organizations view critical security risks as having the utmost importance, project managers constantly struggle to apply risk-management techniques. The first reason for this is a lack of visibility. Even if a technical vulnerability is identified, analysts often don't fully understand its probability and impact. Rarely does an organization use a risk-management framework to consistently calculate a risk's impact at the project-management or portfolio level.

Establish a common risk framework as part of governance efforts to gain business owners' understanding and respect if you want the organization to choose security risk over time-to-market or if you need additional capital when making release decisions.

Tools as the Answer

Companies often believe that an authentication, session management, data encryption, or similar product protects their software completely. Although they serve as lynchpins of an organization's software security proposition, most organizations have a weak adoption of these tools at best. What's worse is that these technologies are often deployed without being properly vetted. Not only do the products themselves possess vulnerabilities, but the organization's development teams weren't consulted to help with deployment, making integration difficult if not infeasible. Even if adoption of these tools were complete, they would not in and of themselves assure that an application could resist attack. Too often, architecture review is reduced to a checklist: "Did you integrate with our single sign-on and directory service tools?" "Yes? Then you're done." It's no wonder these applications still possess exploitable architectural flaws.

Penetration testing and static analysis tools aren't panaceas either. These tools help people find vulnerabilities, but there's a lot more to building security into software applications than running these tools, as we'll see.

7.3.2 Framing the Solution

An enterprise software security framework (ESSF) is a new way of thinking about software security more completely at the enterprise level, targeting the problem directly without demands for massive headcount, role changes, or turning an IT shop upside down to prioritize security ahead of supporting the business that funds it. ESSFs align the necessary people, know-how, technologies, and software development activities to achieve more secure software. Because every organization possesses different strengths and weaknesses and, most important, faces different risks as a result of using software, ESSFs will differ across organizations. There are, however, certain properties that all good ESSFs will possess.

"Who, What, When" Structure

To align each group's role in achieving secure software, an organization's ESSF should possess a "who, what, when" structure—that is, the framework should describe what activities each role is responsible for and at what point the activity should be conducted. Because building security into applications requires the collaboration of a wide variety of disciplines, the framework should include roles beyond the security analysts and application development teams. Figure 7–1 shows column headings under which an ESSF might list each role's responsibility. The boxes outlined in a lighter shade represent each role's first steps.

You might not recognize some of the group names in the figure. One organization's infrastructure group is another's shared services or architecture office, or something else entirely, and that's okay. Another subtlety involves reporting relationships—although they're important, don't get wound up in them when defining an ESSF. Focus on who needs to do what.

Figure 7–2 shows a partial enumeration of activities for which a particular role is responsible. Each group further defines how they accomplish each of their framework activities. For example, the business owner of development might decide to build a handbook to walk developers step-wise through the process of programming securely. It's just as likely this wouldn't get traction, though, so the ESSF could mandate training for developers before they're unleashed into the development organization.

In this relative ordering, teams know which activities depend on others. Providing any more of a detailed "when" diagram can be seen as

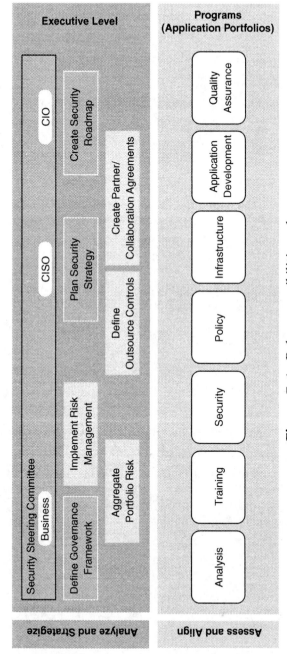

Figure 7-1: *Role responsibilities: who*

231

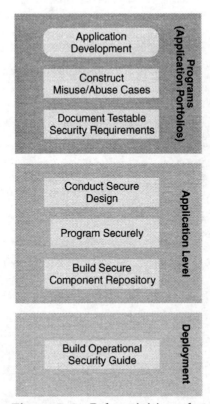

Figure 7–2: *Role activities: what*

offensive and overly constraining to each suborganization. Let people conduct detailed project planning around these activities themselves.

It's unclear what activities will compose your organization's ESSF, but here are a few gotchas to avoid:

- Don't place technologies or products, such as "single sign-on," in the framework's boxes.
- Don't demand that teams begin conducting every activity on day one. Slowly introduce the simplest activities first, then iterate.
- Avoid activities that produce unverifiable artifacts or results, such as "collaborate with security here."

Remember, the framework's primary goal is to align people and their responsibilities, so keep the visuals about who does what activities when.

Focus on Resisting Attack, Not Including Security Features

Security is an emergent property of an application, not just an amalgam of security features. In an attempt to simplify the problem and make initial strides, organizations often get stuck in a feature-centric mode: They tell themselves, "If we just encrypt our HTTP connections and authenticate users, we're doing enough." Thinking about how to leverage the security features of toolkits, languages, and application servers within an application is good and necessary—it just isn't sufficient. To be successful, the philosophy of "resisting attack" must pervade each and every ESSF activity. Avoid the feature trap by establishing a goal of improving attack resistance in each activity from its inception. Here are some guidelines:

- Construct misuse/abuse cases.
- Model the threats each application faces.
- Assess applications against a threat model, including misuse/abuse cases.
- Train using vulnerability case studies.
- Define standards based on risk and vulnerabilities.
- Avoid relying on security-feature checklists.
- Avoid relying solely on API-guide security standards and training.

Like adopting framework activities, attempting to adhere to each of these guidelines on day one can be too onerous. Build on your organization's current strengths, infusing this guidance opportunistically.

Possess Five Competencies

Regardless of how an organization operates, every good ESSF addresses five pursuits in one form or another, as described in Table 7–1. Organizations should iteratively raise their competencies in each of these pursuits gradually as they adopt their ESSF.

Table 7–1: *Competencies for Effective Enterprise Software Security*

Enterprise software security framework	The ESSF defines an organization's approach to software security and describes roles, responsibilities, activities, deliverables, and measurement criteria. It also includes a communication plan for enterprise-wide rollout. Enterprise software and data architectures are essential anchors of the goal-state an ESSF defines. Definition of and migration toward a secure enterprise architecture are thus part of the framework competency.
Knowledge management, training	An organized collection of security knowledge is likely to include policy, standards, design and attack patterns, threat models, code samples, and eventually a reference architecture and secure development framework. Another element of this competency is the development and delivery of a training curriculum. Topics include security knowledge as well as help for conducting assurance activities. This pursuit also includes new courseware, along with retrofitting of existing courseware to software security concepts.
Security touchpoints	The definition of tasks and activities that augment existing development processes (formally or informally) help developers build security into any custom software development process, as well as in-place outsource assurance and commercial off-the-shelf validation processes. This competency defines how to assure software. See [McGraw 2006].
Assurance	The execution of security touchpoint activities provides assurance—conducting a software architectural risk assessment, for example, validates that security requirements were translated into aspects of the software's design and that the design resists attack. Assurance activities rely heavily on the knowledge and training competency to define what to look for. Tool adoption is likely to be part of this pursuit in the short to medium term. It will involve the purchase, customization, and rollout of static analysis tools as well as dynamic analysis aides. Your organization might have already adopted a penetration-testing product, for instance.

Table 7–1: *Competencies for Effective Enterprise Software Security (Continued)*

Governance	In the context of an ESSF, governance is competency in measuring software-induced risk and supporting an objective decision-making process for remediation and software release. This competency involves creating a seat at the project management table for software risk alongside budget and scheduling concerns.
	Governance should also be applied to the rollout and maturation of an organization's ESSF. The framework's owners can measure project coverage and depth of assurance activities, reported risks (and their severity), and the progress of software security knowledge and skill creation, among other things.

7.3.3 Define a Roadmap

Each competency depends somewhat on the others, and growing each effectively demands thoughtful collaboration. It's foolish to attempt to understand all the subtle interdependencies from the start and attempt a "big bang" rollout. Instead, good ESSFs leverage key initial successes in support of iterative adoption and eventual maturation. Keep two things in mind:

- *Patience.* It will take at least three to five years to create a working, evolving software security machine. Initial organization-wide successes can be shown within a year. Use that time to obtain more buy-in and a bigger budget, and target getting each pursuit into the toddler stage within the three-year timeframe.

- *Customers.* The customers are the software groups that support the organization's lines of business. Each milestone in the roadmap should represent a value provided to the development organization, not another hurdle.

Thankfully, the organizations that have been doing this work for a few years now are starting to share some of their experiences. Expert help is increasingly available, too. As always, use your community resources, and good luck being the agent of change in your organization!

7.4 How Much Security Is Enough?

Prior to selecting which security governance and management actions to take and in what order, you must answer the following question: How much security is enough? One way to tackle this question is to formulate and answer the set of security strategy questions presented in Chapter 1 (see Section 1.7.1), identify a means for determining your definition of adequate or acceptable security, and use these as inputs for your security risk management framework.

7.4.1 Defining Adequate Security

Determining adequate security is largely synonymous with determining and managing risk. Where possible, an organization can implement controls that satisfy the security requirements of its critical business processes and assets. Where this is not possible, security risks to such processes and assets can be identified, mitigated, and managed at a level of residual risk that is acceptable to the organization.

Adequate security has been defined as follows: "The condition where the protection strategies for an organization's critical assets and business processes are commensurate with the organization's tolerance for risk" [Allen 2005]. In this definition, *protection strategies* include principles, policies, procedures, processes, practices, and performance indicators and measures—all of which are elements of an overall system of controls.[5]

An *asset* is anything of value to an organization. Assets include information such as enterprise strategies and plans, product information, and customer data; technology such as hardware, software, and IT-based services; supporting facilities and utilities; and items of significant, yet largely intangible value such as brand, image, and reputation. Critical assets are those that directly affect the ability of the organization to meet its objectives and fulfill its critical success factors [Caralli 2004a]. The extent to which software is the means by which digital assets are created, accessed, stored, and transmitted provides one compelling argument for ensuring that such software has been developed with security in mind.

---

5. A system of internal controls often includes categories such as administrative, technical, and physical controls as well as directive, preventive, compensating, detective, and corrective controls [Lousteau 2003].

A *process* is a series of progressive and interdependent actions or steps by which a defined end result is obtained. Business processes create the products and services that an organization offers and can include customer relationship management, financial management and reporting, and management of relationships and contractual agreements with partners, suppliers, and contractors.

Risk Tolerance

An organization's tolerance for risk can be defined as "the amount of risk, on a broad level, an entity is willing to accept in pursuit of value (and its mission)" [COSO 2004]. Risk tolerance influences business culture, operating style, strategies, resource allocation, and infrastructure. It is not a constant, however, but rather is influenced by and must adapt to changes in the environment.

Defining the organization's tolerance for risk is an executive responsibility. Risk tolerance can be expressed as impact (potential consequences of a risk-based event), likelihood of a risk's occurrence, and associated mitigating actions. For identified and evaluated risks, it could be defined as the residual risk the organization is willing to accept after implementing risk-mitigation and monitoring processes [Allen 2005].

Risk tolerance can be expressed both qualitatively and quantitatively. For example, we might define high, medium, and low levels of residual risk. An example is a policy to take explicit and prioritized action for high- and medium-level risks and to accept (monitor) low-level risks as the default condition.

With the benefit of this description, a useful way to address the question "How much security is enough?" is to first ask, "What is our definition of adequate security?" To do so, we can explore the following more detailed questions:

- What are the critical assets and business processes that support achieving our organizational goals? What are the organization's risk tolerances, both in general and with respect to critical assets and processes?
- Under which conditions and with what likelihood are assets and processes at risk? What are the possible adverse consequences if a risk is realized? Do these risks fit within our risk tolerances?

- In cases where risks go beyond these thresholds, which mitigating actions do we need to take and with which priority? Are we making conscious decisions to accept levels of risk exposure and then effectively managing residual risk? Have we considered mechanisms for sharing potential risk impact (e.g., through insurance or with third parties)?

- For those risks we are unwilling or unable to accept, which protection strategies do we need to put in place? What is the cost–benefit relationship or return on investment of deploying these strategies?

- How well are we managing our security state today? How confident are we that our protection strategies will sustain an acceptable level of security 30 days, 6 months, and 1 year from now? Are we updating our understanding and definition of our security state as part of normal planning and review processes?

7.4.2 A Risk Management Framework for Software Security[6]

As introduced in Chapter 1, a necessary part of any approach to ensuring adequate security (including an adequate level of software security) is the definition and use of a continuous risk management process. Software security risks include risks found in the outputs and results produced by each life-cycle phase during assurance activities, risks introduced by insufficient processes, and personnel-related risks. The risk management framework (RMF) described here can be used to implement a high-level, consistent, iterative risk analysis that is deeply integrated throughout the SDLC.

Five Stages of Activity

Figure 7–3 shows the RMF as a closed-loop process with five fundamental activity stages:

1. Understand the business context.
2. Identify the business and technical risks.
3. Synthesize and prioritize the risks, producing a ranked set.
4. Define the risk mitigation strategy.
5. Carry out required fixes and validate that they are correct.

---

6. This material is extracted and adapted from a more extensive article by Gary McGraw of Cigital, Inc. [BSI 33]. Also, see chapter 2 of [McGraw 2006].

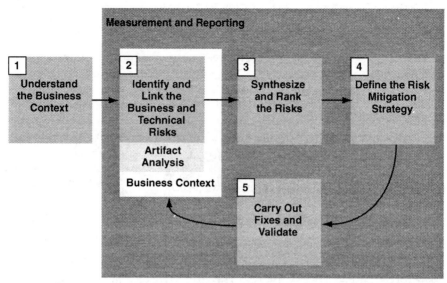

Figure 7–3: *A software security risk management framework*

Each of these stages is briefly summarized below. Critical business decisions, including release readiness, can be made in a more straightforward and informed manner by identifying, tracking, and managing software risks explicitly as described in the RMF.

1. Understand the Business Context

Software risk management occurs in a business context. The increasing integration of business processes and IT systems means that software risks often have serious and specific implications for the organization's mission. Given that resources are rarely unlimited, mitigation of software risks can and should be prioritized according to the severity of the related business risks.

Central to the notion of risk management is the idea of describing impact. Without a clear and compelling tie to either business or mission consequences, technical risks, software defects, and the like are not often compelling enough on their own to warrant action. Unless software risks are described in terms that business people and decision makers understand, they will likely not be addressed.

Risks are unavoidable and are a necessary part of software development. Management of risks, including the notions of risk aversion and technical tradeoff, is deeply affected by the relevant business motivation. Thus the first stage of software risk management involves getting a handle on the business situation. Commonly, business goals are neither obvious nor explicitly stated. In some cases, the risk analyst may even have difficulty expressing these goals clearly and consistently.

During this stage, the analyst must extract and describe business goals, priorities, and circumstances to understand which kinds of software risks are important to care about and which business goals are paramount. Business goals may include, for example, increasing revenue, meeting service-level agreements, reducing development costs, and generating a high return on investment.

2. Identify Business and Technical Risks

Business risks directly threaten one or more of a customer's business goals. The identification of such risks helps to clarify and quantify the possibility that certain events will directly affect business goals. Business risks have impacts that include direct financial loss, damage to brand or reputation, violation of customer or regulatory constraints, exposure to liability, and increased development costs. The severity of a business risk should be expressed in terms of financial or project management metrics. These parameters may include, for example, market share (percentage), direct cost, level of productivity, and cost of rework.

The process of business risk identification helps to define and guide the use of particular technical methods for extracting, measuring, and mitigating software risks for various software artifacts such as requirements, architecture, and design specifications. The identification of business risks provides a necessary foundation that allows software risks (especially their impacts) to be quantified and described in business terms.

Central to this stage of the RMF is the ability to discover and describe technical risks and map them (through business risks) to business goals. A technical risk is a situation that runs counter to the planned design or implementation of the system under consideration. For example, this kind of risk may give rise to the system behaving in an unexpected way, violating its own design constraints, or failing to perform as required. Technical risks can also be related to the process used to develop software—that is, the process an organization follows may offer opportunities for mistakes in design or implementation.

Technical risks involve impacts such as unexpected system crashes, absence or avoidance of controls (audit or otherwise), unauthorized data modification or disclosure, and needless rework of artifacts during development.

Technical risk identification is supported by the practices described in Chapter 4, Secure Software Architecture and Design, which discuss the identification, assessment, prioritization, mitigation, and validation of the risks associated with architectural flaws.

3. Synthesize and Prioritize Risks

Large numbers of risks inevitably become apparent in almost any system. Identifying these risks is important, but it is the prioritization of these risks that leads directly to creation of value. Through the activities of synthesizing and prioritizing risks, the critical "Who cares?" question can (and must) be answered. Synthesis and prioritization should answer questions such as "What shall we do first, given the current risk situation?" and "What is the best allocation of resources, especially in terms of risk mitigation activities?" The prioritization process must take into account which business goals are the most important to the organization, which goals are immediately threatened, and how risks that are likely to be realized may affect the business. The output of this stage is a list of all the risks along with their relative priorities for resolution. Typical risk metrics might include, for example, risk likelihood, risk impact, risk severity, and number of risks emerging and mitigated over time.

4. Define the Risk Mitigation Strategy

Given a set of prioritized risks from stage 3, stage 4 creates a coherent strategy for mitigating the highest-priority risks in a cost-effective manner. Any suggested mitigation activities must take into account cost, time to implement, likelihood of success, completeness, and impact over the entire set of risks. A risk mitigation strategy must be constrained by the business context and should consider what the organization can afford, integrate, and understand. The strategy must also specifically identify validation techniques that can be used to demonstrate that risks are properly mitigated. Typical metrics to consider in this stage are financial in nature and include, for example, estimated cost of mitigation actions, return on investment, method effectiveness in terms of dollar impact, and percentage of risks covered by mitigating actions. Typically, it is not cost-effective to mitigate all possible risks, so some level of residual risk will remain once mitigation actions are taken. Of course, these residual risks need to be regularly reviewed and consciously managed.

5. Fix the Problems and Validate the Fixes

Once a mitigation strategy has been defined, it must be executed. Artifacts in which problems have been identified (such as architectural flaws in a design, requirements collisions, or problems in testing) should be fixed. Risk mitigation is carried out according to the strategy defined in stage 4. Progress at this stage should be measured in terms of completeness against the risk mitigation strategy. Good metrics include, for example, progress against risks, open risks remaining, and any artifact quality metrics previously identified.

This stage also involves application of previously identified validation techniques. The validation stage provides some confidence that risks have been properly mitigated through artifact improvement and that the risk mitigation strategy is working. Testing can be used to demonstrate and measure the effectiveness of risk mitigation activities. The central concern at this stage is to confirm that software artifacts and processes no longer hold unacceptable risks. This stage should define and leave in place a repeatable, measurable, verifiable validation process that can be run from time to time to continually verify artifact quality. Typical metrics employed during this stage include artifact quality metrics as well as levels of risk mitigation effectiveness.

Measurement and Reporting on Risk

The importance of identifying, tracking, storing, measuring, and reporting software risk information cannot be overemphasized. Successful use of the RMF depends on continuous and consistent identification, review, and documentation of risk information as it changes over time. A master list of risks should be maintained during all stages of RMF execution and continually revisited, with measurements against this master list being regularly reported. For example, the number of risks identified in various software artifacts and/or software life-cycle phases can be used to identify problem areas in the software process. Likewise, the number of risks mitigated over time can be used to show concrete progress as risk mitigation activities unfold.

As you converge on and describe software risk management activities in a consistent manner, you'll find that the basis for measurement and common metrics emerges (see Section 7.5.6). Such metrics should help your organization achieve the following ends:

- Better manage business and technical risks, given particular quality goals
- Make more informed, objective business decisions regarding software (such as whether an application is ready to release)
- Improve internal software development processes and thereby better manage software risks

The Multilevel-Loop Nature of the RMF

The RMF shown in Figure 7–3 has a clear loop (a single pass through the stages) that depicts risk management as a continuous and iterative process. Although the five stages are shown in a particular order in Figure 7–3, they may need to be applied over and over again throughout a project, and the order of stage execution may be interleaved.

There are two main reasons for this complication. First, risks can crop up at any time during the software life cycle. One natural way to apply a cycle of the loop is during each software life-cycle phase. For example, software risks should be identified, ranked, and mitigated (one loop) during requirements and again during design (another loop). Second, risks can crop up between stages, regardless of where the software is in its development life cycle or in its development process.

A further complication is that the RMF process can be applied at several levels of abstraction. The top level is the project level, meaning that each stage of the loop clearly must have some representation for an entire project so that risks can be effectively managed and communicated by the project manager. Next comes the software life-cycle phase level: Each stage most likely has a representation for the requirements phase, the design phase, the architecture phase, the test planning phase, and so on. A third level is the artifact level. Each stage has a representation during both requirements analysis and use-case analysis, for example. Fortunately, a generic description of the validation loop is sufficient to capture critical aspects at all of these levels at once.

The risk management process is, by its very nature, cumulative and sometimes arbitrary and difficult to predict (depending on project circumstances). Specific RMF stages, tasks, and methods (described serially here) may occur independently of one another, in parallel, repeatedly, and somewhat randomly as new risks arise.

To summarize, the level of adequate security as defined here is constantly changing in response to business and risk environments and variations in the level of risk tolerance that management is willing to accept. Effectively achieving and sustaining adequate security and the use of a risk management framework demands that this work be viewed as a continuous process, not a final outcome. As a result, processes to plan for, monitor, review, report, and update an organization's security state must be part of normal day-to-day business conduct, risk management, and governance, rather than simply a one-shot occurrence.

In addition to the sources cited here, refer to "Risk-Centered Practices" [BSI 34] and *Software Security: Building Security In* [McGraw 2006] for further implementation details.

7.5 Security and Project Management[7]

This section describes how security influences project plans and management actions and suggests several approaches for inserting security practices into a defined SDLC as described in previous chapters. Continuous risk management and periodic risk assessment are key activities that help guide project managers in determining which security practices to incorporate in each life-cycle activity and to what degree.

Software security requirements affect project planning and monitoring, specifically with respect to the following aspects of the project:

- The project's scope
- The project plan, including the project life cycle, which reflects software security practices
- Tools, knowledge, and expertise
- Estimating the nature and duration of required resources
- Project and product risks

---

7. This material is extracted and adapted from a more extensive article by Robert J. Ellison of Software Engineering Institute [BSI 35].

7.5.1 Project Scope

Security's impact on the scope of the project has several dimensions that need to be considered throughout project planning and execution. These dimensions influence all SDLC activities and need to be specifically addressed in the final software and system before they are approved for release:

- The type and number of threats

  A risk assessment (as described in Section 7.4.2) can help in identifying the highest-priority threats and the profiles of the most likely attackers.

- The sophistication of and resources available to the attacker

  Straightforward preventive measures may offer sufficient protection from the inexperienced attacker. By contrast, protecting against experienced external attackers, those with substantial resources, and "insiders" will require more elaborate tactics.

- The desired response to an attack

  A *passive response* does not depend on the system having knowledge of an attack and is typically preventive in nature. For example, input validation is a passive response that prevents a significant number of attacks. An *active response* is an action that takes place when a fault is detected. For example, an active response that improves reliability in the event of a hardware failure might be automatic failover of processing to a redundant system. A simple active response might be an automatic system shutdown when an attack is detected to protect resources, but a more frequently preferred objective for an active response is to continue to provide essential services during an attack by dynamically changing system behavior. Hence, an active response typically increases software complexity.

- The level of required assurance that the system meets its security requirements

  In practice, the assurance level depends on the consequences of a security failure. Security governance is typically associated with systems that require medium or high assurance. High-assurance systems include those that are important for national defense and for domains such as health care and nuclear power. Medium-assurance systems are those for which the consequences of a risk could reasonably lead to substantial reduction in shareholder value, the leakage of confidential business information, legal liability above normal business liability insurance, or substantial civil action or negative publicity.[8] Medium assurance could, for example, be applicable to corporate financial systems, manufacturing control systems, and the information systems used for critical infrastructure services such as power and water.

Access to sensitive information may have to satisfy legal, regulatory, or fiduciary duties; contractual obligations; or voluntary requirements such as the protection of proprietary data. Those requirements raise the importance of security governance. In particular, regulatory compliance may depend on formalizing governance and risk management and, for each regulation, may require specifying the scope in terms of the responsibilities and roles for personnel and IT systems.

7.5.2 Project Plan

The nature of security risks and their consequences affect both project planning and resources. Actions to mitigate low-consequence and low-likelihood risks can often be left to the discretion of the project leader with limited management review. Conversely, the management of high-probability risks with medium-level consequences would likely require expert assistance and a well-defined, systematic review process.

All too often, software errors that render systems vulnerable to cyberattack are introduced as a result of disconnects and miscommunications during the planning, development, testing, and maintenance of any system or software component. For example:

1. The complexity associated with product development may be a consequence of tight component integration to meet market demands for functionality or performance. Products typically have extensibility requirements so that they can be tailored for a specific customer's operating environment. The complexity induced by those product requirements also increases the risk that those features might be exploited.

2. Shared services typically aggregate risks. A failure in shared software or infrastructure services could affect multiple systems. The level of software assurance required for the shared components

---

8. Cohen, Fred. Burton Group presentation at Catalyst 2005.

should be higher than that required than for the systems in which they are deployed. The higher assurance and aggregation of risks implies that the risks for shared services should include the full spectrum of integrity, confidentiality, and availability issues.

3. System integration has to resolve any mismatches with both internal and outsourced development. One mechanism to encourage better integration might be to specify the software assurance criteria for each component, such as completed code analysis for all delivered software. There will probably be differences in the software assurance requirements among components developed in-house and those commercially available.

Given these concerns, communication and links among life-cycle activities, among multiple development teams, and between the system development and operational use environments need to be addressed by project managers.

Software Security Practices in the Development Life Cycle

As stated earlier, a necessary part of any project planning effort that includes requirements for software security is the use of a continuous risk management process that includes risk assessment. The factors involved with a risk assessment that is done early in the software development process are predominantly business oriented rather than technical. You'll want to ensure that business-knowledgeable stakeholders participate in risk assessment and analysis.

Architectural risk analysis is an example of an important software security practice. The software architecture describes the system structure in terms of components and specified interactions. The increased system specificity provided by this architecture calls for a more detailed description of security threats and desired system responses to them. Thus an architectural risk assessment can review the threats, analyze how the architecture responds to them, and identify additional risks introduced by the architecture. For example, attack patterns would be rather abstract for a preliminary risk assessment, but would become more detailed as the software architecture and detailed design evolve. (See Section 7.4.2 and Section 4.2. Also see Chapter 6 for a more detailed discussion of system development and integration issues, along with recommended mitigations.)

As introduced in Chapter 1, Figure 7–4 depicts one example of how to incorporate security into the SDLC using the concept of touchpoints

[McGraw 2006; Taylor 2005]. Software security best practices (touch-points shown as arrows) are applied to a set of software artifacts that are created during the software development process (the boxes). While Figure 7-4 may convey a traditional waterfall development approach, most of today's organizations actually use an iterative approach and thus cycle through the touchpoints more than once as the software evolves.

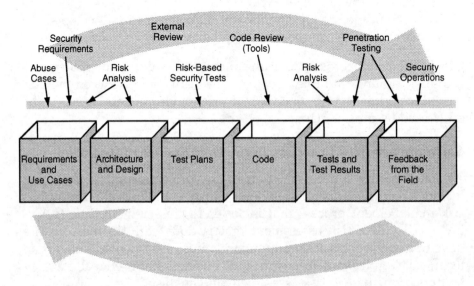

Figure 7–4: *Software development life cycle with defined security touchpoints [McGraw 2006]*

The Security Development Lifecycle—SDL: A Process for Developing Demonstrably More Secure Software [Howard 2006] provides an additional example of a pragmatic way to address security during development; it is being used successfully at Microsoft. CLASP (Comprehensive, Lightweight Application Security Process) [BSI 12], as was mentioned in Chapter 3, is an activity-driven, role-based set of process components guided by formalized best practices. CLASP is designed to help software development teams build security into the early stages of existing and new-start SDLCs in a structured, repeatable, and measurable way. Descriptions of additional secure SDLC processes can be found in *Secure Software Development Life Cycle Processes* [BSI 46; Davis 2005b].

The objective of including security in a defined SDLC is not to over-haul an existing process totally, but rather to add well-defined security practices and security deliverables. The implementation of these prac-tices depends on the characteristics of the software. For example, risk analysis and assessment for an integrated system has different require-ments than the risk assessment of a commercial product or an infra-structure component. The differences in software security issues and project management actions among products, application and inte-grated systems, and systems of systems are discussed in more detail in an article titled "The Influence of System Properties on Software Assurance and Project Management" on the BSI Web site [BSI 36].

Activities Required to Complete Deliverables

Regulatory or contractual compliance may require demonstrating that the software provides the necessary controls when accessing sensitive information (that is, the production of an assurance case— see Section 2.4). Meeting security compliance requirements typically increases the software's complexity. For example, business process com-pliance may require showing that the composition and interactions of multiple applications maintain the required controls and feedback.

Delivering "secure" software requires demonstrating that the desired level of assurance has been achieved. While demonstrating that a sys-tem provides the required functionality is an essential aspect of soft-ware assurance, software security assurance depends more on demonstrating what a system does *not* do. Does improper input lead to a system failure or enable an attacker to bypass authentication or authorization defenses? (See also Section 5.4.) The production of such an assurance case must be planned and managed. An assurance case provides an argument for how the software addresses an identified risk. That argument typically is based on assumptions about how the software behaves under certain operating conditions. Hence, an early step in building an assurance case is to provide evidence that the soft-ware behavior satisfies the assumptions of the assurance argument. Note that the production of an assurance case is an incremental activ-ity: The assurance case should evolve to describe how the architecture contributes to meeting security requirements, and the architectural risk assessment and analysis should provide evidence that the archi-tecture satisfies those requirements.

An assurance case may be part of the requirements for contracted development to address such questions as "How will the assurance of delivered software be demonstrated?" and "Do the assurance cases for the supplied software support the assurance argument for the integrated system?"

7.5.3 Resources

Tools

The software development environment should be at least as secure as the planned security level of the software being produced. Appropriate controls for and configuration management of development artifacts are essential. As part of developing those controls, specific tools may be required to aid in the production or testing of secure software, such as for static code analysis.

The security functionality for authentication, authorization, and encryption is typically composed of commercially supplied components that can be tailored for a specific operational environment. These components must have the required assurance level.

As assurance levels rise, the development process should provide the necessary control and information protection mechanisms. Change management must be conducted according to a defined, repeatable process, with zero tolerance for unauthorized changes. (See the article titled "Prioritizing IT Controls for Effective, Measurable Security" on the BSI Web site [BSI 37].) High-assurance configuration management must support requirements for audit, traceability, and process enforcement. For very sensitive code segments, security governance may require that changes always be made by two developers to limit the ability of an individual to insert malicious code.

Knowledge and Expertise

Security expertise on most projects is limited and may be provided via an internal means or a contracted service. Determining how best to allocate this limited resource is challenging even when security activity involves only networks, authentication, and access control. When security has to be incorporated into application development, this expertise is even more difficult to come by. Also, any increase in the level of assurance can significantly affect the need for security and software engineering expertise.

The security expertise required to develop more secure software can be classified into two categories:

- Knowledge of security functionality and features, such as the specification and implementation of access control, authentication, and encryption. Security functionality specialists should be aware of the security issues associated with development and project management.

- The skills to identify and mitigate exploitable vulnerabilities. Unfortunately, software development teams rarely have the necessary security expertise needed to satisfy this need. Vulnerabilities may reside in the least exercised parts of the system or depend on aspects of system interfaces that are highly unlikely to occur or difficult to predict. Software development teams may miss these types of vulnerabilities because they normally concentrate on the core software and security functionality.

Project managers need to ensure that both types of expertise are available to their development teams throughout the SDLC (see sidebar).

Tasks such as risk assessment, architectural risk analysis, and code review require significant security expertise. Other software security practices can be implemented with somewhat less experience. For example, although extensive security knowledge may be necessary to configure a tool for the static analysis of source code, the use of such a tool may not require the same level of expertise. (See Section 5.2.)

Testing provides a second example. Penetration testing is often part of an acceptance test or certification process. Penetration testing might be implemented by a *red team*—that is, security experts who attempt to breach the system defenses. Fuzz testing is a simple form of penetration testing that finds software defects by purposely feeding invalid and ill-formed data as input to program interfaces [Arkin 2005; Howard 2006]. Fuzz testing does not replace the need for testing that targets explicit security risks, but it is an approach that can be used without detailed knowledge of security vulnerabilities. (See [BSI 23] for a discussion of the effective use of fuzz testing.)

7.5.4 Estimating the Nature and Duration of Required Resources

An increase in the required assurance level can have a significant impact on project cost and schedule, and additional development skills, development practices, and tool support will be required to demonstrate that the desired assurance is in place. Traditional cost-saving strategies such

Deployment of Security Expertise at Microsoft

Microsoft's experience with the implementation of its Security Development Lifecycle suggests that someone with security expertise must be available for frequent interactions with the development team during software design and development. A similar recommendation has been made for projects utilizing agile development [Wäyrynen 2004].

Microsoft created a central security group that drives the development and evolution of security best practices and process improvements, serves as a source of expertise for the organization as a whole, and performs a final security review before software is released. For example, during the requirements phase, the product team requests the assignment of a security advisor from the central group who serves as point of contact, resource, and guide as planning proceeds. This security advisor helps the product team by reviewing plans and ensuring that the central security team plans for and identifies appropriate resources to support the product team's schedule. The security advisor also makes recommendations to the product team on security milestones and exit criteria based on project size, complexity, and risk.

See "Lessons Learned from Five Years of Building More Secure Software" [Howard 2007] for more details on this initiative.

---

as reusing existing components or general-purpose commercial components may not be useful when developing medium- and high-assurance systems. In addition, early estimates for staff effort and schedule are not very reliable until a more detailed description of the software is available, such as that provided by the software architecture and detailed design, along with a more detailed model of attacker actions and possible responses.

Using shared services and a shared IT infrastructure across a number of application development projects can reduce component development costs but typically aggregates risks across all uses. In other words, if a shared service includes a certain risk, this risk needs to be managed by every project that uses the service. Examples of shared services that might be used by multiple applications include Web

---

Mitigations May Create New Risks

Security mechanisms that mitigate a specific risk may create additional ones. For example, security requirements for managing identity for a large distributed system might be met by implementing authentication and authorization as infrastructure services shared by all applications. As noted earlier, the aggregation of authentication and authorization mechanisms into a shared service makes that service a single point of failure and a possible attack target. Such design decisions should involve a risk assessment to identify any new risks that require mediation, as well as the analysis of the operational costs after the system is deployed.

In summary, the requirement for secure systems and software affects many of the "knowledge areas" of project management—specifically, scoping, human resources, communications, risk management, procurement, quality, and integration. Activities such as an architectural risk assessment, threat analysis, and static analysis for the source code provide practices for specific development phases. Development controls and change management are essential development tools. However, the software assurance issues that arise during development are dynamic, meaning that project managers must maintain links between business and technical perspectives, among life-cycle phases, and among development teams. The production of an assurance case can serve as an integrating mechanism by identifying threats and desired responses and then tracing and refining the threats and responses during development.

Providing the necessary level of security assurance requires more than the development of what is typically thought of as a security architecture—that is, perimeter defenses (firewalls), proxies, authentication, and access controls. Software security can be achieved only by integrating software assurance practices into development processes. Such integration happens as an act of project management.

7.5.6 Measuring Software Security[9]

Measurement of both product and development processes has long been recognized as a critical activity for successful software development.

portal interfaces, encryption and public key infrastructure, content management, access control, and authentication. Project estimates need to consider and reflect the increased assurance that will need to be applied to any shared services.

The nature of the required security expertise varies over the development life cycle. General security expertise might be stretched thin in the initial planning and requirements phases, when teams without that experience require the most assistance. Security test planning should start after the architecture is defined. Although risk analysis has to be a continuing activity, the specific expertise required to perform such analysis may vary. The analysis of a detailed design may require in-depth knowledge of a specific technology, while the analysis of an implementation draws on a detailed knowledge of known exploits.

7.5.5 Project and Product Risks

If you are using relatively new protocols such as those for Web services, you may find them to be a moving target, as they continue to change to reflect the experiences of early adopters. Best practices in this context have short lives, and the lack of well-defined and proven practices adversely affects planning. Given this caveat, you might want to include a prototype or use an iterative or incremental approach.

Potential requirements for secure data access during development, secure facilities, or demonstration of capability can add great complexity and schedule concerns to projects.

Software vulnerabilities may be intentionally inserted during in-house or contracted development. These vulnerabilities can be much more difficult to find than those resulting from inadequate software security practices. Change and configuration management procedures provide some assurance for internal development.

Some security risks are inherent in the operational environment or with the desired functionality and hence are unavoidable. For example, it may be very difficult to block a well-resourced denial-of-service attack. Other risks may arise because of tradeoffs made elsewhere in the project. For example, an organization might permit employees to access information assets using personal laptops or PDAs because the need for such access outweighs its perceived risks.

Good measurement practices and data enable realistic project planning, timely monitoring of project progress and status, accurate identification of project risks, and effective process improvement. Appropriate measures and indicators of software artifacts such as requirements, designs, and source code can be analyzed to diagnose problems and identify solutions during project execution and reduce defects, rework (i.e., effort, resources), and cycle time. Unfortunately, useful measurements for software that have been developed to meet security requirements are still in their infancy, and no consensus exists as to which measures constitute best practices. Nonetheless, some measures and practices used in software development can be fruitfully extended to address security requirements.

Effective use of a software development measurement process for security relies first on agreeing on the desired security characteristics and measurement objectives, which can be applied to both the product and the development process. These objectives rely on having explicit system requirements—which means that security aspects must be specified early in the SDLC (see Chapter 3). The organization should assess the risk environment to address probable risks and translate these concerns into specific security requirements, and then design and implement a development process that ensures such requirements are built in.

Measurement objectives can be formulated that will provide insight into the software's security state or condition. Following are some examples of analytical questions that can lead to measurement objectives:

- Which vulnerabilities have been detected in our products? Are our current development practices adequate to prevent the recurrence of the vulnerabilities?

- Which process steps or activities are most likely to introduce security-related risks?

- What proportion of defects relates to security concerns and requirements? Do defect classification schemes include security categories?

- To what extent do developers comply with security-related processes and practices?

---

9. This material is extracted and adapted from a more extensive article by James McCurley, David Zubrow, and Carol Dekkers [BSI 38].

- To what extent are security concerns addressed in intermediate work products (e.g., requirements, architecture and design descriptions, test plans)? Have measures associated with security requirements and their implementation been defined and planned?
- What are the critical and most vulnerable software components? Have vulnerabilities been identified and addressed?

Architectural risk analysis (which helps identify probable types and sources of attacks) can provide significant guidance for the development processes for secure products (see Chapter 4). A thesis by Stuart E. Schechter at Harvard University's Department of Computer Science uses economic models for valuing the discovery of vulnerabilities in the final or end product during development [Schechter 2004]. His measurement of security strength depends most on threat scenarios to assign values to vulnerabilities. Many risk and threat methodologies are publicly available, including [McGraw 2006] and CLASP [BSI 12]. In addition, Microsoft has published extensive materials that delineate its approach to analyzing and mitigating threat risks during the SDLC [Howard 2006].

Process Measures for Secure Development

Process artifacts that implement security measurement objectives for the development process should address the following issues:

- The presence of security policies applicable to the SDLC (e.g., roles and responsibilities, management, procedures, coding rules, acceptance/release criteria)
- Policy compliance
- The efficiency and effectiveness of the policies over time

The security measurement objectives for the development process are identical to the general measurement objectives—and they need to be included in the process implementation. Such measures could be implemented as part of an organization's integrated quality assurance function.

Although targeted for systems development and risk assessment as a whole, the NIST Special Publication *Security Metrics Guide for Information Technology Systems* [Swanson 2003] provides useful guidance for measurements of this type. Risk management can encompass secure coding and provides a familiar framework in which to incorporate new practices and procedures to address software security issues (see also Section 7.4.2).

Defect density is a commonly used measure of product quality. It is often computed as the number of defects discovered during system testing or during the first six months of operational use divided by the size of the system. Estimates of defects remaining in the product (calculated by techniques such as phase containment, defect depletion, and capture–recapture techniques) form a natural analogue to estimate security vulnerabilities remaining in the software. *Phase containment* of defects is an analytical technique that measures the proportion of defects originating in a phase that are detected within that same phase; it provides a good characterization of the ability of the development process to maintain quality throughout the SDLC. Refer to "Team Software Process for Secure Systems Development" [in BSI 46; Over 2002] for additional information on process measures for secure development.

Product Measures for Secure Development

In the product context, security concerns addressed by measurement objectives may take any of the following forms:

- Security requirements, which are based on privacy policies, legal implications, risks identified by threat assessments, and other sources, and can be specified as to extent and completeness
- Security architecture, which reflects the specified security requirements
- Secure design criteria, where security requirements can be traced
- Secure coding practices, where integrity can be assessed and measured

Not all measures need to be complicated. Measures should be as simple as possible while still meeting the project's information needs. For example, in the requirements phase it is useful to know whether security-related concerns have been considered in specifying system requirements. This information could be summarized initially as yes or no. As experience with the measure accrues over time, however, the measure could evolve to characterize the extent to which requirements have been checked and tested against security concerns. Tools, inspections, and reviews can be used to determine the extent to which security measurement objectives are implemented during the design and coding phases.

Inspection measurements often take the form of traditional defect identification checklists, to which security-oriented items have been added. For example, you could track the percentage of sources of input that have validation checks and associated error handling. Check each input source for length, format, and type, and its associated exit flows—either (1) accepted and then executed or (2) recognized as an error or exception and not executed. The target for this measure would be 100 percent, unless performance is unacceptable as a result or this scheme costs too much to implement. Note that while this simple measure represents an improvement over no measurement for this type of vulnerability, it does not address the potentially complex issue of determining the effectiveness of an input validation technique as implemented and whether any particular datum should be counted in the tally. Resolving this issue requires ongoing tracking of this measure's performance to characterize the effectiveness of the input validation techniques used. Over time, you can benchmark these kinds of measures as performance standards.

Simple measures of enumeration and appropriate security handling for vulnerabilities provide insight into the security status of the software during development. For example, a useful list of "Measurable Security Entities" and "Measurable Concepts" has been published by Practical Software and Systems Measurement [PSM 2005]. Questions generated by the PSM/DHS Measurement Technical Working Group address many of the previously mentioned issues and can provide starting points for developing measurement objectives. These questions—which form a solid basis for measurement in most development organizations, regardless of size or methods employed—can be found on the BSI Web site in the article titled "Measures and Measurement for Secure Software Development" [BSI 38]. In addition, a useful description of software security metrics for Web applications is provided in "A Metrics Framework to Drive Application Security Improvement" [Nichols 2007].

This section has described a range of topics that project managers need to pay particular attention to when developing secure software. *Software Project Management for Software Assurance* [Fedchak 2007] is another comprehensive source that presents information on how software assurance and software security affect project management practices, including risk management, size and cost estimation, metrics, quality assurance, and management practices by life-cycle phase.

We close this chapter by highlighting a number of observed shifts and trends, along with supporting evidence, that describe the state of the practice in various communities and market sectors with respect to governing and managing information and software security. This information can be used to help formulate business-based arguments and implementation approaches for developing and deploying more secure software.

7.6 Maturity of Practice

Security's emergence as a governance and management concern is primarily taking place in the parts of the organization that provide and use IT. We currently see minimal attention paid to this topic during the early life-cycle phases of software and system development, but increasing attention being devoted to it during detailed design, coding, and testing. Treating security as a governance and management concern, as a risk management concern, and as a project management concern at the earliest phases of the life cycle will likely produce more robust, less vulnerable software, thereby resulting in a decline in the reactive, fire-fighting mode now observed in most IT and system operations and maintenance organizations.

Consistent governance and management action across the organization is key. This includes attention and participation from business unit leaders, human resources, legal, audit, risk management, and finance, as well as IT and software and system development groups. This section identifies several indicators that organizations are addressing security as a governance and management concern, at the enterprise level. It summarizes how some organizations, trade associations, and market sectors are proceeding in this area. Many of the references cited here provide more detailed implementation guidance.

7.6.1 Protecting Information

One significant shift that is causing leaders to pay increasing attention to security is the need to treat information—and particularly consumer, customer, client, and employee information—with greater care, perhaps with the same care as money. Leaders understand how their organizations' reputations may suffer if this is not done competently and breaches become public.[10] Customers expect that organizations will carefully protect their privacy and their information, and they are becoming more acutely aware of the risk of identity theft posed by unintended data disclosure. U.S. federal laws such as the Sarbanes–Oxley Act for financial reports, along with state laws such as the California Database Protection Act for consumer data, have codified these concerns. The European Union's Directive on the Protection of Personal Data[11] is even more comprehensive with respect to an organization's legal duty and ethical responsibility to protect personal information.

The credit card industry has been proactive in defining a standard for all merchants that accept and process credit card information. Through the efforts of American Express, Discover Financial Services, JCB, MasterCard Worldwide, and Visa International, the Payment Card Industry Security Standards Council was founded and acts as the steward of the Payment Card Industry Data Security Standard [PCI 2006]. As stated on its Web site, "The PCI DSS is a multifaceted security standard that includes requirements for security management, policies, procedures, network architecture, software design, and other critical protective measures. This comprehensive standard is intended to help organizations proactively protect customer account data." The key requirements of DSS are that member organizations will (1) build and maintain a secure network, (2) protect cardholder data, (3) maintain a vulnerability management program, (4) implement strong access control measures, (5) regularly monitor and test networks, and (6) maintain an information security policy. An article on the BSI Web site titled "Plan, Do, Check, Act" [BSI 39] describes how to integrate PCI DSS requirements with other accepted security standards for sustaining software security during deployment and operations.

7.6.2 Audit's Role

As part of the U.S. Critical Infrastructure Assurance Project, the Institute of Internal Auditors (IIA) held six summit conferences in

---

10. Refer to the Privacy Rights ClearingHouse Web site for a chronology of all publicly reported privacy breaches that have occurred since the ChoicePoint breach in 2005 (http://www.privacyrights.org/ar/ChronDataBreaches.htm).

11. http://ec.europa.eu/justice_home/fsj/privacy/index_en.htm.

2000 to better understand the role of governance with respect to information security management and assurance. The IIA also provided guidance in 2001 in the document titled "Information Security Governance: What Directors Need to Know." This report includes case studies from General Motors, IBM, BellSouth, Intel, Sun Microsystems, the Federal Reserve Bank in Chicago, and Home Depot. Useful questions to ask that resulted from this work are listed in "Maturity of Practice and Exemplars" on the BSI Web site [IIA 2001; BSI 40].

The Information Systems Audit and Control Association (ISACA) and its partner organization, the IT Governance Institute (ITGI), have published extensive guidance on information technology and information security governance. Their report titled "Information Security Governance: Guidance for Boards of Directors and Executive Management" [ITGI 2006] addresses these questions:

1. What is information security governance?
2. Why is it important?
3. Who is responsible for it?

The same report also describes how to measure an organization's maturity level relative to information security governance.

7.6.3 Operational Resilience and Convergence

In its work with the Financial Services Technology Consortium (FSTC), CERT is examining the convergence of security, business continuity, and IT operations management given their critical roles in operational risk management.[12] The intent is "to improve the operational resiliency of the organization—the ability to adapt to a changing operational risk environment as necessary" [Caralli 2006]. In their technical reports *Sustaining Operational Resilience: A Process Improvement Approach to Security Management* [Caralli 2006] and *Introducing the CERT Resiliency Engineering Framework: Improving the Security and Sustainability Processes* [Caralli 2007], the authors offer an initial process improvement framework for business continuity and security. This framework is being pilot-tested with members of the FSTC and other collaboration partners.

---

12. http://www.cert.org/resiliency_engineering

A number of other organizations are describing their efforts to achieve organizational resilience through the integration of business continuity, operational and technology risk management, compliance, and information security and privacy, supported by audit. These integrating activities occur across products and business lines and take into account people, business processes, infrastructure, applications, information, and facilities. Indicators of success include the following outcomes:

- Reduced risk of a business interruption
- Shorter recovery time when an interruption occurs
- Improved ability to sustain public confidence and meet customer expectations
- Increased likelihood of complying with regulatory and internal service level requirements

The Alliance for Enterprise Security Risk Management is a coalition formed by ASIS International (representing the physical security community), ISACA (representing the IT audit community), and ISSA (Information Systems Security Association, representing the information security community). It is addressing "the integration of traditional and information security functions to encourage board and senior executive level attention to critical security-related issues" [AESRM 2005]. In its study titled "Convergence of Enterprise Security Organizations," the Alliance quotes the ASIS definition of convergence:

> The identification of security risks and interdependencies between business functions and processes within the enterprise and the development of managed business process solutions to address those risks and interdependencies.

The report goes on to describe five imperatives driving convergence[13] and the organizational implications with supporting examples. These efforts are providing evidence of the value of addressing security as part of a broader convergence effort and in support of organizational preparedness.

---

13. Rapid expansion of the enterprise ecosystem, value migration from the physical to information-based and intangible assets, new protective technologies blurring functional boundaries, new compliance and regulatory regimes, continuing pressure to reduce cost [AESRM 2005].

7.6.4 A Legal View

The American Bar Association's Privacy and Computer Crime Committee has published a "Roadmap to an Enterprise Security Program" [Westby 2005]. The preface to the Roadmap states the following:

> This publication was developed by a multidisciplinary team of industry representatives, government personnel, policy specialists, attorneys, technical experts, and academicians. They came together to provide a roadmap that links the various pieces of the cyber security "puzzle" into an orderly process that conforms with global standards and best practices, helps meet compliance requirements, facilitates cooperation with law enforcement, and promotes public-private sector cooperation.

The Roadmap presents a structure that includes governance, security integration and security operations, implementation and evaluation, and capital planning and investment controls. The steps for governance include these [Westby 2005]:

- Establish governance structure, exercise oversight, and develop policies.
- Inventory digital assets (networks, applications, information).
- Establish ownership of networks, applications, and information; designate security responsibilities for each.
- Determine compliance requirements with laws, regulations, guidance, standards, and agreements (privacy, security, and cybercrime).
- Conduct threat and risk assessments and security plan reviews (for internal and contractor operations). This may include certification and accreditation.
- Conduct risk management based on digital asset categorization and level of risk.

7.6.5 A Software Engineering View

An emerging body of knowledge describes aspects of how to apply governance and management thinking to the engineering and development of secure software. In addition to John Steven's article "Adopting an Enterprise Software Security Framework" provided in Section 7.3, several other articles on the BSI Web site that were previously published in a series in *IEEE Security & Privacy* address aspects of this issue. "Adopting a Software Security Improvement Program" [BSI 41; Taylor 2005] provides several concrete steps and a progression of phases for improvement. "Bridging the Gap Between Software Development and Information Security" [BSI 42; van Wyk 2005] describes a range of secure software development activities and practices to conduct during a software development life cycle.

Chapter 10 of *Software Security: Building Security In* [McGraw 2006] elaborates on several of the *IEEE Security & Privacy* articles. It describes elements of an enterprise software security program, addressing the following concerns:

- The business climate
- Building blocks of change, including four common pitfalls:
  - Over-reliance on late-life-cycle testing
  - Management without measurement
  - Training without assessment
  - Lack of high-level commitment (particularly relevant for governance and management)
- Building an improvement program
- Establishing a metrics program, including a three-step enterprise rollout:
  - Assess and plan
  - Build and pilot
  - Propagate and improve
- Continuous improvement
- COTS (and existing software applications), including an enterprise information architecture
- Adopting a secure development life cycle

Part I of *The Security Development Lifecycle—SDL: A Process for Developing Demonstrably More Secure Software* [Howard 2006] describes the need for a Secure Development Lifecycle (SDL). According to Michael Howard and Steve Lipner, "The biggest single factor in the success of SDL is executive support." Effective commitment to an SDL includes making a statement, being visible, providing resources, and stopping the delivery of products that do not meet their security and SDL requirements. Part II of the same book describes the 12-stage SDL.

7.6.6 Exemplars

On the BSI Web site, the article titled "Maturity of Practice and Exemplars" [BSI 40] provides 12 examples of principles, guidelines, frameworks, and roadmaps that can assist organizations in implementing a governance-based enterprise security program. This article summarizes the efforts of several professional associations and selected market sectors and organizations, describing how they have successfully addressed security at governance and management levels. Many use strategic questions and guiding principles as starting points. Summaries are provided for the following organizations and events:

- Aberdeen Group
- American Chemistry Counsel
- Audit Associations (Institute of Internal Auditors, Information Technology Governance Institute)
- BITS
- Corporate Governance Task Force
- Corporate Information Security Working Group
- Federal Financial Institutions Examination Council
- Health Information and Management Systems Society
- ISO/IEC 27001 and ISO/IEC 17799
- National Association of Corporate Directors
- National Institute of Standards and Technology
- Payment Card Industry Data Security Standard
- Veterans Administration Data Breach

Several of these examples and their supporting references provide sufficient detail to help you start implementing a security governance and management program.

Clearly, many sectors, organizations, and organizational functions (including risk management, IT, business continuity, audit, legal, and software development) are making progress and producing results by treating security as an enterprise issue. They are taking governance and management actions to integrate security into ongoing business councils and steering groups, decision-making processes, plans, business and development processes, and measures of success.

7.7 Summary

Regardless of the extent of security practices included as part of the SDLC, software security and system security cannot be accomplished without informed, knowledgeable, committed leaders—business leaders, project managers, and technical leaders. This chapter presented recommendations and practices to aid software project managers in the management tasks of producing more secure software as well as actions to take to engage their business leaders and senior executives at the governance level.

Key recommendations and practices are as follows:

- Recognize that being security aware and understanding the importance of addressing security during software development needs to be a cultural norm.
- Engage leaders to better appreciate and understand the characteristics and actions necessary to address security as governance and management concerns, and the consequences of not doing so.
- Establish a framework and roadmap for addressing software security as an enterprise-wide undertaking and for tackling some of the pitfalls and barriers head on.
- Identify ways to determine what constitutes adequate security practice based on risk management, established levels of risk tolerance, and risk assessment.
- Put a continuous, business-driven risk management framework in place, and assess for acceptable and unacceptable levels of risk throughout the SDLC.
- Follow the recommendations for inserting security into the SDLC as part of traditional project management activities, including the use of defined security touchpoints at each life-cycle phase.
- Include security as part of the software development measurement process, including implementing suggested process and product measures.

As the examples offered in this chapter demonstrate, security is being effectively tackled today, at the enterprise level, from several points of view, representing a growing community of practice across a wide range of roles, disciplines, and market sectors.

Chapter 8

Getting Started

Ideally, by now we will have convinced you that software security is a topic worthy of your attention. As software and security professionals, we will never be able to get ahead of the game by addressing security solely as an operational issue. Attackers are creative, ingenious, and increasingly motivated by financial gain. They have been learning how to exploit software for several decades; the same is not true for software engineers and we need to change this. Given the extent to which our nations, our economies, our businesses, and our families rely on software to sustain and improve our quality of life, we must make significant progress in putting higher-quality and more secure software into production. The practices described in this book serve as an excellent starting point for this journey.

To aid you in getting started, this chapter summarizes all of the practices presented in the preceding chapters. Practices described in each chapter are summarized here in tabular form (Tables 8–1 through 8–6), listed in the order of which practice to tackle first, then second, then third, and so forth. The practice order is established either by an author's assessment of which practice makes most sense to do first based on its serving as a prerequisite for or a useful precursor to subsequent practices or by listing first those practices that are most mature and in widespread use.

For example, Table 8–2 lists "Establish a defined process for identifying and documenting security requirements" as the first practice. Without a defined process, all of the other requirements engineering practices are deployed out of context; the defined process serves as the foundation for their implementation. Once this is in place, the practice order is then determined based on its ability to produce the best results from the process. With respect to Table 8–4, the practice order is more obvious. Clearly, you cannot review source code until it is developed (by using secure coding practices!), and you cannot test that code until you understand the unique aspects of software security testing.

Each chapter practice table identifies the designated "maturity level" for each practice as follows:

L1 The practice serves as guidance for how to think about a topic for which there is no proven or widely accepted approach. The intent of the description is to raise awareness and assist you in thinking about the problem and candidate solutions. The content may also describe promising research results that may have been demonstrated in a constrained setting.

L2 The practice is in early pilot use and demonstrating some successful results.

L3 The practice is in limited use in industry or government organizations, perhaps for a particular market sector.

L4 The practice has been successfully deployed and is in widespread use. You can start using this practice today with confidence. Experience reports and case studies are typically available for it as well.

The tables identify the relevant reader audiences called out in the chapters:

E Executive and senior managers

M Project and mid-level managers

L Technical leaders, engineering managers, first-line managers, and supervisors

They also identify other relevant roles that need to understand a practice and are typically involved in its deployment.

8.1 Where to Begin

Each project manager needs to carefully consider the knowledge, skills, and competencies of his or her development team, the organizational culture's tolerance (and attention span) for change, and the degree to which sponsoring executives have bought in (a prerequisite for sustaining any improvement initiative). In some cases, it may be best to start with coding and testing practices (Table 8–4) given that these are the most mature, have a fair level of automated support, and can demonstrate some early successes, thereby providing visible benefit to help software security efforts gain support and build momentum. By contrast, requirements engineering (Table 8–2) and architecture and design practices (Table 8–3) offer opportunities to address more substantive root cause issues early in the life cycle that, if left unaddressed, will show up in code and testing. Practice selection and tailoring are specific to each organization and project, being based on the objectives, constraints, and criticality of the software under development. Software criticality is based on the functionality it provides and the information it processes.

Project managers and software engineers need to better understand what constitutes secure software and develop their skills to think like an attacker—and then apply this mindset throughout the SDLC. The practices listed in Table 8–1 get this ball rolling and are the best place to start in terms of awareness, training, and education. Alternatively, if you have access to experienced security analysts, adding a few of them to your development team can jump-start this effort.

With respect to the context within which software lives, it is essential to consider the practices, processes, and mitigations identified in Table 8–5 (and Chapter 6), because they inform the practice selection process and help set expectations as to what is realistically achievable given the current state of the practice.

Two of the key project management practices are (1) defining and deploying a risk management framework to help inform practice selection and determine where best to devote scarce resources and (2) identifying how best to integrate software security practices into the organization's current software development life cycle. These and other governance and management practices are described in Table 8–6 and Chapter 7.

Table 8–1: *Software Security Practices That Span the SDLC (Chapter 2)*

Practices in Recommended Order	Description	Maturity	Audience	Relevant for These Roles
Properties of secure software	Core and influential properties of software that enable the understanding and description of its security characteristics	L4	E, M, L	• Executive responsible for software development • Project manager • All software engineering roles • Security analyst
Attack patterns	Formalized capture of common methods of attacking software to serve as guides for improving software attack resistance and resilience	L3	M, L	• Requirements engineer • Architect • Designer • Developer • Quality assurance engineer • Security analyst
Assurance cases	Structured mechanism for capturing, communicating, and validating desired or attained levels of software security assurance in terms of the properties of secure software	L2	M, L	• Project manager • Quality assurance engineer • Security analyst • Acquisition manager • Software supplier

Table 8–2: *Requirements Engineering Practices (Chapter 3)*

Practices in Recommended Order	Description	Maturity	Audience	Relevant for These Roles
Standard security requirements engineering process	Establish a defined process for identifying and documenting security requirements, such as SQUARE	L3	E, M, L	• Project manager
Security risk assessment	Perform a risk assessment aimed at security exposures, either as part of a project risk assessment or as a stand-alone activity	L3 for security; L4 for projects in general	M, L	• Project manager • Lead requirements engineer
Threat identification	Use techniques such as misuse/abuse cases, threat modeling, attack patterns, or attack trees to identify security threats	L3	L	• Lead requirements engineer • Security analyst

Continues

Table 8–2: *Requirements Engineering Practices (Chapter 3) (Continued)*

Practices in Recommended Order	Description	Maturity	Audience	Relevant for These Roles
Security requirements elicitation	Conduct a security requirements elicitation activity to identify potential security requirements	L2	L	• Lead requirements engineer Stakeholders
Security requirements categorization and prioritization	Categorize and prioritize security requirements to separate true requirements from architectural recommendations and to optimize cost–benefit considerations	L2	L	• Lead requirements engineer Stakeholders
Security requirements inspection	Inspect security requirements in conjunction with other requirements to ensure they are correct and complete	L2 for security; L4 for inspections in general	L	• Lead requirements engineer

Table 8–3: *Architecture and Design Practices (Chapter 4)*

Practices in Recommended Order	Brief Description	Maturity	Audience	Relevant for These Roles
Security principles	High-level perspectives/practices to provide prescriptive guidance for architecture and design	L3	M, L	• Architect • Designer • Security analyst
Attack patterns	Formalized capture of common methods of attacking software to serve as guides for improving the attack resistance and resilience of the software architecture	L3	M, L	• Requirements engineer • Architect • Designer • Developer • Quality assurance engineer • Security analyst
Architectural risk analysis	Perform a detailed risk assessment of the software architecture and design and its ability to securely support the requirements of the software	L3	M, L	• Architect • Designer • Security analyst
Security guidelines	Technology-specific prescriptive guidance founded on demonstrated experience to guide integrating security concerns into architecture and design	L3	M, L	• Architect • Designer • Developer • Security analyst

Table 8–4: *Coding and Testing Practices (Chapter 5)*

Practices in Recommended Order	*Brief Description*	*Maturity*	*Audience*	*Relevant for These Roles*
Secure coding practices	Use sound and proven secure coding practices to aid in reducing software defects introduced during implementation	L4	M, L	• Project manager • Security analyst • Developer
Source code review for security vulnerabilities	Perform source code review using static code analysis tools, metric analysis, and manual review to minimize implementation-level security bugs	L4	M, L	• Project manager • Security analyst • Developer
Unique aspects of software security testing	Understand the differences between software security testing and traditional software testing, and plan how best to address these (including thinking like an attacker and emphasizing how to exercise what the software should *not* do)	L3/4	M, L	• Project manager • Security analyst • Test engineer
Functional test cases for security	Construct meaningful functional test cases (using a range of techniques) that demonstrate the software's adherence to its functional requirements, including its security requirements (positive requirements)	L4	M, L	• Project manager • Security analyst • Test engineer

Table 8–4: *Coding and Testing Practices (Chapter 5) (Continued)*

Practices in Recommended Order	Brief Description	Maturity	Audience	Relevant for These Roles
Risk-based test cases for security	Develop risk-based test cases (using, for example, misuse/abuse cases, attack patterns, or threat modeling) that exercise common mistakes, suspected software weaknesses, and mitigations intended to reduce or eliminate risks to ensure they cannot be circumvented (negative requirements)	L3/4	M, L	• Project manager • Security analyst • Test engineer
Test cases using a range of security test strategies	Use a complement of testing strategies including white-box testing (based on deep knowledge of the source code), black-box testing (focusing on the software's externally visible behavior), and penetration testing (identifying and targeting specific vulnerabilities at the system level)	L4	M, L	• Project manager • Security analyst • Test engineer

Table 8–5: *Security Analysis for System Complexity and Scale: Mitigations (Chapter 6)*

Practices in Recommended Order	Brief Description	Maturity	Audience	Relevant for These Roles
Tackle known interface vulnerabilities first	With systems having more interfaces to less trusted systems, developers should concentrate first on known interface vulnerabilities such as those in Web services.	L3	M, L	• Project manager • Security analyst • Developer
Conduct end-to-end analysis of cross-system work processes	With increasing complexity, vulnerability analysis of individual systems is not sufficient. The security analysis of work processes that cross multiple systems has to consider the risks for those processes (including end-to-end analysis) as well as the risks that each work process creates for the systems that support it. Security analysis has to consider a wider spectrum of errors.	L3	M, L	• System architect • Security analyst
Attend to containing and recovering from failures	Assume the existence of discrepancies of some form, whether in systems, operations, or users, during the execution of work processes, particularly as usage evolves. Give increased attention to containment and recovery from failures. These should be considered in the context of business continuity analysis.	L4	M, L	• System architect • Software architect • Security analyst • Designer

Table 8–5: *Security Analysis for System Complexity and Scale: Mitigations (Chapter 6) (Continued)*

Practices in Recommended Order	Brief Description	Maturity	Audience	Relevant for These Roles
Explore failure analysis and mitigation to deal with complexity	The multiplicity of systems and increasing number of possible error states arising from their interactions can overwhelm analysis or generate too many point solutions that mitigate narrowly specified events. Explore how security could take advantage of a consolidated failure analysis and mitigation effort.	L2	M, L	• Chief information officer • System architect • Security analyst • Designer
Coordinate security efforts across organizational groups	Security is typically treated as a separate concern, with responsibility often being assigned to independent parts of the organization. It is not unusual to find that an organization's development, operational, and business groups are tackling common problems with little coordination or that some security problems have fallen through the cracks. This separation becomes even more problematic as the scope and scale of systems expand. Vulnerability analysis and mitigations should be integrated across organization units, users, technology, systems, and operations.	L4	E, M, L	• Chief information officer • Chief information security officer • System architect

Table 8–6: *Governance and Management Practices (Chapter 7)*

Practices in Recommended Order	Brief Description	Maturity	Audience	Relevant for These Roles
Risk-based definition of adequate security	Identify ways to determine what constitutes adequate security practice based on risk management, established levels of risk tolerance, and risk assessment	L4 for information security; L3 for software security	E, M, L	• Executive responsible for software development • Project manager • Lead software engineer • Lead security analyst
Continuous risk management framework	Put a continuous, business-driven risk management framework in place and periodically assess for acceptable and unacceptable levels of risk throughout the SDLC	L4	M, L	• Project manager • Lead software engineer • Lead security analyst
Software security practices integrated with SDLC	Provide recommendations for inserting security practices into the SDLC as part of traditional project management activities, including the use of defined security touchpoints at each life-cycle phase	L3	M, L	• Project manager • Lead software engineer • Lead security analyst

Table 8–6: *Governance and Management Practices (Chapter 7) (Continued)*

Practices in Recommended Order	Brief Description	Maturity	Audience	Relevant for These Roles
Software security as a cultural norm	Recognize that being security aware and understanding the importance of addressing security during software development needs to be a cultural norm (beliefs, behaviors, capabilities, actions)	L4 for information security; L3 for software security	E, M, L	• Executive responsible for software development • Project manager • Lead software engineer • Lead security analyst
Characteristics of software security at the governance/management level	Engage leaders to better appreciate and understand the characteristics and actions necessary to address software security as governance and management concerns, and the consequences of not doing so	L4 for information security; L3 for software security	E, M, L	• Executive responsible for software development • Project manager • Lead software engineer • Lead security analyst

Continues

Table 8–6: *Governance and Management Practices (Chapter 7) (Continued)*

Practices in Recommended Order	Brief Description	Maturity	Audience	Relevant for These Roles
Enterprise software security framework	Establish a framework and road-map for addressing software security as an enterprise-wide undertaking, and identify some of the pitfalls and barriers to tackle head on	L3	E, M, L	• Executive responsible for software development • Project manager • Lead software engineer • Lead security analyst
Software security included in software development measurement process	Determine how to include security as part of a software development measurement process, including suggested process and product measures, and implement, track, and report such measures	L1	M, L	• Project manager • Lead software engineer • Lead security analyst

John Steven states [Steven 2006]:

> Don't demand teams to begin conducting every activity on day one. Slowly introduce the simplest activities first, then iterate.

> [Have] patience. It will take at least three to five years to create a working, evolving software security machine. Initial organization-wide successes can be shown within a year. Use that time to obtain more buy-in and a bigger budget.

Clearly, there is no one-size-fits-all approach to software security. Project managers and their teams need to think through the choices, define their tradeoff and decision criteria, learn as they go, and understand that this effort requires continuous refinement and improvement.

The U.S. Department of Homeland Security Software Assurance Program has sponsored and provided access to a number of reports that contain additional guidance on software assurance practices in general and for project management, acquisition, and workforce competency development in particular. Downloadable current versions and drafts for review are available on the BSI Web site [BSI 47].

8.2 In Closing

We'll leave you with the five key take-away points introduced in the preface. We trust you now better understand these and can use them to build a sense of urgency and a better business case for software security engineering:

1. Software security is about more than eliminating vulnerabilities and conducting penetration tests. Project managers need to take a systematic approach to incorporate the sound practices discussed in this book into their development processes.
2. Network security mechanisms and IT infrastructure security services do not sufficiently protect application software from security risks.
3. Software security initiatives should follow a risk management approach to identify priorities and determine what is good enough, understanding that software security risks will change throughout the SDLC.

4. Building secure software depends on understanding the operational context in which it will be used.

5. Project managers and software engineers need to learn to think like an attacker to address the range of things that software should *not* do and how software can better resist, tolerate, and recover from attack.

Glossary

Accountability
For software entities that act as users (e.g., proxy agents, Web services, peer processes), the ability to record and track security-relevant actions of the software-as-user, with attribution of responsibility.

Ambiguity analysis
Identification and elimination of ambiguities in the software architecture and design due to ambiguous requirements or insufficiently specified architecture and design.

Architectural risk analysis
A high-level evaluation of a software system involving (1) characterization of the system to clearly understand its nature; (2) the identification of potential **threats** to the system; (3) an assessment of the system's vulnerability to attack; (4) an estimate of the likelihood of potential threats; (5) identification of the assets at risk and the potential impact if threats are realized; and (6) risk **mitigation** planning.

Assurance case
A structured set of arguments and a corresponding body of evidence demonstrating that a system satisfies specific claims with respect to its security, safety, or reliability properties.

Attack pattern
A pattern abstraction describing common approaches that attackers might use to attack certain kinds of software for a certain purpose. It is used to capture and represent the attacker's perspective in software security engineering.

Attack resilience
The ability to recover from **failures** that result from successful attacks by resuming operation at or above some predefined minimum acceptable level of service in a timely manner.

Attack resistance
The ability of the software to prevent the capability of an attacker to execute an attack against it.

Attack resistance analysis
The process of examining software architecture and design for common weaknesses that might lead to **vulnerabilities** and for susceptibility to common attack patterns.

Attack surface
The set of ways (functionalities, APIs, interfaces, resources, data stores, etc.) in which an attacker can attempt to enter and potentially cause damage to a system. The larger the attack surface, the more insecure the system [Manadhata 2007].

Attack tolerance
The ability of software to "tolerate" **errors** and **failures** that result from successful attacks and, in effect, continue to operate as if the attacks had not occurred.

Attack tree
A representation of the ways that an attacker could cause an event to occur that could significantly harm a system's mission. Each path through an attack tree represents a unique intrusion.

Authentication
The process of determining whether someone or something (such as a computer or software process) is, in fact, who or what it is declared to be. Methods for human authentication typically include something you know (a password), something you have (a token), or something you are (fingerprint).

Availability
The extent to which a software component, product, or system is operational and accessible to its intended, authorized users (humans and processes) whenever it is needed and, at the same time, when availability is considered as a property of software security, its functionality and privileges are inaccessible to unauthorized users (humans and processes) at all times.

Best practice; sound practice
The most efficient (least amount of effort) and effective (best results) way of accomplishing a task, based on repeatable procedures that have proven themselves over time for large numbers of people [http://en.wikipedia.org/wiki/Best_practice].

Black-box testing
Software testing using methods that do not require access to source code. Such testing usually focuses on the externally visible behavior of the software, such as requirements, protocol specifications, and interfaces.

Botnet
A number of Internet computers that, although their owners are unaware of it, have rogue software that forwards transmissions (including spam or viruses) to other computers on the Internet. Any such computer is referred to as a zombie—in effect, it is a computer "robot" or "bot" that serves the wishes of some master spam or virus originator [http://searchsecurity.techtarget.com].

Buffer overflow
An attack that targets improper or missing bounds checking on buffer operations, typically triggered by input injected by an attacker. As a consequence,

an attacker is able to write past the boundaries of allocated buffer regions in memory, causing a program crash or redirection of execution [http://capec.mitre.org/data/definitions/100.html].

Bug
A software security defect that is introduced during software implementation and can be detected locally through static and manual analysis [BSI 48].

Cache poisoning
A technique that tricks a domain name server (DNS server) into believing it has received authentic information when, in reality, it has not. If the server does not correctly validate DNS responses to ensure that they have come from an authoritative source, the server will end up caching the incorrect entries locally and serve them to users that make the same request [http://en.wikipedia.org/wiki/DNS_cache_poisoning].

Confidentiality
The extent to which the characteristics of a software component, product, or system—including its relationships with its execution environment and its users, its managed assets, and its content—are obscured or hidden from unauthorized entities.

Conformance
Planned, systematic, and multidisciplinary activities that ensure software components, products, and systems conform to requirements and applicable standards and procedures for specified uses.

Correctness
The property of software behaving exactly as specified.

Cross-site scripting (XSS)
An attack in which an attacker embeds malicious scripts in content that will be served to Web browsers. The goal of the attack is for the target software (i.e., the client-side browser) to execute the script with the user's privilege level [http://capec.mitre.org/data/definitions/63.html].

Defect
A software fault, typically either a **bug** or a **flaw.**

Defense in depth
Using multiple types and layers of security to defend an application or system so as to avoid having a single point of failure.

Denial-of-service attack
An attempt to make a computer resource unavailable to its intended users, usually to prevent an Internet site or service from functioning efficiently or at all, either temporarily or indefinitely [http://en.wikipedia.org/wiki/Denial_of_service].

Dependability
The property of software that ensures the software always operates as intended.

Dependency analysis
Analysis of the vulnerabilities and associated risk present in the underlying software platforms, operating systems, frameworks, and libraries that the software under analysis relies on in its operational environment. The software you are writing almost never exists in total isolation.

DNS cache poisoning
See **cache poisoning.**

Elevation (escalation) of privilege
A situation in which a user obtains privileges that he or she is not authorized to have.

Error
For a software system, an internal state leading to **failure** if the system does not handle the situation correctly.

Exploit
A piece of software, a chunk of data, or sequence of commands that takes advantage of a **bug,** glitch, or **vulnerability** in an effort to cause unintended or unanticipated behavior to occur [http://en.wikipedia.org/wiki/Exploit_%28computer_security%29].

Fagan inspection
A structured process set forth by M. E. Fagan [Fagan 1999] for trying to find **defects** in development documents such as programming code, specifications, designs, and others during various phases of the software development life cycle [http://en.wikipedia.org/wiki/Fagan_inspection].

Failure
For a software system, a situation in which the system does not deliver its expected service as specified or desired. Such a failure is externally observable.

Fault
The cause of an **error,** which may lead to a **failure.**

Flaw
A software security defect that originates at the architecture or design level and is instantiated in the code [BSI 48].

Hardening
Securing a system to defend it against attackers by, for example, removing unnecessary usernames or logins and removing or disabling unnecessary services [http://en.wikipedia.org/wiki/Hardening].

Identity spoofing
A situation in which one person or program successfully masquerades as another by falsifying data and thereby gains an illegitimate advantage [http://en.wikipedia.org/wiki/Spoofing_attack].

Illegal pointer values
A situation in which a software function returns a pointer to memory outside the bounds of the buffer to be searched. This can occur when an attacker controls the contents of the buffer to be searched or an attacker controls the value for which to search [http://www.owasp.org/index.php/Illegal_Pointer_Value].

Integer overflow
An attack that forces an integer variable to go out of range, leading to unexpected program behavior and possibly execution of malware by the attacker [CAPEC 2007].

Integrity
The extent to which the code, managed assets, configuration, and behavior of a software component, product, or system are resistant and resilient to unauthorized modification by authorized entities or any modification by unauthorized entities.

Malware
Malicious software (e.g., viruses, worms, and Trojan horses) that is created to do intentional harm to a computer system.

Misuse/abuse cases
Descriptive statements of the undesirable, nonstandard conditions that software is likely to face during its operation from either unintentional misuse or intentional and malicious misuse or abuse.

Mitigation
An action that can be taken to reduce the likelihood and/or impact of a risk to a software system.

Non-repudiation
For software entities that act as users (e.g., proxy agents, Web services, peer processes), the ability to prevent the software-as-user from disproving or denying responsibility for actions it has performed.

Phishing
An attempt to acquire sensitive information criminally and fraudulently, such as usernames, passwords, and credit card details, by masquerading as a trustworthy entity in an electronic communication [http://en.wikipedia.org/wiki/Phishing].

Predictable execution
Justifiable confidence that the software, when executed, functions as intended. The ability of malicious input to alter the execution or outcome in a way favorable to the attacker is significantly reduced or eliminated.

Protection profile
In the Common Criteria, a set of security requirements that a product can be evaluated and certified against.

Reasonable degree of certainty
The amount of assurance needed that security requirements have been met given a specific perceived threat, the consequences of a security breach, and the costs of security measures.

Recognize
As a property that can be used to measure software security, the ability of a software component or system to identify known **attack patterns.**

Recover
As a property that can be used to measure software security, the ability of a software component or system to isolate, contain, and limit the damage resulting from any failures caused by attack-triggered **faults** that it was unable to resist or tolerate and to resume operation as quickly as possible.

Red teaming
In the software security engineering context, red teaming is creative software penetration testing in which the test team takes a defined adversarial role and uses doctrine, tactics, techniques, and procedures appropriate to that role.

Replay attack
A form of network attack in which a valid data transmission is maliciously or fraudulently repeated or delayed. It is carried out either by the originator or by an adversary who intercepts the data and retransmits it [http://en.wikipedia.org/wiki/Replay_attack].

Repudiation
The ability of an attacker to deny performing some malicious activity because the system does not have sufficient proof otherwise [Howard 2002].

Resist
As a property that can be used to measure software security, the ability of a software component or system to prevent the capability of an attacker to execute an attack against it.

Security architecture
A framework that enables the interoperability of security features such as access control, permissions, and cryptography and integrates them with the broader software architecture.

Security governance
Directing and controlling an organization to establish and sustain a culture of security in the organization's conduct and treating adequate security as a non-negotiable requirement of being in business.

Security profile
The degree to which software meets its security requirements.

Social engineering
A collection of techniques used to manipulate people into performing actions or divulging confidential information, typically for information

gathering or computer system access [http://en.wikipedia.org/wiki/
Social_engineering_%28security%29].

Software assurance
The level of confidence that software is free from **vulnerabilities,** either intentionally designed into the software or accidentally inserted at any time during its
life cycle, and that the software functions in the intended manner [CNSS 2006].

Software reliability
The probability of **failure**-free (or otherwise satisfactory) software operation
for a specified/expected period/interval of time, or for a specified/expected
number of operations, in a specified/expected environment under specified/
expected operating conditions [Goertzel 2006, 94].

Software safety
Persistence of dependability in the face of accidents or mishaps—that is,
unplanned events that result in death, injury, illness, damage to or loss of
property, or environmental harm [Goertzel 2006, 94].

Software security
Engineering software so that it is as vulnerability and defect free as possible
and continues to function correctly in spite of attack or misuse.

Spoofing
An attack in which the identity of a person or resource is impersonated.

SQL injection
An attack exploiting software that constructs SQL statements based on user
input. An attacker crafts input strings so that when the target software constructs
SQL statements based on the input, the resulting SQL statement performs
actions other than those the application intended [http://capec.mitre.org/data/
definitions/66.html].

Stack smashing attack
Causing a stack in a computer application or operating system to overflow,
which makes it possible to subvert the program or system or cause it to crash.
The stack is a form of buffer that holds the intermediate results of an operation or data that is awaiting processing. If the stack receives more data than it
can hold, the excess data is lost [http://searchsecurity.techtarget.com].

Tampering
Modification of data within a system to achieve a malicious goal [Howard
2002].

Threat
An actor or agent that is a source of danger, capable of violating the confidentiality, integrity, and availability of information assets and security policy.

Threat analysis
The identification of relevant threats for a specific architecture, functionality,
and configuration.

Threat modeling
Combining software characterization, threat analysis, vulnerability analysis, and likely attack analysis to develop a gestalt picture of the risk posed to the software under analysis by anticipated threats.

Tolerate
As a property that can be used to measure software security, the ability of a software component or system to withstand the **errors** and **failure** that result from successful attacks and, in effect, to continue to operate as if the attacks had not occurred.

Touchpoints
Lightweight software security **best practice** activities that are applied to various software artifacts, such as requirements and code [McGraw 2006].

Trust boundaries
The boundaries between system zones of trust (areas of the system that share a common level and management mechanism of privilege—Internet, dmz, hosting LAN, host system, application server, database host, and so forth). These trust boundaries are often ripe with vulnerabilities because systems fail to properly segregate and manage differing levels of privilege.

Trustworthiness
A situation in which the number of exploitable **vulnerabilities** in a software product is intentionally minimized to the greatest extent possible. The goal is no exploitable vulnerabilities.

Use case
In requirements elicitation, a description of a complete transaction between one or more actors and a system in normal, expected use of the system.

Vulnerability
A software **defect** that an attacker can exploit.

White-box testing
Performing security analysis of software, including its deployed environment, with knowledge of the architecture, design, and implementation of the software.

Whitelist
A list of all known good inputs that a system is permitted to accept.

Zone of trust
Elements of a software system that share a specific level and management mechanism of privilege.

References

[AESRM 2005]
Alliance for Enterprise Security Risk Management. "Convergence of Enterprise Security Organizations." Booz Allen Hamilton, November 8, 2005. http://www.asisonline.org/newsroom/alliance.pdf

[Ahl 2005]
Ahl, V. "An Experimental Comparison of Five Prioritization Methods." Master's thesis, School of Engineering, Blekinge Institute of Technology, Ronneby, Sweden, 2005.

[Alberts 2003]
Alberts, Christopher J., & Dorofee, Audrey J. *Managing Information Security Risks: The OCTAVE^SM Approach.* Boston, MA: Addison-Wesley, 2003.

[Aleph One 1996]
Aleph One. "Smashing the Stack for Fun and Profit." *Phrack Magazine 7,* 49 (1996): file 14 of 16. http://www.phrack.org/issues.html?issue=49

[Alexander 1964]
Alexander, Christopher. *Notes on the Synthesis of Form.* Cambridge, MA: Harvard University Press, 1964.

[Alexander 1977]
Alexander, Christopher, Ishikawa, Sara, & Silverstein, Murray. *A Pattern Language.* New York: Oxford University Press, 1977.

[Alexander 1979]
Alexander, Christopher. *A Timeless Way of Building.* New York: Oxford University Press, 1979.

[Alexander 2002]
Alexander, Ian. "Misuse Cases Help to Elicit Non-Functional Requirements." http://easyweb.easynet.co.uk/~iany/consultancy/misuse_cases/misuse_cases.htm

[Alexander 2003]
Alexander, Ian. "Misuse Cases: Use Cases with Hostile Intent." *IEEE Software 20,* 1 (2003): 58–66.

[Allen 2005]
Allen, Julia. *Governing for Enterprise Security* (CMU/SEI-2005-TN-023, ADA441250). Pittsburgh, PA: Software Engineering Institute, Carnegie

Mellon University, June 2005. http://www.sei.cmu.edu/publications/documents/05.reports/05tn023.html

[Allen 2007]
Allen, Julia H., & Westby, Jody R. "Characteristics of Effective Security Governance." *Governing for Enterprise Security Implementation Guide*, 2007. http://www.cert.org/governance/ges.html

[Anderson 2001]
Anderson, Ross. *Security Engineering: A Guide to Building Dependable Distributed Systems*. New York: John Wiley & Sons, 2001.

[Anton 2001]
Anton, A. I., Dempster, J. H., & Siege, D. F. "Deriving Goals from a Use Case Based Requirements Specification for an Electronic Commerce System," 10–19. *Proceedings of the Sixth International Workshop on Requirements Engineering: Foundation for Software Quality (REFSQ 2000)*. Stockholm, Sweden, June 5–6, 2000. London, UK: Springer-London, 2001.

[Arkin 2005]
Arkin, Brad, Stender, Scott, & McGraw, Gary. "Software Penetration Testing." *IEEE Security & Privacy Magazine 3*, 1 (January/February 2005): 84–87.

[Avizienis 2004]
Avizienis, Algirdas, Laprie, Jean-Claude, Randell, Brian, & Landwehr, Carl. "Basic Concepts and Taxonomy of Dependable and Secure Computing." *IEEE Transactions on Dependable and Secure Computing 1*, 1 (January–March 2004): 11–33.

[Beck 2004]
Beck, Kent, & Andres, Cynthia. *Extreme Programming Explained: Embrace Change* (2nd ed.). Boston, MA: Addison-Wesley, 2004.

[Beizer 1995]
Beizer, Boris. *Black-Box Testing: Techniques for Functional Testing of Software and Systems*. New York: John Wiley & Sons, 1995.

[Berinato 2002]
Berinato, Scott. "Finally, a Real Return on Security Spending." *CIO Magazine (Australia)*, April 8, 2002. http://www.cio.com.au/index.php/id;557330171

[Binder 1999]
Binder, R. V. *Testing Object-Oriented Systems: Models, Patterns, and Tools* (Addison-Wesley Object Technology Series). Reading, MA: Addison-Wesley, 1999.

[Bishop 1996]
Bishop, Matt, & Dilger, M. "Checking for Race Conditions in File Accesses." *The USENIX Association, Computing Systems*, Spring 1996: 131–152.

[Bishop 2002]
Bishop, Matt. *Computer Security: Art and Science*. Boston, MA: Addison-Wesley, 2002.

[Black 2002]
Black, Rex. *Managing the Testing Process: Practical Tools and Techniques for Managing Hardware and Software Testing* (2nd ed.). New York: John Wiley & Sons, 2002.

[Blum 2006]
Blum, D. *Making Business Sense of Information Security, Security and Risk Management Strategies*, Version 1.0. Burton Group, February 10, 2006.

[Boehm 1987]
Boehm, Barry W. "Improving Software Productivity." *Computer 20*, 9 (September 1987): 43–57.

[Boehm 1988]
Boehm, Barry W., & Papaccio, Philip N. "Understanding and Controlling Software Costs. *IEEE Transactions on Software Engineering 14*, 10 (October 1988): 1462–1477.

[Boehm 1989]
Boehm, B., & Ross, R. "Theory-W Software Project Management: Principles and Examples." *IEEE Transactions on Software Engineering 15*, 4 (July 1989): 902–916.

[Boehm 2007]
Boehm, Barry, & Lane, Jo Ann. *Using the Incremental Commitment Model to Integrate System Acquisition, Systems Engineering, and Software Engineering* (USC-CSSE-2007-715). Los Angeles, CA: University of Southern California Center for Systems and Software Engineering, 2007.

[Booch 2005]
Booch, Grady. Architecture Web Log. http://www.booch.com/architecture/blog.jsp (2005).

[Bowen 2006]
Bowen, Pauline, Hash, Joan, & Wilson, Mark. *Information Security Handbook: A Guide for Managers* (NIST Special Publication 800-100). Gaithersburg, MD: Computer Security Division, Information Technology Laboratory, National Institute of Standards and Technology, October 2006. http://csrc.nist.gov/publications/nistpubs/800-100/SP800-100-Mar07-2007.pdf

[Brackett 1990]
Brackett, J. W. *Software Requirements* (SEI-CM-19-1.2, ADA235642). Pittsburgh, PA: Software Engineering Institute, Carnegie Mellon University, 1990. http://www.sei.cmu.edu/publications/documents/cms/cm.019.html

[Butler 2002]
Butler, Shawn. "Security Attribute Evaluation Method: A Cost–Benefit Approach," 232–240. *Proceedings of the 24th International Conference on Software Engineering.* Orlando, FL, May 19–25, 2002. New York: ACM Press, 2002.

[Cameron 2005]
Cameron, Kim. *The Laws of Identity.* http://www.identityblog.com/stories/2004/12/09/thelaws.html (2005).

[CAPEC 2007]
MITRE Corporation. *Common Attack Pattern Enumeration and Classification.* http://capec.mitre.org (2007).

[Cappelli 2006]
Cappelli, Dawn, Trzeciak, Randall, & Moore, Andrew. "Insider Threats in the SDLC." Presentation at SEPG 2006. Carnegie Mellon University, Software Engineering Institute, 2006. http://www.cert.org/insider_threat/

[Caralli 2004a]
Caralli, Richard. *The Critical Success Factor Method: Establishing a Foundation for Enterprise Security Management* (CMU/SEI-2004-TR-010, ADA443742). Pittsburgh, PA: Software Engineering Institute, Carnegie Mellon University, 2004. http://www.sei.cmu.edu/publications/documents/04.reports/04tr010.html

[Caralli 2004b]
Caralli, Richard. *Managing for Enterprise Security* (CMU/SEI-2004-TN-046, ADA430839). Pittsburgh, PA: Software Engineering Institute, Carnegie Mellon University, 2004. http://www.sei.cmu.edu/publications/documents/04.reports/04tn046.html

[Caralli 2006]
Caralli, Richard. *Sustaining Operational Resiliency: A Process Improvement Approach to Security Management.* (CMU/SEI-2006-TN-009, ADA446757). Pittsburgh, PA: Software Engineering Institute, Carnegie Mellon University, 2006. http://www.sei.cmu.edu/publications/documents/06.reports/06tn009.html

[Caralli 2007]
Caralli, Richard, Stevens, James F., Wallen, Charles M., White, David W., Wilson, William R., & Young, Lisa R. *Introducing the CERT Resiliency Engineering Framework: Improving the Security and Sustainability Processes* (CMU/SEI-2007-TR-009). Pittsburgh, PA: Software Engineering Institute, Carnegie Mellon University, 2006. http://www.sei.cmu.edu/publications/documents/07.reports/07tr009.html

[Carey 2006]
Carey, Allan. "2006 Global Information Security Workforce Study." Framingham, MA: IDC, 2006. https://www.isc2.org/download/workforcestudy06.pdf

[CERT 2007]
CERT Insider Threat Research. http://www.cert.org/insider_threat/ (2007).

[CCMB 2005a]
Common Criteria Management Board. *Common Criteria for Information Technology Security Evaluation Version 2.3*, Parts 1–3 (CCMB-2005-08-001/002/003), August 2005. http://www.commoncriteriaportal.org/public/thecc.html

[CCMB 2005b]
Common Criteria Management Board. *Common Methodology for Information Technology Security Evaluation* (CCMB-2005-08-004), August 2005. http://www.commoncriteriaportal.org/public/thecc.html

[Charette 2005]
Charette, R. N. "Why Software Fails." *IEEE Spectrum 42*, 9 (September 2005): 42–49.

[Checkland 1990]
Checkland, Peter. *Soft Systems Methodology in Action*. Toronto, Ontario, Canada: John Wiley & Sons, 1990.

[Chen 2004]
Chen, P., Dean, M., Ojoko-Adams, D., Osman, H., Lopez, L., & Xie, N. *Systems Quality Requirements Engineering (SQUARE) Methodology: Case Study on Asset Management System* (CMU/SEI-2004-SR-015, ADA431068). Pittsburgh, PA: Software Engineering Institute, Carnegie Mellon University, 2004. http://www.sei.cmu.edu/publications/documents/04.reports/04sr015.html

[Chess 2004]
Chess, Brian, & McGraw, Gary. "Static Analysis for Security." *IEEE Security & Privacy 2*, 6 (November/December 2004): 76–79.

[Chess 2007]
Chess, Brian, & West, Jacob. *Secure Programming with Static Analysis*. Boston, MA: Addison-Wesley, 2007.

[Christel 1992]
Christel, M., & Kang, K. *Issues in Requirements Elicitation* (CMU/SEI-92-TR-012, ADA258932). Pittsburgh, PA: Software Engineering Institute, Carnegie Mellon University, 1992. http://www.sei.cmu.edu/publications/documents/92.reports/92.tr.012.html

[Chung 2006]
Chung, L., Hung, F., Hough, E., & Ojoko-Adams, D. *Security Quality Requirements Engineering (SQUARE): Case Study Phase III* (CMU/SEI-2006-SR-003). Pittsburgh, PA: Software Engineering Institute, Carnegie Mellon University, 2006. http://www.sei.cmu.edu/publications/documents/06.reports/06sr003.html

[CNSS 2006]
Committee on National Security Systems. "National Information Assurance (IA) Glossary, Instruction No. 4009." Ft. Meade, MD: CNSS Secretariat, June 2006. http://www.cnss.gov/Assets/pdf/cnssi_4009.pdf

[Cornford 2004]
Cornford, Steven L., Feather, Martin S., & Hicks, Kenneth A. *DDP—A Tool for Life-Cycle Risk Management.* http://ddptool.jpl.nasa.gov/docs/f344d-slc.pdf (2004).

[COSO 2004]
Committee of Sponsoring Organizations of the Treadway Commission. "Enterprise Risk Management—Integrated Framework." September 2004. The executive summary and ordering information are available at http://www.coso.org.

[CVE 2007]
MITRE Corporation. *Common Vulnerabilities and Exposures.* http://cve.mitre.org (2007).

[CWE 2007]
MITRE Corporation. *Common Weakness Enumeration.* http://cwe.mitre.org (2007).

[Davis 2003]
Davis, A. "The Art of Requirements Triage." *IEEE Computer, 36,* 3 (March 2003): 42–49.

[Davis 2005a]
Davis, A. *Just Enough Requirements Management: Where Software Development Meets Marketing.* New York: Dorset House, 2005.

[Davis 2005b]
Davis, Noopur. *Secure Software Development Life Cycle Processes* (CMU/SEI-2005-TN-024, ADA447047). Pittsburgh, PA: Software Engineering Institute, Carnegie Mellon University, 2005. http://www.sei.cmu.edu/publications/documents/05.reports/05tn024.html

[Deloitte 2007]
Deloitte Touche Tohmatsu. *2007 Global Security Survey: The Shifting Security Paradigm.* September 2007. http://www.deloitte.com/

[Denning 1998]
Denning, Dorothy E. *Information Warfare and Security.* Reading, MA: Addison-Wesley, 1998.

[DHS 2003]
Department of Homeland Security. *National Strategy to Secure Cyberspace.* Action-Recommendation 2-14, February 2003. http://www.whitehouse.gov/pcipb/cyberspace_strategy.pdf

[Dijkstra 1970]
Dijkstra, E. W. "Structured Programming," 84–88. *Software Engineering Techniques.* Edited by J. N. Buxton and B. Randall. Brussels, Belgium: NATO Scientific Affairs Division, 1970.

[Dustin 1999]
Dustin, E., Rashka, J., & Paul, J. *Automated Software Testing*. Reading, MA: Addison-Wesley, 1999.

[Ellison 2003]
Ellison, Robert J., & Moore, Andrew. P. *Trustworthy Refinement Through Intrusion-Aware Design* (CMU/SEI-2003-TR-002, ADA414865). Pittsburgh, PA: Software Engineering Institute, Carnegie Mellon University, 2003. http://www.sei.cmu.edu/publications/documents/03.reports/03tr002.html

[Fagan 1999]
Fagan, Michael E. "Design and Code Inspections to Reduce Errors in Program Development." *IBM Systems Journal 38*, 2 & 3 (1999): 258–287. http://www.research.ibm.com/journal/sj/382/fagan.pdf

[Fedchak 2007]
Fedchak, Elaine, McGibbon, Thomas, & Vienneau, Robert. *Software Project Management for Software Assurance: A DACS State-of-the-Art Report*. DACS Report Number 34717, 30 September 2007. https://buildsecurityin.us-cert.gov/daisy/bsi/resources/dhs/906.html

[Fewster 1999]
Fewster, Mark, & Graham, Dorothy. *Software Test Automation*. Reading, MA: Addison-Wesley, 1999.

[Fink 1997]
Fink, G., & Bishop, M. "Property-Based Testing: A New Approach to Testing for Assurance." ACM SIGSOFT *Software Engineering Notes 22*, 4 (July 1997): 74–80.

[Fyodor 2006]
Fyodor. "Top 100 Network Security Tools." Insecure.org, http://sectools.org/ (2006).

[Gamma 1995]
Gamma, E., Helm, R., Johnson, R., & Vlissides, J. *Design Patterns: Elements of Reusable Object-Oriented Software*. Reading, MA: Addison-Wesley, 1995.

[GAO 1999]
U.S. General Accounting Office. "Information Security Risk Assessment: Practices of Leading Organizations, A Supplement to GAO's May 1998 Executive Guide on Information Security Management." Washington, DC: U.S. General Accounting Office, 1999.

[Gaudin 2007]
Gaudin, Sharon. "TJX Breach Costs Hit $17M." *Information Week*, May 18, 2007.

[Gilb 1988]
Gilb, Tom. *Principles of Software Engineering Management*. Reading, MA: Addison-Wesley, 1988.

[Goertzel 2006]
Goertzel, Karen Mercedes, Winograd, Theodore, McKinley, Holly Lynne, & Holley, Patrick. *Security in the Software Lifecycle: Making Software Development Processes—and Software Produced by Them—More Secure*, Draft version 1.2. U.S. Department of Homeland Security, August 2006. http://www.cert.org/books/secureswe/SecuritySL.pdf

[Goertzel 2007]
Goertzel, Karen Mercedes, Winograd, Theodore, McKinley, Holly Lynne, et al. *Software Security Assurance: A State-of-the-Art Report (SOAR)*. Herndon, VA: Information Assurance Technology Analysis Center (IATAC) and Defense Technical Information Center (DTIC), 2007. http://iac.dtic.mil/iatac/download/security.pdf

[Goldenson 2003]
Goldenson, Dennis R., & Gibson, Diane L. *Demonstrating the Impact and Benefits of CMMI: An Update and Preliminary Results* (CMU/SEI-2003-SR-009, ADA418481). Pittsburgh, PA: Software Engineering Institute, Carnegie Mellon University, October 2003. http://www.sei.cmu.edu/publications/documents/03.reports/03sr009.html

[Gong 2003]
Gong, Li, Ellison, Gary, & Dageforde, Mary. *Inside Java 2 Platform Security: Architecture, API Design, and Implementation* (2nd ed.). Boston, MA: Addison-Wesley, 2003.

[Goodman 2007]
Goodman, Seymour E., Aucsmith, David, Bellovin, Steven M., et al. *Towards a Safer and More Secure Cyberspace*. Edited by Seymour E. Goodman and Herbert S. Lin. Washington, DC: National Academy Press, 2007 (draft). http://books.nap.edu/catalog.php?record_id=11925

[Gordon 2005]
Gordon, D., Mead, N. R., Stehney, T., Wattas, N., & Yu, E. *System Quality Requirements Engineering (SQUARE): Case Study on Asset Management System, Phase II* (CMU/SEI-2005-SR-005, ADA441304). Pittsburgh, PA: Software Engineering Institute, Carnegie Mellon University, 2005. http://www.sei.cmu.edu/publications/documents/05.reports/05sr005.html

[Gordon 2006]
Gordon, L. A., & Loeb, M. P. "Budgeting Process for Information Security Expenditures." *Communications of the ACM 49*, 1 (January 2006): 121–125.

[Graff 2003]
Graff, Mark G., & Van Wyk, Kenneth R. *Secure Coding: Principles and Practices*. Sebastopol, CA: O'Reilly, 2003.

[Haimes 2004]
Haimes, Yacov Y. *Risk Modeling, Assessment, and Management* (2nd ed.). Hoboken, NJ: John Wiley & Sons, 2004.

[Heitmeyer 2002]
Heitmeyer, Constance. "Software Cost Reduction," 1374–1380. *Encyclopedia of Software Engineering.* Edited by John J. Marciniak. 2 vols. New York: John Wiley & Sons, 2002.

[Hickey 2003]
Hickey, A., Davis, A., & Kaiser, D. "Requirements Elicitation Techniques: Analyzing the Gap Between Technology Availability and Technology Use." *Comparative Technology Transfer and Society 1*, 3 (December 2003): 279–302.

[Hickey 2004]
Hickey, A., & Davis, A. "A Unified Model of Requirements Elicitation." *Journal of Management Information Systems 20*, 4 (Spring 2004): 65–84.

[Hoglund 2004]
Hoglund, Greg, & McGraw, Gary. *Exploiting Software: How to Break Code.* Boston, MA: Addison-Wesley, 2004.

[Hope 2004]
Hope, Paco, McGraw, Gary, & Anton, Annie I. "Misuse and Abuse Cases: Getting Past the Positive." *IEEE Security & Privacy 2*, 3 (May/June 2004): 90–92.

[Howard 2002]
Howard, Michael, & LeBlanc, David C. *Writing Secure Code* (2nd ed.). Redmond, WA: Microsoft Press, 2002.

[Howard 2005]
Howard, Michael, LeBlanc, David, & Viega, John. *19 Deadly Sins of Software Security.* Emeryville, CA: McGraw-Hill/Osborne Media, 2005.

[Howard 2006]
Howard, Michael, & Lipner, Steve. *The Security Development Lifecycle—SDL: A Process for Developing Demonstrably More Secure Software.* Redmond, WA: Microsoft Press, 2006.

[Howard 2007]
Howard, Michael. "Lessons Learned from Five Years of Building More Secure Software." *MSDN Magazine,* November 2007. http://msdn2.microsoft.com/en-us/mazagine/cc163310.aspx

[Huang 2006]
Huang, C. Derrick, Hu, Qing, & Behara, Ravi S. "Economics of Information Security Investment in the Case of Simultaneous Attacks." *Fifth Workshop on the Economics of Information Security (WEIS 2006).* University of Cambridge, Cambridge, UK, June 26–28, 2006. http://weis2006.econinfosec.org/docs/15.pdf

[Hubbard 1999]
Hubbard, R. "Design, Implementation, and Evaluation of a Process to Structure the Collection of Software Project Requirements." Ph.D. dissertation, Colorado Technical University, 1999.

[Hubbard 2000]
Hubbard, R., Mead, N., & Schroeder, C. "An Assessment of the Relative Efficiency of a Facilitator-Driven Requirements Collection Process with Respect to the Conventional Interview Method." *Proceedings of the International Conference on Requirements Engineering*. June 2000. Los Alamitos, CA: IEEE Computer Society Press, 2000.

[IEEE 1990]
IEEE Standards Coordinating Committee (IEEE). *IEEE Standard Glossary of Software Engineering Terminology* (IEEE Std 610.12-1990). Los Alamitos, CA: IEEE Computer Society, 1991.

[IIA 2001]
Institute of Internal Auditors. "Information Security Governance: What Directors Need to Know." IIA, 2001. http://www.theiia.org/index.cfm

[ITGI 2006]
IT Governance Institute. "Information Security Governance: Guidance for Boards of Directors and Executive Management, Second Edition." ITGI, 2006. http://www.isaca.org (downloads).

[Jacobson 1992]
Jacobson, Ivar. *Object-Oriented Software Engineering: A Use Case Driven Approach*. Reading, MA: Addison-Wesley, 1992.

[Jaquith 2002]
Jaquith, Andrew. *The Security of Applications: Not All Are Created Equal* (@atstake Security Research Report) (2002). http://www.securitymanagement.com/archive/library/atstake_tech0502.pdf

[Johansson 2005]
Johansson, Olof, & Torvalds, Linus. "Fix Possible futex mmap_sem Deadlock." http://linux.bkbits.net:8080/linux-2.6/cset@421cfc11zFsK9gxvSJ2t__FCmuUd3Q (2005).

[Jones 1986a]
Jones, Capers (Ed.). *Tutorial: Programming Productivity: Issues for the Eighties* (2nd ed.). Los Angeles, CA: IEEE Computer Society Press, 1986.

[Jones 1986b]
Jones, Capers. *Programming Productivity*. New York: McGraw-Hill, 1986.

[Jones 1991]
Jones, Capers. *Applied Software Measurement: Assuring Productivity and Quality*. New York: McGraw-Hill, 1991.

[Jones 1994]
Jones, Capers. *Assessment and Control of Software Risks*. Englewood Cliffs, NJ: Prentice Hall, 1994.

[Jones 2005]
Jones, Jack. "An Introduction to Factor Analysis of Information Risk (FAIR): A Framework for Understanding, Analyzing, and Measuring Information Risk." Jack A. Jones, 2005. http://journals.sfu.ca/nujia/index.php/nujia/article/download/9/9

[Kaner 1999]
Kaner, Cem, Falk, Jack, & Nguyen, Hung Quoc. *Testing Computer Software* (2nd ed.). New York: John Wiley & Sons, 1999.

[Kang 1990]
Kang, K., Cohen, S., Hess, J., Novak, W., & Peterson, A. *Feature-Oriented Domain Analysis (FODA) Feasibility Study* (CMU/SEI-90-TR-021, ADA235785). Pittsburgh, PA: Software Engineering Institute, Carnegie Mellon University, 1990. http://www.sei.cmu.edu/publications/documents/90.reports/90.tr.021.html

[Karlsson 1995]
Karlsson, J. "Towards a Strategy for Software Requirements Selection. Licentiate." Thesis 513, Linkping University, October 1995.

[Karlsson 1996]
Karlsson, J. "Software Requirements Prioritizing," 110–116. *Proceedings of the Second International Conference on Requirements Engineering (ICRE '96).* Colorado Springs, CO, April 15–18, 1996. Los Alamitos, CA: IEEE Computer Society, 1996.

[Karlsson 1997]
Karlsson, J., & Ryan, K. "Cost–Value Approach for Prioritizing Requirements." *IEEE Software 14,* 5 (September/October 1997): 67–74.

[Kean 1997]
Kean, L. "Feature-Oriented Domain Analysis." *Software Technology Roadmap.* (1997). http://www.sei.cmu.edu/str/descriptions/foda_body.html

[Kelly 2004]
Kelly, Tim P., & Weaver, Rob A. "The Goal Structuring Notation: A Safety Argument Notation." *Proceedings of the Dependable Systems and Networks 2004 Workshop on Assurance Cases,* July 2004. http://www.aitcnet.org/Assurance-Cases/agenda.html

[Kitson 1993]
Kitson, David H., & Masters, Stephen. "An Analysis of SEI Software Process Assessment Results, 1987–1991," 68–77. *Proceedings of the Fifteenth International Conference on Software Engineering.* Baltimore, MD, May 17–21, 1993. Washington, DC: IEEE Computer Society Press, 1993.

[Koizol 2004]
Koizol, Jack, Litchfield, D., Aitel, D., Anley, C., Eren, S., Mehta, N., & Riley. H. *The Shellcoder's Handbook: Discovering and Exploiting Security Holes.* Indianapolis, IN: Wiley, 2004.

[Kunz 1970]
Kunz, Werner, & Rittel, Horst. "Issues as Elements of Information Systems." http://www-iurd.ced.berkeley.edu/pub/WP-131.pdf (1970)

[Leffingwell 2003]
Leffingwell, D., & Widrig, D. *Managing Software Requirements: A Use Case Approach* (2nd ed.). Boston, MA: Addison-Wesley, 2003.

[Leveson 2004]
Leveson, Nancy. "A Systems-Theoretic Approach to Safety in Software-Intensive Systems." *IEEE Transactions on Dependable and Secure Computing 1,* 1 (January–March 2004): 66–86. http://sunnyday.mit.edu/papers/tdsc.pdf

[Lipner 2005]
Lipner, Steve. & Howard, Michael. *The Trustworthy Computing Security Development Lifecycle.* http://msdn2.microsoft.com/en-us/library/ms995349.aspx

[Lipson 2001]
Lipson, Howard F., Mead, Nancy R., & Moore, Andrew P. *A Risk-Management Approach to the Design of Survivable COTS-Based Systems.* http://www.cert.org/research/isw/isw2001/papers/Lipson-29-08-a.pdf (2001).

[Lipson 2002]
Lipson, Howard, Mead, Nancy, & Moore, Andrew. "Can We Ever Build Survivable Systems from COTS Components?" *Proceedings of the 14th International Conference on Advanced Information Systems Engineering (CAiSE '02).* Toronto, Ontario, Canada, May 27–31, 2002. Heidelberg, Germany: Springer-Verlag (LNCS 2348), 2002.

[Lousteau 2003]
Lousteau, Carolyn L., & Reid, Mark E. "Internal Control Systems for Auditor Independence." *CPA Journal,* January 2006. http://www.nysscpa.org/cpa-journal/2003/0103/features/f013603.htm

[Manadhata 2007]
Manadhata, Pratyusa K., Kaynar, Dilsun K., & Wing, Jeannette M. *A Formal Model for a System's Attack Surface* (CMU-CS-07-144). Pittsburgh, PA: School of Computer Science, Carnegie Mellon University, 2007. http://reports-archive.adm.cs.cmu.edu/anon/2007/CMU-CS-07-144.pdf

[Manson 2001]
Manson, J., & Pugh, W. "Core Semantics of Multithreaded Java," 29–38. *Proceedings of the 2001 Joint ACM–ISCOPE Conference on Java Grande.* Palo Alto, CA, 2001. New York: ACM Press, 2001. DOI= http://doi.acm.org/10.1145/376656.376806

[Manson 2005]
Manson, J., Pugh, W., & Adve, S. V. "The Java Memory Model," 378–391. *Proceedings of the 32nd ACM SIGPLAN–SIGACT Symposium on Principles of Programming Languages.* Long Beach, CA, January 12–14, 2005. New York: ACM Press, 2005. DOI= http://doi.acm.org/10.1145/1040305.1040336

[Marick 1994]
Marick, Brian. *The Craft of Software Testing: Subsystems Testing Including Object-Based and Object-Oriented Testing.* Upper Saddle River, NJ: Prentice Hall, 1994.

[McCollum 2004]
McCollum, Tim. "MacLean: Auditors Play Key Role Against IT Threats." *IT Audit 7.* Institute of Internal Auditors, May 2004. http://www.theiia.org/itaudit/index.cfm?fuseaction=forum&fid=5514

[McConnell 1996]
McConnell, Steve. "Software Quality at Top Speed." *Software Development,* August 1996. http://www.stevemcconnell.com

[McConnell 2001]
McConnell, Steve. "From the Editor—An Ounce of Prevention." *IEEE Software 18,* 3 (May 2001): 5–7.

[McGraw 2006]
McGraw, Gary. *Software Security: Building Security In.* Boston, MA: Addison-Wesley, 2006.

[Mead 2002]
Mead, N. R. *Survivable Systems Analysis Method.* http://www.cert.org/archive/html/analysis-method.html (2002).

[Mead 2005]
Mead, N. R., Hough, E., & Stehney, T. *Security Quality Requirements Engineering (SQUARE) Methodology* (CMU/SEI-2005-TR-009, ADA452453). Pittsburgh, PA: Software Engineering Institute, Carnegie Mellon University, 2005. http://www.sei.cmu.edu/publications/documents/05.reports/05tr009.html

[Meunier 2006]
Meunier, Pascal. "What Is Secure Software Engineering?" CERIAS Weblogs, 2006. http://www.cerias.purdue.edu/weblogs/pmeunier/secure-it-practices/post-29/what-is-secure-software-engineering/

[Moffett 2004]
Moffett, Jonathan D., Haley, Charles B., & Nuseibeh, Bashar. *Core Security Requirements Artefacts* (Technical Report 2004/23). Milton Keynes, UK: Department of Computing, Open University, June 2004. http://computing.open.ac.uk

[Moisiadis 2000]
Moisiadis, F. "Prioritising Scenario Evolution," 85–94. *Proceedings of the Fourth International Conference on Requirements Engineering (ICRE 2000).* June 19–23, 2000. Los Alamitos, CA: IEEE Computer Society, 2000.

[Moisiadis 2001]
Moisiadis, F. "A Requirements Prioritisation Tool." *6th Australian Workshop on Requirements Engineering (AWRE 2001).* Sydney, Australia, November 2001.

[Moore 2001]
Moore, A. P., Ellison, R. J., & Linger, R. C. *Attack Modeling for Information Security and Survivability* (CMU/SEI-2001-TN-001, ADA388771). Pittsburgh, PA: Software Engineering Institute, Carnegie Mellon University, 2001. http://www.sei.cmu.edu/publications/documents/01.reports/01tn001.html

[Nagaratnam 2005]
Nagaratnam, N., Nadalin, A., Hondo, M., McIntosh, M., & Austel, P. "Business-Driven Application Security: From Modeling to Managing Secure Applications." *IBM Systems Journal 44*, 4 (2005): 847–867.

[Neumann 2004]
Neumann, Peter G. "Principled Assuredly Trustworthy Composable Architectures" (Final Report to DARPA, CDRL A001). Menlo Park, CA: Computer Science Laboratory, SRI International, December, 28, 2004. http://www.csl.sri.com/users/neumann/chats4.html

[NIAC 2005]
National Infrastructure Advisory Council. "Risk Management Approaches to Protection, Final Report and Recommendations by the Council." NIAC, October 11, 2005. http://www.dhs.gov/xlibrary/assets/niac/NIAC_RMWG_-_2-13-06v9_FINAL.pdf

[Nichols 2007]
Nichols, Elizabeth, & Peterson, Gunnar. "A Metrics Framework to Drive Application Security Improvement." *IEEE Security & Privacy 5*, 2 (March/April 2007): 88–91.

[NIST 2002]
National Institute of Standards and Technology. *Risk Management Guide for Information Technology Systems* (NIST 800-30). http://csrc.nist.gov/publications/nistpubs/800-30/sp800-30.pdf (2002).

[NIST 2007]
NIST. *National Vulnerability Database*. http://nvd.nist.gov (2007).

[NSA 2004]
National Security Agency. *INFOSEC Assessment Methodology*. http://www.iatrp.com/iam.php (2004).

[Over 2002]
Over, James. "Team Software Process for Secure Systems Development." Pittsburgh, PA: Software Engineering Institute, Carnegie Mellon University, 2002. http://www.sei.cmu.edu/tsp/tsp-secure-presentation/tsp-secure.pdf

[Park 1999]
Park, J., Port, D., & Boehm B. "Supporting Distributed Collaborative Prioritization for Win-Win Requirements Capture and Negotiation," 578–584. *Proceedings of the International Third World Multi-conference on Systemics,*

Cybernetics and Informatics (SCI99), Vol. 2. Orlando, FL, July 31–August 4, 1999. Orlando, FL: International Institute of Informatics and Systemics (IIIS), 1999.

[PCI 2006]
Payment Card Industry. *Payment Card Industry (PCI) Data Security Standard, Version 1.1.* PCI Security Standards Council, September 2006. https://www.pcisecuritystandards.org/tech/

[Perillo 1997]
Perillo, Robert J. "AT&T Database Glitch Caused '800' Phone Outage." *Telecom Digest 17,* 253 (September 18, 1997). http://massis.lcs.mit.edu/archives/back.issues/1997.volume.17/vol17.iss251-300

[PITAC 2005]
President's Information Technology Advisory Committee. *Cyber Security: A Crisis of Prioritization.* Arlington, VA: National Coordination Office for Information Technology Research and Development, PITAC, February 2005. http://www.nitrd.gov/pitac/reports/20050301_cybersecurity/cybersecurity.pdf

[PSM 2005]
Practical Software and Systems Measurement (PSM). *Security Measurement, White Paper v2.0* (2005). http://www.psmsc.com/Downloads/Other/Security%20White%20Paper%202.0.pdf

[Pugh 1999]
Pugh, W. "Fixing the Java Memory Model," 89–98. *Proceedings of the ACM 1999 Conference on Java Grande.* San Francisco, CA, June 12–14, 1999. New York: ACM Press, 1999. DOI= http://doi.acm.org/10.1145/304065.304106

[QFD 2005]
QFD Institute. *Frequently Asked Questions About QFD.* http://www.qfdi.org/what_is_qfd/faqs_about_qfd.htm (2005).

[Reifer 2003]
Reifer, D., Boehm, B., & Gangadharan, M. "Estimating the Cost of Security for COTS Software," 178–186. *Proceedings of the Second International Conference on COTS-Based Software Systems.* Ottawa, Ontario, Canada, February 2003. Springer, Lecture Notes in Computer Science, 2003.

[Rumbaugh 1994]
Rumbaugh, J. "Getting Started: Using Use Cases to Capture Requirements." *Journal of Object-Oriented Programming 7,* 5 (September 1994): 8–23.

[Saaty 1980]
Saaty, T. L. *The Analytic Hierarchy Process.* New York: McGraw-Hill, 1980.

[SAE 2004]
SAE. *JA 1002 Software Reliability Program Standard.* Society of Automotive Engineers, January 2004. http://www.sae.org/technical/standards/JA1002_200401

[Saltzer 1975]
Saltzer, Jerome H., & Schroeder, Michael D. "The Protection of Information in Computer Systems," 1278–1308. *Proceedings of the IEEE 63*, 9 (September 1975).

[Schechter 2004]
Schechter, Stuart Edward. "Computer Security Strength and Risk: A Quantitative Approach." PhD dissertation, Harvard University, 2004. http://www.eecs.harvard.edu/~stuart/papers/thesis.pdf

[Schiffrin 1994]
Schiffrin, D. *Approaches to Discourse*. Oxford, UK: Blackwell, 1994.

[Schneider 1999]
Schneider, Fred B. (Ed.). *Trust in Cyberspace*. Washington, DC: National Academies Press, 1999. http://www.nap.edu/books/0309065585/html/R1.html

[Schneier 2000]
Schneier, Bruce. *Secrets and Lies: Digital Security in a Networked World*. New York, NY: John Wiley & Sons, 2000.

[Schneier 2003]
Schneier, Bruce. *Beyond Fear*. New York: Copernicus Books, 2003.

[Schwartz 2007]
Schwartz, John. "Who Needs Hackers?" *New York Times*, September 12, 2007.

[SDS 1985]
Systems Designers Scientific. *CORE—The Method: User Manual*. London, UK: SD-Scicon, 1986.

[Seacord 2005]
Seacord, Robert C. *Secure Coding in C and C++*. Boston, MA: Addison-Wesley, 2005.

[SecurityFocus 2007]
SecurityFocus. *BugTraq*. http://www.securityfocus.com/archive/1 (2007).

[Shirey 1994]
Shirey, Robert W. "Security Architecture for Internet Protocols: A Guide for Protocol Designs and Standards." Internet Draft: draft-irtf-psrg-secarch-sect1-00.txt, November 1994.

[Sindre 2000]
Sindre, Guttorm, & Opdahl, Andreas L. "Eliciting Security Requirements by Misuse Cases," 120–131. *Proceedings of the 37th International Conference on Technology of Object-Oriented Languages and Systems* (TOOLS-37 '00). New York: IEEE Press, 2000.

[Sindre 2001]
Sindre, Guttorm, & Opdahl, Andreas L. "Templates for Misuse Case Description." *Seventh International Workshop on Requirements Engineering: Foundation*

for Software Quality, 2001. http://swt.cs.tu-berlin.de/lehre/saswt/ws0506/unterlagen/TemplatesforMisuseCaseDescription.pdf

[Soo Hoo 2001]
Soo Hoo, Kevin, Sudbury, Andrew W., & Jaquith, Andrew R. "Tangible ROI Through Secure Software Engineering." *Secure Business Quarterly 1*, 2 (2001). http://www.musecurity.com/assets/files/Tangible%20ROI%20Secure%20SW%20Engineering.pdf

[Steven 2006]
Steven, John. "Adopting an Enterprise Software Security Framework." *IEEE Security & Privacy 4*, 2 (March/April 2006): 84–87. https://buildsecurityin.us-cert.gov/daisy/bsi/resources/published/series/bsi-ieee/568.html

[Stoneburner 2002]
Stoneburner, Gary, Goguen, Alice, & Feringa, Alexis. *Risk Management Guide for Information Technology Systems* (Special Publication 800-30). Gaithersburg, MD: National Institute of Standards and Technology, 2002. http://csrc.nist.gov/publications/nistpubs/800-30/sp800-30.pdf

[Swanson 2003]
Swanson, Marianne, Bartol, Nadya, Sabato, John, Hash, Joan, & Graffo, Laurie. *Security Metrics Guide for Information Technology Systems* (NIST Special Publication 800-55). Gaithersburg, MD: Computer Security Division, Information Technology Laboratory, National Institute of Standards and Technology, July 2003. http://csrc.nist.gov/publications/nistpubs/800-55/sp800-55.pdf

[Taylor 2005]
Taylor, Dan, & McGraw, Gary. "Adopting a Software Security Improvement Program." *IEEE Security & Privacy 3*, 3 (May/June 2005): 88–91.

[Telang 2004]
Telang, R., & Wattal, S. "Impact of Software Vulnerability Announcements on the Market Value of Software Vendors." Carnegie Mellon University, 2004. http://www.infosecon.net/workshop/pdf/telang_wattal.pdf

[Tsipenyuk 2005]
Tsipenyuk, Katrina, Chess, Brian, & McGraw, Gary. "Seven Pernicious Kingdoms: A Taxonomy of Software Security Errors." *IEEE Security & Privacy 3*, 6 (November/December 2005): 81–84.

[van Wyk 2005]
van Wyk, Kenneth, & McGraw, Gary. "Bridging the Gap between Software Development and Information Security." *IEEE Security & Privacy 3*, 5 (September/October 2005): 64–68.

[Viega 2001]
Viega, John, & McGraw, Gary. *Building Secure Software: How to Avoid Security Problems the Right Way*. Boston, MA: Addison-Wesley, 2001.

[Voas 1997]
Voas, Jeffrey M., & McGraw, Gary. *Software Fault Injection: Inoculating Programs Against Errors.* New York: John Wiley & Sons, 1998.

[Wayner 1997]
Wayner, Peter. "Human Error Cripples the Internet." *New York Times*, July 17, 1997. http://www.nytimes.com/library/cyber/week/071797dns.html

[Wäyrynen 2004]
Wäyrynen, J., Bodén, M., & Boström, G. "Security Engineering and eXtreme Programming: An Impossible Marriage?" *Proceedings of the 4th Conference on Extreme Programming and Agile Methods.* Calgary, Alberta, Canada, August 15–18, 2004. Published as *Extreme Programming and Agile Methods: XP/Agile Universe 2004.* Berlin, Germany: Springer-Verlag, 2004.

[Westby 2005]
Westby, Jody (Ed.). "Roadmap to an Enterprise Security Program." American Bar Association, Privacy and Computer Crime Committee, Section of Science and Technology Law. American Bar Association, 2005. Ordering information available at http://www.abanet.org/abastore/index.cfm?section=main&fm=Product.AddToCart&pid=5450039

[Westby 2007]
Westby, Jody R., & Allen, Julia H. *Governing for Enterprise Security (GES) Implementation Guide* (CMU/SEI-2007-TN-020). Pittsburgh, PA: Software Engineering Institute, Carnegie Mellon University, August 2007.

[Whittaker 2002]
Whittaker, James A. *How to Break Software: A Practical Guide to Testing.* Boston MA: Addison-Wesley, 2002.

[Whittaker 2003]
Whittaker, James A., & Thompson, Herbert H. *How to Break Software Security.* Boston MA: Addison-Wesley, 2003.

[Whitten 1999]
Whitten, A., & Tygar, J. "Why Johnny Can't Encrypt: A Usability Evaluation of PGP 5.0." *Proceedings of Usenix Security Symposium,* Usenix Association, 1999.

[Wiegers 2003]
Wiegers, Karl E. *Software Requirements* (2nd ed.). Redmond, WA: Microsoft Press, 2003.

[Wood 1989]
Wood, Jane, & Silver, Denise. *Joint Application Design: How to Design Quality Systems in 40% Less Time.* New York: John Wiley & Sons, 1989.

[Wood 1995]
Wood, J., & Silver, D. *Joint Application Development* (2nd ed.). New York: Wiley, 1995.

[Woody 2005]
Woody, C. *Eliciting and Analyzing Quality Requirements: Management Influences on Software Quality Requirements* (CMU/SEI-2005-TN-010, ADA441310). Pittsburgh, PA: Software Engineering Institute, Carnegie Mellon University, 2004. http://www.sei.cmu.edu/publications/documents/05.reports/05tn010.html

[Woody 2007]
Woody, Carol, & Alberts, Christopher. "Considering Operational Security Risk During System Development." *IEEE Security & Privacy 5,* 1 (January/February 2007): 30–35.

[Wysopal 2006]
Wysopal, Chris, Nelson, Lucas, Dai Zovi, Dino, & Dustin, Elfriede. *The Art of Software Security Testing.* Cupertino, CA: Symantec Press, 2006.

[Xie 2004]
Xie, Nick, & Mead, Nancy R. *SQUARE Project: Cost/Benefit Analysis Framework for Information Security Improvement Projects in Small Companies* (CMU/SEI-2004-TN-045, ADA31118). Pittsburgh, PA: Software Engineering Institute, Carnegie Mellon University, 2004. http://www.sei.cmu.edu/publications/documents/04.reports/04tn045.html

[Zowghi 2005]
Zowghi, D., & Coulin, C. "Requirements Elicitation: A Survey of Techniques, Approaches, and Tools." In *Engineering and Managing Software Requirements,* edited by Aybuke Aurum and Claes Wohlin. Heidelberg, Germany: Springer-Verlag, 2005.

Build Security In Web Site References

The Build Security In Web site URL is https://buildsecurityin.us-cert.gov/. The following BSI documents are cited in this book.

[BSI 01]
Deployment & Operations content area
https://buildsecurityin.us-cert.gov/daisy/bsi/articles/best-practices/deployment.html

[BSI 02]
Attack Patterns content area
https://buildsecurityin.us-cert.gov/daisy/bsi/articles/knowledge/attack.html

[BSI 03]
Assurance Cases content area
https://buildsecurityin.us-cert.gov/daisy/bsi/articles/knowledge/assurance.html

[BSI 04]
Coding Practices content area
https://buildsecurityin.us-cert.gov/daisy/bsi/articles/knowledge/coding.html

[BSI 05]
Coding Rules content area
https://buildsecurityin.us-cert.gov/daisy/bsi-rules/home.html

[BSI 06]
Guidelines content area
https://buildsecurityin.us-cert.gov/daisy/bsi/articles/knowledge/guidelines.html

[BSI 07]
Code Analysis content area
https://buildsecurityin.us-cert.gov/daisy/bsi/articles/best-practices/code.html

[BSI 08]
Runtime Protection
https://buildsecurityin.us-cert.gov/daisy/bsi/articles/knowledge/coding/310.html

[BSI 09]
Risk Management content area
https://buildsecurityin.us-cert.gov/daisy/bsi/articles/best-practices/risk.html

[BSI 10]
Requirements Elicitation Case Studies
https://buildsecurityin.us-cert.gov/daisy/bsi/articles/best-practices/requirements/532.html

[BSI 11]
Requirements Prioritization Case Study Using AHP
https://buildsecurityin.us-cert.gov/daisy/bsi/articles/best-practices/requirements/534.html

[BSI 12]
Introduction to the CLASP Process
https://buildsecurityin.us-cert.gov/daisy/bsi/articles/best-practices/requirements/548.html

[BSI 13]
The Common Criteria
https://buildsecurityin.us-cert.gov/daisy/bsi/articles/best-practices/requirements/239.html

[BSI 14]
Using Integer Programming to Optimize Investments in Security Counter-measures
https://buildsecurityin.us-cert.gov/daisy/bsi/articles/best-practices/requirements/552.html

[BSI 15]
Architectural Risk Analysis content area
https://buildsecurityin.us-cert.gov/daisy/bsi/articles/best-practices/architecture.html

[BSI 16]
Architectural Risk Analysis
https://buildsecurityin.us-cert.gov/daisy/bsi/articles/best-practices/architecture/10.html

[BSI 17]
Principles content area
https://buildsecurityin.us-cert.gov/daisy/bsi/articles/knowledge/principles.html

[BSI 18]
Business Case
https://buildsecurityin.us-cert.gov/daisy/bsi/articles/best-practices/code/212.html

[BSI 19]
Code Analysis
https://buildsecurityin.us-cert.gov/daisy/bsi/articles/best-practices/code/214.html

[BSI 20]
Coding Practices
https://buildsecurityin.us-cert.gov/daisy/bsi/articles/knowledge/coding/305.html

[BSI 21]
Risk-Based and Functional Security Testing
https://buildsecurityin.us-cert.gov/daisy/bsi/articles/best-practices/testing/255.html

[BSI 22]
White Box Testing
https://buildsecurityin.us-cert.gov/daisy/bsi/articles/best-practices/white-box/259.html

[BSI 23]
Black Box Security Testing Tools
https://buildsecurityin.us-cert.gov/daisy/bsi/articles/tools/black-box/261.html

[BSI 24]
Adapting Penetration Testing for Software Development Purposes
https://buildsecurityin.us-cert.gov/daisy/bsi/articles/best-practices/penetration/655.html

[BSI 25]
Penetration Testing Tools
https://buildsecurityin.us-cert.gov/daisy/bsi/articles/tools/penetration/657.html

[BSI 26]
Building Security In *IEEE Security & Privacy* Series
https://buildsecurityin.us-cert.gov/daisy/bsi/resources/published/series/bsi-ieee.html

[BSI 27]
Identity in Assembly and Integration
https://buildsecurityin.us-cert.gov/daisy/bsi/articles/best-practices/assembly/207.html

[BSI 28]
Application Firewalls and Proxies—Introduction and Concept of Operations
https://buildsecurityin.us-cert.gov/daisy/bsi/articles/best-practices/assembly/30.html

[BSI 29]
Correctness by Construction
https://buildsecurityin.us-cert.gov/daisy/bsi/articles/knowledge/sdlc/
613.html

[BSI 30]
Assessing Security Risk in Legacy Systems
https://buildsecurityin.us-cert.gov/daisy/bsi/articles/best-practices/leg-
acy/624.html

[BSI 31]
Security Considerations in Managing COTS Software
https://buildsecurityin.us-cert.gov/daisy/bsi/articles/best-practices/leg-
acy/623.html

[BSI 32]
Security Is Not Just a Technical Issue
https://buildsecurityin.us-cert.gov/daisy/bsi/articles/best-practices/man-
agement/563.html

[BSI 33]
Risk Management Framework
https://buildsecurityin.us-cert.gov/daisy/bsi/articles/best-practices/risk/
250.html

[BSI 34]
Risk-Centered Practices
https://buildsecurityin.us-cert.gov/daisy/bsi/articles/best-practices/
deployment/575.html

[BSI 35]
Security and Project Management
https://buildsecurityin.us-cert.gov/daisy/bsi/articles/best-practices/
project/38.html

[BSI 36]
The Influence of System Properties on Software Assurance and Project Management
https://buildsecurityin.us-cert.gov/daisy/bsi/articles/best-practices/
project/228.html

[BSI 37]
Prioritizing IT Controls for Effective, Measurable Security
https://buildsecurityin.us-cert.gov/daisy/bsi/articles/best-practices/
deployment/577.html

[BSI 38]
Measures and Measurement for Secure Software Development
https://buildsecurityin.us-cert.gov/daisy/bsi/articles/best-practices/mea-
surement/227.html

[BSI 39]
Plan, Do, Check, Act
https://buildsecurityin.us-cert.gov/daisy/bsi/articles/best-practices/
deployment/574.html

[BSI 40]
Maturity of Practice and Exemplars
https://buildsecurityin.us-cert.gov/daisy/bsi/articles/best-practices/man-
agement/567.html

[BSI 41]
Adopting a Software Security Improvement Program
https://buildsecurityin.us-cert.gov/daisy/bsi/resources/published/series/
bsi-ieee/113.html

[BSI 42]
Bridging the Gap Between Software Development and Information Security
https://buildsecurityin.us-cert.gov/daisy/bsi/resources/published/series/
bsi-ieee/109.html

[BSI 43]
Misuse and Abuse Cases: Getting Past the Positive
https://buildsecurityin.us-cert.gov/daisy/bsi/resources/published/series/
bsi-ieee/125.html

[BSI 44]
Adopting an Enterprise Software Security Framework
https://buildsecurityin.us-cert.gov/daisy/bsi/resources/published/series/
bsi-ieee/568.html

[BSI 45]
Making the Business Case for Software Assurance
https://buildsecurityin.us-cert.gov/daisy/bsi/articles/knowledge/busi-
ness/685.html

[BSI 46]
Secure Software Development Life Cycle Processes
https://buildsecurityin.us-cert.gov/daisy/bsi/articles/knowledge/sdlc/
326.html

[BSI 47]
Additional Resources—DHS SwA WG Output
https://buildsecurityin.us-cert.gov/daisy/bsi/resources/dhs.html

[BSI 48]
Risk Management Framework Glossary
https://buildsecurityin.us-cert.gov/daisy/bsi/articles/best-practices/risk/
248.html

Index

Index terms should be read within the context of software security engineering. For example, "requirements engineering" refers to *security* requirements engineering.